MAPPING CONTRACTS

Keyed to: **CASES AND MATERIALS: CONTRACTS, 8th Edition**
Farnsworth, Sanger, Cohen, Brooks, and Garvin

Suzanne Darrow-Kleinhaus
Professor of Law
Touro College,
Jacob D. Fuchsberg Law Center

Sidney Kwestel
Professor of Law
Touro College,
Jacob D. Fuchsberg Law Center

WEST ACADEMIC PUBLISHING

Mat #41251094

© 2015 LEG, Inc. d/b/a West Academic
444 Cedar Street, Suite 700
St. Paul, MN 55101
1-877-888-1330

West, West Academic Publishing, and West Academic are trademarks of West Publishing Corporation, used under license.

Printed in the United States of America

ISBN: 978-0-314-28044-2

To our students, who never fail to surprise and challenge us

—Suzanne Darrow-Kleinhaus and Sidney Kwestel

■ CONTENTS

Acknowledgments ix

How To Use This Book xi

CHAPTER 1. BASES FOR ENFORCING PROMISES 1

■ **Section 1.** Enforceable Promises: An Introduction 1

■ **Section 2.** Remedying Breach 2

■ **Section 3.** Consideration as a Basis for Enforcement 4
    (A) Fundamentals of Consideration 4
    (B) The Requirement of Exchange: Action in the Past 7
    (C) The Requirement of Bargain 8
    (D) Promises as Consideration 9

■ **Section 4.** Reliance as a Basis of Enforcement 12

■ **Section 5.** Restitution as an Alternative Basis for Recovery 15

CHAPTER 2 : CREATING CONTRACTUAL OBLIGATIONS 19

■ **Section 1.** The Nature of Assent 19

■ **Section 2.** The Offer 20

■ **Section 3.** The Acceptance 24

■ **Section 4.** Termination of the Power of Acceptance 29
    (A) Lapse of an Offer 30
    (B) Revocation of Offers 30
    (C) Death of an Offeror 32
    (D) The Consequences of Rejection 33
    (E) The "Mailbox Rule": Contracts by Correspondence 33

■ **Section 5.** Acceptance Varying Offer: Contract Formation and
Contract Terms 34
    (A) The Common Law Approach and the Mirror Image Rule Concepts . . 34
    (B) The "Battle of the Forms" 35
    (C) UCC §2-207: Transcending the Mirror Image Rule 35

■ **Section 6.** Precontractual Liability 41

■ **Section 7.** The Requirement of Definiteness 46

CHAPTER 3. STATUTES OF FRAUDS 49

- **Section 1.** Introduction 49
  - (A) What a Statute of Frauds Does and Does Not Do 49
  - (B) Background 50
  - (C) Why a Statute of Frauds? 50

- **Section 2.** Scope 50
  - (A) Duration of Performance: The One-Year and Lifetime Clauses 50
  - (B) Interests in Real Property 51
  - (C) The Suretyship Clause 52

- **Section 3.** Satisfying the Statute of Frauds 54
  - (A) The Content of a Writing 54
  - (B) Issues of Form 54
  - (C) The Statute of Frauds in the Digital Age 56

- **Section 4.** The Statute of Frauds and the Sale of Goods 57

- **Section 5.** Exceptions to the Statute of Frauds 57
  - (A)(1) Part Performance Exceptions 57
  - (A)(2) Reliance-based Exceptions 58
  - (B) UCC §2-201(2): The Sounds of Silence 60
  - (C) UCC §2-201(3)(b): The Judicial Admissions Exception 62

- **Section 6.** Assessing the Statute of Frauds 63
  - (A) Ethical Practices and the Statute of Frauds 63
  - (B) W(h)ither the Statute of Frauds? 63

CHAPTER 4. POLICING THE BARGAINING PROCESS 65

- **Section 1.** Capacity 65

- **Section 2.** Overreaching 69
  - (A) Pressure in Bargaining 70
  - (B) Concealment and Misrepresentation 75

CHAPTER 5. DETERMINING THE PARTIES' OBLIGATIONS UNDER THE CONTRACT 81

- **Section 1.** The Parol Evidence Rule 81

- **Section 2.** The Use of Extrinsic Evidence of the Parties' Intent 86

- **Section 3.** The Use of Extrinsic Evidence From Commercial Context 92

- **Section 4.** The Use of Extrinsic Evidence to Supplement or Qualify the Agreement: Course of Dealing, Usage of Trade and Course of Performance 95

- **Section 5.** Objective Interpretation and Its Limits 98

- **Section 6.** Supplementing the Agreement with Terms Supplied by Law: Gap Fillers, Warranties, and Mandatory Terms 100
  - (A) Filling Contractual Gaps—Generally 100
  - (B) Filling Common Contractual Gaps by Statute 100
  - (C) Gap Filling With Respect to Product Quality— Implied Warranties in Article 2 100
  - (D) Express Warranties 106
  - (E) Supplementing the Contract With Mandatory Terms— Good Faith 107

CHAPTER 6. LIMITS ON THE BARGAIN AND ITS PERFORMANCE

CHAPTER 6. LIMITS ON THE BARGAIN AND ITS PERFORMANCE 109

- **Section 1.** Unfairness 109

- **Section 2.** Standard Form and Adhesion Contracts.................... 111

- **Section 3.** Unconscionability.. 114

- **Section 4.** Performing in Good Faith................................. 118

- **Section 5.** Public Policy... 122
  - (A) Illegal Contracts 122
  - (B) Judicially Created Public Policy 124

CHAPTER 7. REMEDIES FOR BREACH

CHAPTER 7. REMEDIES FOR BREACH 131

- **Section 1.** Specific Relief 131

- **Section 2.** Measuring Expectation 136

- **Section 3.** Limitation on Damages 144
  - (A) Avoidability 144
  - (B) Foreseeability 146
  - (C) Certainty 150

- **Section 4.** "Liquidated Damages" and "Penalties" 151

CHAPTER 8. PERFORMANCE AND BREACH 155

■ **Section 1.** Conditions 155
(A) Effects of Conditions 158
(B) Problems of Interpretation 161
(C) Mitigating Doctrines 163

■ **Section 2.** Constructive Conditions of Exchange 164

■ **Section 3.** Mitigating Doctrines 167
(A) Substantial Performance 167
(B) Divisibility 169
(C) Restitution 170

■ **Section 4.** Suspending Performance and Terminating the Contract 172

■ **Section 5.** Prospective Nonperformance 175
(A) Anticipatory Repudiation 178
(B) Assurance of Due Performance 182

CHAPTER 9. BASIC ASSUMPTIONS:
MISTAKE, IMPRACTICABILITY, AND FRUSTRATION 185

■ **Section 1.** Unilateral Mistake 186

■ **Section 2.** Mutual Mistake 188

■ **Section 3.** Impracticability of Performance 190

■ **Section 4.** Frustration of Purpose 198

■ **Section 5.** Half Measures 203

CHAPTER 10. THIRD PARTIES:
RIGHTS AND RESPONSIBILITIES 205

■ **Section 1.** Third-Party-Beneficiary Contracts 205

■ **Section 2.** Delegation of Duties 210

■ **Section 3.** Assignment of Rights 212
(A) Assignability of Rights; Means of Assignment 212
(B) Obligor's Duty to Assignee: Some Variations 215
(C) Assignees in Contests With Third Parties.................... 217

Table of Cases 219

ACKNOWLEDGMENTS

This project has been a major enterprise and would not have happened without the support and assistance of others. We are indebted to Jacqueline Hudson and Sue Mori for their patient and thorough administrative support. We are grateful to Joy Gary, Frances Bowdre, and Ashleigh Televandos for their careful proofreading and comments on the manuscript. And a very special thank you to Irene Crisci, Head of Public Services, and to Isaac Samuels, Reference Librarian and Educational Technology Specialist, for their helpfulness and support throughout this project.

No writing project becomes real without the vision and support of a publisher and this one is no exception. We are grateful to Louis Higgins and Staci Herr at West Academic. It is a pleasure to know them and work with them. Suzanne is especially grateful to Staci for her confidence in her ideas and encouragement of her work.

Suzanne Darrow-Kleinhaus & Sidney Kwestel
May, 2014

I owe a very special thank you to Sidney Kwestel, my former Contracts professor and now my writing partner. I realized early as a student in his class that what was important was learning to ask the right questions. It is wholly appropriate to recognize his enormous contribution to a book which shows how to organize the rules into a framework of questions to guide a legal analysis.

This is the first time that I have had a true partner in a writing endeavor and I am hopeful that it will result in a long and productive association for us both. I know that I am already the beneficiary. I hope the same will be true for him.

Suzanne Darrow-Kleinhaus
May, 2014

Special thanks to Suzanne for graciously giving me the opportunity to participate in her project. Her willingness to share is reflective of the modesty she exhibits in her professional life. May she continue in good health to teach, inspire, and support Touro's students to whom she is so dedicated.

Sidney Kwestel
May, 2014

HOW TO USE THIS BOOK

YOU WILL NOTICE AS SOON AS YOU PICK UP *Mapping the Law* that it looks unlike any other law school supplement or review text. Maybe that's because it is based on a law student's class outlines. When one of your authors was a student, she realized that she needed something different from the typical outline to help her learn the material. She needed to know the cases and the rules from those cases, but she also needed to know the steps of analysis involved in applying those rules to solve a legal problem. In figuring out how to do this, she created an outline in a table format that let her see the connection between legal concepts and the cases from which they were derived. When this approach worked well for one of her classes, she began to use it for all of her other classes—always careful to follow the casebook's table of contents in conjunction with the professor's syllabus. Classmates with whom she shared her outlines thought they were incredibly helpful.

Using the casebook's table of contents as the structure of the book, *Mapping Contracts* provides:

- Capsule case summaries of the relevant facts:, holding, and reasoning for every case in the book.

- A conceptual framework for each legal principle as derived from the cases.

- A format which makes the connection between cases and concepts "visible" and thus easier to learn.

- The foundation for your own course outline—just add material from class and your professor's individual "take" on the cases and the law.

As you progress through your Contracts course, use *Mapping Contracts* to help you develop your core knowledge and reasoning skills. We suggest that you begin your studies with the overview provided by the Contracts TimeLine. It is an excellent starting point to get a sense of the whole subject. When you look at the big picture, it does not matter where your professor begins the course—whether with promises, formation, or remedies—you can see where all the pieces fit and it is much easier not to get lost in the details.

We have tried to be consistent throughout *Mapping*. All references to the Restatement are to the Restatement Second unless otherwise indicated. We use the terms "Code" and "UCC" interchangeably throughout the text to refer to Article 2 of the Uniform Commercial Code.

As you will soon learn, a threshold question for contracts analysis is whether the transaction involves a sale of goods: if it does, then the UCC applies, otherwise, it does not. For example, a construction contract, an employment contract and a contract for the sale of land are covered by the state's common law and not the UCC. While we are sure that you will learn this from your professor, we want to make sure that you hear this from us as well: the UCC applies to both consumers and merchants. Article 2 governs contracts for the sale of goods whether the seller is a merchant or not. There are some provisions which treat merchants differently, but it is not a requirement that one be a merchant for the provisions of the Code to apply to the transaction.

Although Article 2 is applicable only to transactions involving the sale of goods, it has been highly influential in the transformation of the common law. As you will see, the Restatement Second has adopted many provisions of Article 2 in formulating its own rules. Courts often apply the UCC by analogy to non-sales transactions in view of the underlying policies to be served. Sometimes a case involves both goods and services. These are referred to as "hybrid cases." Here, a court has several options: a minority of courts apply Article 2 to only the sale of goods aspect of the transaction whereas a majority of courts apply Article 2 only if the predominant purpose of the whole transaction was a sale of goods, and in that event, the majority applies Article 2 to the whole. If the sale of goods is not the predominant purpose, then Article 2 does not apply at all.

We hope that this book will enhance your understanding of Contracts. We welcome your feedback and wish you the best of luck in your studies.

— SDK & SK

MAPPING
CONTRACTS

CONTRACTS TIMELINE

FORMATION			AVOIDING THE DEAL
Do we have a deal?			**We have a deal, but**
Mutual Assent + Consideration			
Offer +	**Acceptance**	**+ Consideration**	
Objective Test	Power of acceptance	"Peppercorn" theory	Statute of Frauds
"Master" of offer	Unilateral contract	Benefit/detriment	Misunderstanding
Contractual intent	• Acceptance by promised performance only	Illusory promises	Mistake:
Certainty of terms		Gratuitous promises	• Unilateral
Preliminary Negotiations	Bilateral contract	Past consideration	• Mutual
Terminating an offer:	• Acceptance by promise	Moral obligation	Incapacity
• Revocation		Promissory estoppel	Fraud/Misrepresentation
• Rejection	"Mirror-image Rule"	Modifications:	Duress
• Counteroffer	"Mail Box Rule"	• Pre-existing Duty Rule	Undue influence
• Lapse of time	"Battle of the Forms"	• UCC 2-209	Unconscionability:
• Death or incapacity	Irrevocable offers:	Requirements/output contract	• Procedural
	• Option contract		• Substantive
	• "Firm offer"		Illegality
			Public policy

Additional formation concepts:

      Implied-in-fact contracts

      Implied-in-law or "quasi contracts"

Notes: These terms and category delineations represent a way of looking and thinking about contract law; they are not definitive, nor by any means the only way to look at the subject. The chart is meant as a way to begin looking at the parts and trying to make sense of the whole. But know that the whole is greater than the sum of these parts.

PERFORMANCE/NONPERFORMANCE	THIRD PARTIES		REMEDIES
Who has to do what and when or maybe not?	**Is there another party to the deal?**		**Someone failed to perform when required, now what?**
	At formation?	**Subsequently?**	

Establishing the Contract Terms
• Parol Evidence Rule
• Interpretation
• Ambiguity
Implied Terms
• Good faith
Warranties
Conditions
• Express/Implied-in-Fact
• Constructive
Excuse/waiver of non-occurrence of condition
Modification
Impossibility/Impracticability
Frustration of purpose
Anticipatory Repudiation
Breach
• Substantial Performance or Material Breach
• UCC Perfect Tender Rule
• Right to Cure
• Avoiding forfeiture: divisibility
	3rd Party Beneficiaries
	• Intended
	• Incidental
		Assignment
		Delegation
		Novation
			Measuring money damages:
			• Expectation interest
			  Loss in value
			  Cost of repair/completion
			  Diminution in value
			• Reliance interest
			• Restitution interest
			Consequential damages
			Incidental damages
			Liquidated damages
			
			Limitations on money damages:
			• Foreseeability
			• Mitigation/Avoidability
			• Certainty
			
			Equitable remedies:
			• Specific performance
			• Injunctive relief

■ CHAPTER 1. BASES FOR ENFORCING PROMISES

Section 1. Enforceable Promises: An Introduction

Concepts: Determining the bases for contract liability

- Contract liability is based on the parties' voluntary agreement.

- A basic question for contract law is whether a promise or set of promises will be legally enforceable:

  1. Why are some promises legally enforceable while others are not?

  2. Is there particular language, circumstances, or other factors to consider in determining whether a promise has been made? (*Hawkins v. McGee; Bayliner*)

- The law is careful to recognize only such relationships as the parties manifest an intent to create because a contract creates a legal relationship resulting in rights and obligations for the parties.

- A threshold question for contracts analysis is whether the transaction involves a sale of goods: if it does, then Article 2 of the Uniform Commercial Code ("UCC") applies. If it does not, then the common law applies. (*Bayliner*)

CASES	SUMMARIES
Hawkins v. McGee (1929) →(CB pg. 2)*	**FACTS:** A doctor allegedly told a patient that the doctor would make the patient's injured hand "a hundred per cent good hand." The patient agreed to the surgery. When the surgery did not result in a "good hand," the patient brought suit. **HOLDING:** The court found that there was a reasonable basis for the jury to determine that if the doctor spoke these words, that he did so with the intent that the patient accept them at their face value (a promise to make a good hand) as an inducement to consent to the operation. The court further found that there was evidence that the plaintiff accepted. Thus, the court found that whether the doctor's assurance was a legally enforceable promise was a matter properly submitted to the jury. **QUESTION TO THINK ABOUT:** *Concept of "promise": would there be a legally enforceable promise if a doctor said he would make an injured hand "one hundred percent perfect"?*

CASES	SUMMARIES
Bayliner Marine Corp. v. Crow (1999) →(CB pg. 4)	**FACTS:** A buyer of a sport fishing boat brought suit against the seller alleging breach of express warranty and implied warranties of merchantability and fitness for a particular purpose when the boat failed to achieve the maximum speed of 30 miles per hour described in the dealer's "prop matrixes." Instead, its maximum was only 23 to 25 miles per hour. **HOLDING:** The court held that the manufacturer's statements in the "prop matrixes" did not relate to the particular boat purchased by the plaintiff and therefore could not constitute an express warranty about the performance capabilities of the boat actually purchased. Statements made in the sales brochure were expressions of the manufacturer's opinion about the quality of the boat's performance but did not create an express warranty that the boat was capable of speeds of 30 mph. The court also found that Bayliner did not violate the implied warranties of merchantability provided under UCC § 2-314. Discussion of implied warranties is to be found in Chapter 5.

Section 2. Remedying Breach

Concepts: Making the injured party whole through compensation

- Enforcing a promise is accomplished by awarding remedies for its breach.

- Our system of contract remedies does not seek to punish the breaching party but instead is concerned with compensating the non-breaching party for its loss; punitive damages are generally not recoverable for breach of a contract. (*White v. Benkowski*)

FRAMEWORK FOR ANALYSIS: Protecting one or more of the promisee's three interests

ASK: If the promise has been breached, which measure of damages best protects the interests of the aggrieved party?

1. Can she recover her "**expectation interest**" which represents what the injured party expected to receive if the breaching party had fully performed its promise and is often referred to as the "benefit of the bargain"? (*Naval Institute*)

2. Can she recover her "**reliance interest**" which represents the injured party's loss for expenditures made in reliance on the other party's promise to perform and seeks to place her in as good a position as she would have been in had the contract not been made?

3. Can she recover her "**restitution interest**" which represents her interest in having restored to her any benefit she has conferred on the other party? The objective is to put the party in breach back in the position that party would have been in if the contract had not been made.

ASK: Even if the party cannot prove any loss under one of these theories, is she able to recover nominal damages? Can she seek specific performance?

CASES	SUMMARIES
United States Naval Institute v. Charter Communications Inc. (1991) →(CB pg. 10)	**FACTS:** A licensing agreement between the parties granted the publisher the exclusive license to publish a paperback edition of *The Hunt for Red October*, "not sooner than October 1985." The publisher nevertheless began sales of the paperback book on September 15, 1985 and it climbed to the top of the bestseller lists before the end of September. Plaintiff brought an action for copyright infringement and for contract damages. The court rejected the infringement claim because an exclusive licensee cannot be liable for infringing the copyright conveyed to it but considered the claim for damages for breach of contract. **HOLDING:** The court affirmed the district court's award to plaintiff of $35,380.50 in damages as appropriate for its loss of profits from hardcover sales it would have made absent defendant's breach. In measuring the loss, the court used the August 1985 hardcover sales as a basis to determine what, "but for" defendant's premature release of the soft cover edition, would have been the resulting profits from the lost September hardcover sales. The court further stated that any uncertainty in the calculation would come at the wrongdoer's expense.
Sullivan v. O'Connor (1973) →(CB pg. 15)	**FACTS:** A professional entertainer brought suit against her doctor for breach of contract when plastic surgery which was promised "to enhance her beauty and improve her nose" required a third surgery, caused pain and suffering, and worsened her appearance. The jury awarded $13,500 for breach of contract. Both parties appealed, with the woman objecting to the judge's refusal to instruct the jury that she was entitled to the difference in value between the present nose and the nose as promised. **HOLDING:** The court upheld the jury verdict but did not decide whether the expectation or reliance measure of damages was appropriate because the woman waived her claims to expectation damages (she waived her claim to the difference in value between the present and promised nose). However, the court explained that an expectancy recovery might be excessive while a limitation to restitution might be too meager. It concluded that a reliance measure might be best in this situation and she would be entitled to recover "her out-of-pocket expenditures," damages for the "worsening of her condition," and for the "pain and suffering and mental distress involved in the third operation."

CASES	SUMMARIES
White v. Benkowski (1967) →(CB pg. 24)	**FACTS:** White and Benkowski entered into a written contract where the Benkowskis agreed to supply water to the Whites home for $3 per month and half the cost of future well repairs. After a while, the parties' relationship soured and the Benkowskis shut off the water supply to the White home on nine occasions for short periods of time. The Whites brought suit for breach of contract, seeking compensatory and punitive damages. The jury awarded the Whites $10 in compensatory damages and $2000 in punitive damages. The trial court reduced the award to $1 in compensatory damages and no punitive damages. The Whites appealed. **HOLDING:** On appeal, the court stated that in a breach of contract action, a party is entitled to such damages as she sustains which resulted naturally and directly from the breach. Compensatory damages include pecuniary loss suffered as a natural result of the breach. When a breach has been established, nominal damages are recoverable even where there have been no actual damages. Here, plaintiffs were entitled to the $10 set by the jury. Although the pecuniary loss was only 25 cents based on the contract rate, the trial court failed to include the plaintiffs' inconvenience. This was an actual injury and compensable. The award of punitive damages, however, was inappropriate since the general rule is that punitive damages are not recoverable in breach of contract actions even when the breach is willful.

Section 3. Consideration as a Basis for Enforcement

(A) Fundamentals of Consideration

CONCEPTS: Finding the bargain

- For a promise to be enforceable, the other party must furnish "consideration" to the promisor in the form of a performance or promise.

- Consideration doctrine requires a "bargained for exchange."

- The question is whether a performance or return promise is sought by the promisor in exchange for her promise and given by the promisee in exchange for that promise.

- Courts will not inquire into the adequacy of the consideration unless there is such a disparity in the exchange that it is questionable whether it was in fact bargained for.

Contractual Settings:

ASK: Since agreements typically fall within certain categories where specialized practices and rules develop, when reading a fact pattern, ask which of the following categories is at issue:

- Contract for the sale of goods (UCC Article 2)?
- Real estate transaction?
- Employment agreement?
- Construction contract?
- Family contract?

FRAMEWORK FOR ANALYSIS: Finding the exchange element

ASK: Is there a "bargained for" exchange? Has something, either a promise or a performance, been sought by the promisor in return for the promisor's promise?

- Consideration can be forbearance from doing that which one has a legal right to do. (*Hamer v. Sidway*)

- Consideration can be forbearance from enforcing a doubtful or uncertain claim or even one which proves to be invalid if it is brought on an objective good faith belief. (*Dyer v. National By-Products, Inc., Fiege v. Boehm*) R2d §74(1)(b)

If yes, then the consideration requirement is met. Or is it one of the following where there may have been bargaining but the promise is still not enforceable?

- Is the promise illusory?

- Is there a pre-existing duty?

If the promise is not bargained for, then what type of promise is it?

- Is it a gratuitous promise? Is the promise one to make a future gift where the promisor asks for and receives nothing in exchange? If so, then the promise is not legally enforceable.

- Is it past consideration where the promisee has already taken the action before the promise is made? (*Feinberg v. Pfeiffer Co.*)

- Is it a promise made in recognition of a moral obligation arising out of a benefit previously received? If so, then it is not enforceable under the common law. (*Mills v. Wyman*)

Does an exception apply?

- Was the promise made in recognition of a benefit previously received by the promisor from the promisee where enforcement is necessary to prevent injustice? (*Webb v. McGowin*) R2d §86(1)
- Is it a promise to pay a debt no longer legally enforceable because the Statute of Limitations has run?
- Is it a promise made by a minor upon reaching majority reaffirming a previous promise which the minor could have set aside upon reaching majority?
- Is it a promise to pay a debt that has been discharged in bankruptcy?

CASES	SUMMARIES
Hamer v. Sidway (1891) →(CB pg. 35)	**FACTS:** An uncle promised his nephew that he would pay him $5,000 if the nephew refrained from drinking, using tobacco, swearing, and playing cards or billiards for money until he became 21. The nephew refrained from these activities until he was 21 and when the $5,000 was not paid, brought suit. The issue was whether there was consideration to support the uncle's promise. The defense claimed that there was no consideration because the nephew was not harmed but benefitted by not engaging in these activities, that what he did was best for him to do independent of his uncle's promise, and that unless the promisor was benefitted, the contract lacked consideration. **HOLDING:** The NY Ct of Appeals held that the nephew's forbearance from doing that which he had a legal right to do—drinking and smoking tobacco—was consideration to support the uncle's promise. It was a detriment to the promisee and possibly a benefit to the uncle.
Dyer v. National By-Products, Inc. (1986) →(CB pg. 43)	**FACTS:** Dyer, an employee of National By-Products, lost his right foot in a job-related accident and brought an action against his employer for breach of an oral contract to provide lifetime employment. Dyer claimed that he held a good faith belief that he had a valid claim against his employer for Dyer's personal injury. He further claimed that his forbearance from litigating his claim was made in exchange for a promise from his employer that he would have lifetime employment. The district court determined, as a matter of law, that consideration for the alleged settlement was lacking because the forborne claim was not a viable cause of action because the employee's sole remedy against his employer was to pursue workers' compensation benefits so that he had no basis for a tort suit. Upon grant of summary judgment for the employer, the employee appealed. **HOLDING:** The issue on appeal was whether good faith forbearance to litigate a claim, which proves to be invalid and unfounded, is consideration to uphold a contract of settlement. The court held that the invalidity of the employee's claim against his employer did not preclude him, as matter of law, from asserting forbearance as consideration and that there was material issue of fact as to whether the employee's forbearance to assert the claim was in made in good faith, thus precluding summary judgment for the employer.
Fiege v. Boehm (1956) →(CB pg. 46: Note 2)	**FACTS:** Plaintiff, a woman who had an out-of-wedlock child brought a breach of contract claiming the child's father had agreed to pay her medical expenses, compensation for lost salary, and $10 per week in child support. He paid her $480 and stopped when a blood test revealed that he was not the child's father. Plaintiff filed a charge of bastardy with the State's Attorney who brought suit. Defendant was found not guilty of the criminal charge based on the blood test. Plaintiff brought a civil suit and was awarded $2,145.80. **HOLDING:** The court affirmed on appeal. It held that there was consideration because when the woman made the charge of bastardy against the defendant, she believed in good faith that he was the child's father; and that the claim had a reasonable basis of support.

(B) The Requirement of Exchange: Action in the Past

CASES	SUMMARIES
Feinberg v. Pfeiffer Co. (1959) →(CB pg. 48)	**FACTS:** An employer decided to pay an employee who had been working for him for 37 years $200 per month for life upon her retirement. She continued working for a while and then retired. She was paid for a number of years and then the payment was reduced. The employee brought suit. **HOLDING:** The court held that a promise based on past services is not supported by consideration. Since the employee was not required to do anything in return for the pension, there was no mutuality of obligation and the promise was unenforceable for lack of consideration. However, the court found in favor of the employee on a reliance basis since the employee relied on the promise of payment for life when she retired and gave up her opportunity to continue working.
Mills v. Wyman (1825) →(CB pg. 52)	**FACTS:** Wyman promised to pay Mills after he learned that Mills had incurred expenses in caring for Wyman's sick son, age 25. Mills brought suit when the father decided not to do so. **HOLDING:** The court held that while the father may have incurred a moral obligation to make good on his promise, the law will not enforce such a promise where nothing was promised or paid for it in return. The father did not ask Mills to care for his adult son; the promise was made after the father learned what Mills had done, and so the father's promise to pay cannot be said to be in exchange for Mills' performance of caring for his son.
Webb v. McGowin (1935) →(CB pg. 54)	**FACTS:** Employee saved the life of his employer by throwing himself in the path of a 75 pound pine block and was permanently injured in the process. After the incident, the employer promised to pay the employee $15 every two weeks for the rest of his life. Payments were made for almost ten years. After the employer's death, however, the executor refused to continue the payments. The employee brought suit. **HOLDING:** The court held that there was sufficient consideration to support the subsequent promise to pay for a service where the promisor has received a material benefit.
Harrington v. Taylor (1945) →(CB pg. 57)	**FACTS:** A man was assaulting his wife when she knocked him down with an axe and was about to cut his head open or decapitate him when plaintiff intervened. The ax fell on plaintiff's hand, mutilating it but saving the man's life. Subsequently, the man promised to pay plaintiff her damages. The man paid plaintiff a small sum and then stopped. Plaintiff brought suit to recover on the man's promise and the defendant moved to dismiss. **HOLDING:** The court granted the defendant's motion, finding that plaintiff's humanitarian act, which was voluntarily performed, was not consideration for the defendant's promise.

(C) The Requirement of Bargain

CASES	SUMMARIES
Kirksey v. Kirksey (1845) →(CB pg. 58)	**FACTS:** A widow abandoned the land she had been living on with her children and moved about 60 miles to live on her brother-in-law's property when he wrote, "if you will come down and see me, I will let you have a place to raise your family." After a couple of years, he required her to leave. She brought suit. **HOLDING:** On appeal, the court held that the brother-in-law's promise was a mere gift and unenforceable. Gratuitous promises lack the bargain element necessary for a legally enforceable promise. The court did not discuss whether the promise should be enforced based on plaintiff's reliance on her brother-in-law's promise.
Lake Land Employment Group of Arkron, LLC v. Columber (2004) →(CB pg. 62)	**FACTS:** After working at Lake Land for several years, an at-will employee was asked to sign a non-compete agreement. The at-will relationship continued for another ten years when the employee left Lake Land and formed a corporation that was engaged in a similar business. Lake Land brought suit alleging a breach of the non-compete agreement. The issue was whether the employee's promise not to compete was supported by consideration. The trial court found that the non-compete agreement was unenforceable because it lacked consideration: the employee received no increase in benefits or salary or change in employment status in exchange for signing the agreement. The issue of whether subsequent employment alone was sufficient consideration to support a non-compete agreement with an at-will employee entered into after employment had already begun was certified for appeal. **HOLDING:** The court held that there was consideration to support the non-compete agreement because the parties continued their at-will relationship even though each had the right to terminate it. The court reasoned that an employer's presentation of a non-compete agreement to an at-will employee is a proposal to renegotiate the terms of the parties' at-will agreement. Where an employer makes such a proposal by presenting his employee with a non-compete agreement and the employee assents by continuing employment on the new terms there is consideration: the employee's assent to the agreement is given in exchange for the employer's forbearance from terminating the employee. While the court found that the agreement did not lack consideration, it nonetheless reversed the judgment of the lower court and remanded the case for further proceedings to determine whether the non-compete agreement was reasonable.

(D) Promises as Consideration

CONCEPTS: Bilateral and unilateral contracts

- **Unilateral contract:** a contract where a promisor seeks only a performance in exchange for her promise; an offer for a unilateral contract can be accepted only by performance or by tendering or beginning the invited performance or by tendering a beginning of it (see R2d §45) and not a return promise.

- **Bilateral contract:** a contract in which the parties exchange a promise for a promise—the offeror's promise is contained in the offer and the offeree makes a return promise by the acceptance.

FRAMEWORK FOR ANALYSIS: Identifying a legally enforceable promise

ASK: Does the promise satisfy the bargain requirement of consideration: has the promise been sought by the promisor and given in exchange for that promise? If yes, then the promise was given as part of a bargain and generally would be legally enforceable if broken.

Exception: Has the promise been bargained for but it is still not enforceable? Consider the following:

- Is there a pre-existing duty? Here, the promise may be bargained for, but the party is promising to perform a duty that she already owes to the promisee. In this case, the promise may not be enforceable. See Chapter 4.

- Is it an illusory promise? Does the promise by its terms make performance entirely optional with the promisor? If so, then even if the promise has been bargained for, there is no commitment as to future behavior and the promise is illusory. (*Strong v. Sheffield*)

- If the promisor has limited its discretion in some way, then the promise is not illusory. In this case, ask: are there limits to the party's discretion?

  - Is it a requirements or output contract where the quantity term is measured by the buyer's requirements or the seller's output? If so, it means such requirements or output as may occur in good faith and thus the promise is not illusory.

  - Is there an implied promise to use "best efforts" as in an "exclusive dealings" agreement? If so, then the obligation to use best efforts prevents the promise from being illusory. (UCC § 2-306(2)) ("Reasonable efforts" in *Wood v. Lucy, Lady Duff-Gordon*)

  - Is the party entitled to exercise discretion over its performance as in a satisfaction clause? This is also considered a conditional promise where the promisor's obligation to perform is conditioned on its satisfaction with the other party's performance. If so, then the promisor's discretion is not unlimited because it must be done reasonably or in good faith, depending on the circumstances. (*Mattei v. Hopper*)

CASES	SUMMARIES
Strong v. Sheffield *(1895)* →(CB pg. 73)	**FACTS:** A wife endorsed a promissory note for her husband, the maker of the note, where she promised to pay the debt if he did not. She was reluctant to endorse the note and the debt was past due at the time. The holder of the note said that he would "hold it until such time as I want my money." The holder did in fact forebear for two years. The holder brought an action against the wife seeking to enforce the note. **HOLDING:** On appeal, the court found for the endorser of the note because the endorser's promise was not supported by consideration. The court stated that here the note was payable on demand and there was nothing to prevent the holder from bringing immediate suit against the maker to recover the debt. The holder did not promise to forebear for a fixed period of time or a reasonable time, but only for such time as he should decide. Even though the holder waited two years before collecting the debt, the court stated that whether there is "consideration is to be tested by the agreement, and not by what was done under it."
Mattei v. Hopper *(1958)* →(CB pg. 76)	**FACTS:** A real estate developer entered into an agreement with a landowner to buy her property. Among other terms, the developer's promise to complete the purchase was subject to him obtaining "satisfactory" leases. Thereafter, the landowner refused to sell her land, claiming that the developer's promise was illusory and the agreement lacked mutuality. **HOLDING:** The court held that the agreement was supported by consideration because the developer was bound to exercise good faith in determining his satisfaction with the leases. The court stated that while a commercial contract such as one involving manufacturing or construction required objective satisfaction (the satisfaction of a reasonable person), a contract involving a lease falls within the type of contract involving fancy, taste, or judgment such that the judgment of the individual is involved. In this case, the individual's subjective satisfaction is required and the "criterion becomes one of good faith."
Structural Polymer Group, Ltd. v. Zoltek Corp. *(2008)* →(CB pg. 81)	**FACTS:** Zoltek and Structural Polymer (SP) entered into a Supply Agreement under which Zoltek promised to manufacture and sell to SP all of SP's requirements of large carbon fibers between November 6, 2000 and December 31, 2010. In turn, SP promised to purchase its requirements in an amount not to exceed what SP purchased in the preceding contract year plus 1 million pounds. SP placed two orders in 2005 and 2006 which Zoltek did not fill and SP sued to recover lost profits. **HOLDING:** Zoltek argued that the Supply Agreement was unenforceable because it lacked mutuality of obligation—a claim that the contract, more particularly Zoltek's promise to sell, was not supported by consideration. Zoltek argued that when the contract was entered into SP had zero requirements. However, under UCC §2-306(1), SP had an implied obligation of good faith to order product from Zoltek and therefore SP's promise was not illusory. If SP acted in bad faith, Zoltek would have a claim that SP breached the contract—not that there was no consider-

CASES	SUMMARIES
Structural Polymer Group, continued	ation at the outset to support Zoltek's promise. Zoltek also argued that the agreement's price protection clause which gave SP the right to purchase carbon fibers from third parties made SP's promise to purchase its requirements from Zoltek illusory. However, the court noted that the price protection clause gave Zoltek the right to match any offer SP had from another supplier and if it did, SP was obligated to purchase from Zoltek. Thus, SP was bound to buy from Zoltek if Zoltek met the third party's price and if it did not, then SP could buy elsewhere. In essence, therefore, SP's promise was not illusory since it did not have an unfettered option to buy from third parties.

Finally, Zoltek argued that small tow and large tow fibers were interchangeable and that SP could buy small tow fibers from other parties rendering its supply contract with Zoltek illusory. Aside from the fact that there was substantial evidence that small and large fibers were not interchangeable, the court noted that even if they were interchangeable, any SP purchase of an interchangeable product from a third party without a good faith basis to do so, would constitute a breach of its requirements contract with Zoltek. SP had an obligation under the requirements contract to purchase in good faith from Zoltek and it could not arbitrarily purchase interchangeable products from a third party. The court concluded its opinion with a discussion of the jury's award of damages for SP. |
| *Wood v. Lucy, Lady Duff-Gordon (1917)*

→ (CB pg. 86) | **FACTS:** Lucy, Lady Duff-Gordon, a famous fashion designer, gave Wood exclusive rights to endorse designs with her name and to market and license her designs. In exchange, she was to receive half of all the profits and revenues from any contracts that Wood made. The exclusive right was for a period of one year. During this period, Lucy placed her own endorsement on fabrics, dresses, and millinery without Wood's knowledge and withheld the profits. Wood brought suit. Lucy claimed that the agreement was not binding because Wood did not bind himself to anything.

HOLDING: The court found that in exchange for Lucy's giving Woods an exclusive privilege to market her fashions, Wood promised to use "reasonable efforts to bring profits and revenues into existence." The parties' arrangement as evidenced by its terms was "instinct with obligation" for Wood to use reasonable efforts so that Lucy would get something because without such an implied promise, the transaction would not have such business "efficacy as both parties must have intended that at all events it should have." |

Section 4. Reliance as a Basis of Enforcement

CONCEPTS: Promissory estoppel

- There are some promises which, although the promisor makes them without bargaining for anything in return, nonetheless induce the promisee to rely to her detriment. While this promise would be otherwise unenforceable because of a lack of consideration, the doctrine of promissory estoppel offers some relief.

- Distinguish promissory estoppel from equitable estoppel: equitable estoppel is where a misrepresentation of fact is made by one party and relied on by the other, the party making the representation is precluded ("estopped") from denying such fact if the other party has justifiably relied on it.

FRAMEWORK FOR ANALYSIS: Determining whether a promise is enforceable based on reliance

ASK: If there is no consideration to support the promise, has there been reliance by the promisee on it? There are some promises which, although the promisor makes them without bargaining for anything in return, nonetheless induce the promisee to rely to her detriment. In such circumstances, recovery may be available on a reliance basis. R2d §90(1)

If yes, then ask: Has a promise been made?

- Was it foreseeable to the promisor that the promisee would rely on the promise?

- Did the promise induce actual reliance and was the reliance justified? (*Feinberg v. Pfeiffer Co.*)

- Are the circumstances such that injustice can be avoided only by enforcement of the promise? (*Cohen v. Cowles Media Co.*)

If the answer is "yes" to all of the above, then the promise is enforceable on a reliance theory and the promisee is entitled to relief. (*Ricketts v. Scothorn*)

Now ask, what is the appropriate form of relief?

> The remedy may be limited as justice requires. This means that the promisee may not receive full contractual relief which would include her expectation damages but may be limited to reimbursement of the actual loss expended in reliance on the promise. This would include opportunity costs. (*D&G Stout, Inc. v. Bacardi Imports, Inc.*)
>
> Note: If the promise is for a charitable subscription, then it may be binding without proof that the promise induced action or forbearance. R2d §90(2)

This topic is revisited in Chapter 2, Section 6, *Precontractual Liability*, where reliance as a basis for recovery is considered in circumstances where a party may incur liability for conduct occurring before a contract has been formed.

CASES	SUMMARIES
Ricketts v. Scothorn (1898) →(CB pg. 92)	**FACTS:** Katie Scothorn received a written promissory note from her grandfather that he would pay her "on demand, $2,000 to be at 6 per cent. per annum." When he gave her the note, the grandfather said that he had "fixed out something that you have not got to work any more. . . none of my grandchildren work, and you don't have to." Katie quit her job. The grandfather died after paying only one year's interest on the note and expressing regret that he had not been able to pay the balance. Katie brought an action seeking the balance of the note from the executor of the estate. The executor claimed a lack of consideration. **HOLDING:** The court found that while the note was not given in exchange for Katie's promising, doing, or refraining from doing anything, the executor was "estopped" from alleging a lack of consideration. Having done what her grandfather induced her to do—quit her job—the court held that "it would be grossly inequitable" to permit "the maker, or his executor, to resist payment on the ground that the promise was given without consideration."
Feinberg v. Pfeiffer Co. (1959) →(CB PG. 97)	**FACTS:** An employer decided to pay an employee who had been working for him for 37 years $200 per month for life upon her retirement. She continued working for a while and then retired. She was paid for a number of years and then the payment was stopped. The employee brought suit. **HOLDING:** The court held that the employee's past services were not valid consideration to support the employer's promise of a pension but the employee's reliance on that promise by retiring and giving up her opportunity to continue working made it enforceable.
Wright v. Newman (1996) →(CB pg. 101)	**FACTS:** Newman sued Wright seeking child support for her son. Although Wright was not the father nor had he adopted the boy, the trial court ordered him to pay support because he had listed himself on the birth certificate, given the child his last name, and established a parent-child relationship which had deterred Newman from establishing the paternity of the child's natural father. **HOLDING:** On appeal, the court noted that although Wright was neither the natural nor adoptive father, this did not mean that he had no legal obligation to pay child support. The issue was whether Wright was liable for child support under state contract law. The court noted that Wright had not agreed in a formal written contract to support Newman's son but under Georgia contract law—more particularly the state's codification of the promissory estoppel doctrine—a "promise which the promisor should reasonably expect to induce action or forbearance on the part of the promisee or a third person and which does induce such action or forbearance is binding if injustice can be avoided only by enforcement of the promise." Here the court said that the evidence—such as Wright listing himself as the father on the birth certificate and giving the child his surname—would justify a conclusion that Wright promised Newman that he would assume all fatherhood obligations. At the time, Wright knew he was not the natural father and nevertheless made a commitment and held himself out to others as the child's father for ten years. Newman and her son detrimentally

CASES	SUMMARIES

Wright, continued

relied on Wright's promise in refraining from trying to identify and obtain support from the child's natural father. The court concluded that Newman and her son would suffer an injustice if Wright were allowed to evade the voluntary commitment he had made ten years earlier and thus his commitment was enforceable under the promissory estoppel doctrine.

CONCURRING: Under promissory estoppel, the injured party need not "exhaust all other possible means of obtaining the benefit of the promise from any and all sources before being able to enforce the promise against the promisor." After reasonably relying on Wright's promise for ten years, it was not rational to say that Newman can now identify and secure support from the biological father. Such a task "would be an imposing, if not impossible, burden, and would require Newman not only to identify the father (if possible), but also to locate him, bring a costly legal action against him, and succeed in that action." Since it was unlikely for Newman to successfully do so, Newman and her son would suffer an injustice unless Wright's promise was enforced. Moreover, Newman's child, who was told that he would be able to depend upon Wright for parenting and sustenance would suffer if Wright's commitment was not enforced.

DISSENT: The dissent disagreed with the majority's finding that Newman and her son incurred a detriment: it noted that Newman did not allege and the record did not show that she did not know the natural father's identity nor that he was dead or unable to be found. Further, Newman severed all relationship with Wright when her son was three years old and that Wright did not support the child for the past seven years. Thus any detriment Newman incurred because of the passage of ten years since her son's birth, at least for the past seven years, was not due to anything Wright had done.

Cohen v. Cowles Media Co. (1992)

→(CB pg. 104)

FACTS: Cohen supplied information about a candidate for lieutenant governor to reporters for the *Minneapolis Star* and the *Pioneer Press* who promised to keep Cohen's identity confidential when publishing the story. The reporters' editors failed to honor their promise and Cohen's identity was revealed. Cohen was fired by his advertising agency when the stories were published. He sued the publishers for breach of contract. The jury awarded $200,000 in compensatory damages but the Minnesota Supreme Court held that because the parties were not likely thinking that they were forming a contract at the time, the reporter has no claim based on contract even though there was an offer, acceptance and consideration. Further, recovery under a theory of promissory estoppel would violate the papers' First Amendment rights. The Supreme Court granted cert and held that the First Amendment was not offended by use of the doctrine to enforce confidentiality agreements simply because it had "incidental effects" on its ability to gather and report the news.

CASES	SUMMARIES
Cohen, continued	**HOLDING:** On remand, the Supreme Court of Minnesota affirmed the jury's award of damages on a theory of promissory estoppel because it would be unjust to deny Cohen a remedy for the breaking of the reporters' promise. Cohen relied on the journalistic tradition of the confidentiality of sources in asking for and receiving a promise of anonymity.
D&G Stout, Inc. v. Bacardi Imports, Inc. (1991) →(CB pg. 106)	**FACTS:** D&G, known as "General," was a liquor distributor in Indiana. The industry was facing difficult times and General faced a decision of whether to sell the business or continue operating on a smaller scale. General relied on a promise from Bacardi, one of General's major suppliers, that it would continue to be Bacardi's distributor, and turned down an offer to sell at a negotiated price. Although Bacardi promised that General would continue to act as Bacardi's distributor, the relationship remained terminable-at-will, as it had been for over 35 years. A week later, Bacardi withdrew its account and General had to settle for selling at an amount $550,000 below the first offer. General brought suit against Bacardi for the price difference on a promissory estoppel theory. **HOLDING:** The court held that opportunity costs are reliance costs and are recoverable in an at-will relationship. General had a reliance interest in Bacardi's promise since General had been in lively negotiations with National for the sale of General and Bacardi was aware of this fact. General had a business opportunity that all parties knew would be devalued once Bacardi withdrew from General. The extent of that devaluation represents a reliance injury. Note: Lost opportunity costs may also be considered reliance damages; example is "forgone wages" which an at-will employee gives up while preparing to relocate to a new job. Moving expenses, which are out-of-pocket expenses, are reliance costs.

Section 5. Restitution as an Alternative Basis for Recovery

Concepts: Unjust enrichment

- **Restitution:** an umbrella term encompassing all claims for recovery based on a claim of unjust enrichment.

- **Unjust enrichment: a** doctrine based on the equitable principle that a person should not be allowed to enrich herself unjustly at the expense of another. (*Pyeatte v. Pyeatte*)

- **Quasi-contract:** refers to any money claim for the redress of unjust enrichment. To recover on this basis, plaintiff must prove that defendant received a benefit (was enriched) and that retention of that benefit without payment would be unjust. (*Callano v. Oakwood Park Homes Corp.*)

- *Quantum meruit:* "as much as the claimant deserved."
- **Contract implied-in-law:** a contract implied-in-law is not really a contract at all. Instead, the court creates an obligation in law (quasi-contract) to do justice even though no promise was ever made or intended. (*Cotnam v. Wisdom*)

CASES	SUMMARIES
Cotnam v. Wisdom (1907) →(CB pg. 114)	**FACTS:** Doctors were called by a bystander to a street car accident and provided emergency services to an unconscious patient who died without regaining consciousness. The doctors brought suit against the patient's estate for payment for their services. When the judgment was for the plaintiffs, the estate appealed, claiming that the patient did not and could not have expressly or impliedly assented to the doctors' actions because he was unconscious. **HOLDING:** The court held that it was well-settled law that an implied contract, while not an actual contract, is a legal fiction implied-in-law for the sake of providing a remedy. While there was no actual promise or mutual understanding, the law will imply a contract to provide a remedy based on a legal obligation and a legal right. The court creates an obligation in law (quasi-contract) to do justice even though no promise was ever made or intended. Here, the doctors were entitled to be reasonably compensated for the services they provided.
Callano v. Oakwood Park Homes Corp. (1966) →(CB pg. 117)	**FACTS:** Oakwood contracted to sell to Pendergast a lot with a house to be built on it and, under a separate contract, contracted with Callano to plant shrubbery on the lot. Pendergast died before paying for the shrubbery and his estate cancelled the contract with Oakwood. Oakwood then resold the lot, including the shrubbery on it, not knowing that the Callanos had not been paid. Callano brought suit against Oakwood on a quasi-contract theory claiming that Oakwood was unjustly enriched at the Callanos' expense because the shrubbery increased the value of the property. **HOLDING:** The court held Callano could not recover in quasi-contract because it had an express contract with the homeowner Pendergast for the shrubbery and never expected to be paid by Oakwood. Although Oakwood was enriched, its retention of the benefit was not unjust. Further, recovery on the theory of quasi-contract is appropriate to provide a remedy where no other exists—here, Callano may bring an action against the homeowner's estate because it had a contract with him.

CASES	SUMMARIES
Pyeatte v. Pyeatte (1982) →(CB pg. 121)	**FACTS:** A couple agreed that the wife would work and put her husband through law school and when he graduated he would put her through graduate school. He finished law school, passed the bar, and became an associate at a law firm. A year later, he asked for a divorce. The wife had not started grad school yet. She sued for breach of the agreement. The trial court found a valid contract and awarded the wife $23,000. The husband appealed, claiming the agreement was too indefinite to be enforced. The wife claimed she was entitled to recover in restitution. The appellate court granted her claim and the husband again appealed.

HOLDING: On appeal, the court found that while the parties' agreement failed for indefiniteness to be enforceable as a contract, it was relevant for the wife's claim of unjust enrichment to show her expectation of payment and that the husband's retention of the benefits of her efforts would be unjust. Generally, unjust enrichment is not available in a marital relationship where the claim is for the usual activities of the marriage but here the wife's extra efforts inured solely to the husband's benefit. |

■ CHAPTER 2 : CREATING CONTRACTUAL OBLIGATIONS

Section 1. The Nature of Assent

Concepts: The "Objective Test"

- The two essential elements of a contract are **agreement** (mutual assent) and **consideration**.

- The consideration doctrine's requirement of a bargain means that the parties' manifestations of assent to the exchange must be reciprocal.

- Both parties must intend to contract and must agree to the same terms. Typically, mutual assent is found through the process of offer and acceptance.

- In determining the parties' intent, courts apply an "objective test" which looks to the parties' words and actions (outward manifestations) and not to what they may have subjectively believed. The test of a party's intent is viewed from the perspective of a reasonable person in the position of the other party. (*Lucy v. Zehmer*)

CASES	SUMMARIES
Lucy v. Zehmer (1954) →(CB pg. 126)	**FACTS:** Lucy brought suit against Zehmer for specific performance of a contract to sell Lucy the Ferguson farm for $50,000. The Zehmers had written, "We hereby agree to sell to W.O. Lucy the Ferguson Farm complete for $50,000, title satisfactory to buyer," and signed it. The Zehmers refused to go through with the deal claiming that they were only joking and drunk when they signed the document and that they never intended to sell. **HOLDING:** The court held that the Zehmers were bound by their agreement even if they subjectively did not intend to sell because the evidence indicates that Lucy took them seriously and he was not unreasonable in doing so. In contracts, we "look to the outward expression of a person [here the Zehmers' outward expression] as manifesting his intention rather than to his secret and unexpressed intention."
Specht v. Netscape Communications Corp. (2002) →(CB pg. 131)	**FACTS:** Plaintiffs brought a class action alleging that their use of Netscape's Smart-Download software transmitted private information to Netscape about plaintiffs' downloading files from the internet. Netscape moved to compel arbitration based on an arbitration clause contained in SmartDownload's license terms. The court held that, under the circumstances of the case, plaintiffs' act of downloading the free software at Netscape's invitation did not amount to an agreement to be bound by the license terms which included the arbitration clause. **HOLDING:** Before downloading SmartDownload, all of the named plaintiffs except one, allegedly arrived at a webpage entitled "SmartDownload Communicator" that urged plaintiffs to download SmartDownload. Toward the bottom of the screen, there was a prompt stating "Start Download" and a button marked "Download."

CASES	SUMMARIES
Specht, continued	Plaintiffs clicked on the download button. From the time plaintiffs clicked on the download button until the downloading of SmartDownload finished, no information appeared on the screen regarding any license. In this case, there was no clickwrap presentation accompanying the download. Had plaintiffs' scrolled down, they would have seen a statement reading, "Please review and agree to the terms of the SmartDownload software license agreement before using downloading and using the software." But plaintiffs did <u>not</u> scroll down. Instead plaintiffs, at Netscape's invitation, clicked the download button and therefore never saw the licensing provision. Plaintiffs testified, without contradiction, that they were unaware that Netscape intended to attach licensing terms to the use of SmartDownload. The Second Circuit concluded that "in circumstances such as these, where consumers are urged to download free software at the immediate click of a button, a reference to the existence of license terms on a submerged screen is not sufficient to place consumers on inquiry or constructive notice of those terms. . . . We hold that a reasonably prudent offeree in plaintiffs' position would not have known or learned, prior to acting on the invitation to download, of the reference to SmartDownload's license terms hidden below the "Download" button on the next screen." Plaintiffs' therefore, were not bound by any licensing agreement and thus, the Second Circuit affirmed the District Court's denial of Netscape's motion to compel arbitration.

Section 2. The Offer

Concepts:

- An offer is the manifestation of willingness to enter into a bargain, so made as to justify the offeree in understanding that her assent to the bargain is invited and, if given, would conclude it. R2d §24

- While a contract may be formed after a single set of communications between the parties, more often there is a series of communications over a period of time. In some instances, a contract may be formed only after considerable "dickering" over the terms and negotiations back and forth between the parties.

- Not every expression qualifies as an offer; for example, it might be an expression of opinion, a statement of intent, an inquiry, or an invitation to deal.

- Unless the parties have agreed otherwise, where a subcontractor submits a bid to the general contractor, for use by the general contractor in its bid submission for a project, the subcontractor's offer is irrevocable until the general contractor has had a reasonable opportunity to notify the subcontractor of the award and accept the subcontractor's offer. R2d §87 ill. 6

FRAMEWORK FOR ANALYSIS: Determining whether an offer has been made

ASK: Has the offeror made a manifestation of willingness to enter a bargain so as to justify the offeree in understanding that her assent to the bargain is invited and, if given, would conclude it? In determining whether an offer was made, ask the following:

- What words were used? Were they words of commitment or invitations to negotiate? (*Owen v. Tunison*)

- Were there any prior communications between the parties? If so, then all should be considered in determining whether an offer has been made. (*Fairmont Glass Works v. Crunden-Martin Woodenware Co.*)

- To whom was the offer made? Advertisements to the public or a large group of persons are likely to be considered invitations to make an offer unless the ad is clear, definite, and explicit, leaving nothing open to negotiation in which case, the ad may be an offer. (*Lefkowitz v. Great Minneapolis Surplus Store*)

CASES	SUMMARIES
Owen v. Tunison (1932) →(CB pg. 142)	**FACTS:** Owen wrote to Tunison asking, "Will you sell me your store property . . . for the sum of $6,000.00?" to which Tunison replied that "it would not be possible for me to sell it unless I was to receive $16,000.00 cash." Owen wrote back that he accepted the offer. When Tunison notified him that he did not wish to sell, Owen brought suit for damages. **HOLDING:** The court held that Tunison's letter of December 5 in response to Owen's offer to purchase the property was not a proposal to sell but "may have been written with the intent to open negotiations that might lead to a sale." If there was no offer to sell, then there can be no contract for the sale of the property.
Harvey v. Facey (1893) →(CB pg. 144)	**FACTS: :** Harvey telegraphed Facey, the owner of a property and asked two questions: whether he was willing to sell the property and the lowest price. When Facey telegraphed his answer, indicating only the lowest price, Harvey treated it as an offer and telegraphed his acceptance. **HOLDING:** The Lordships found that the statement of the lowest price was not an offer. It was only an answer to the question regarding price and all other terms were left open. Instead, Harvey's last telegram to Facey was an offer which Facey could accept.
Fairmont Glass Works v. Crunden-Martin Woodenware Co. (1899) →(CB pg. 145)	**FACTS:** Fairmont wrote in a letter of April 23 in response to an inquiry from Crunden for the lowest price for ten car loads of jars that "we quote you Mason jars . . . for immediate acceptance." By telegram on April 24, Crunden wrote "enter order." Fairmont responded that it could not book the order. Crunden claims that it had a contract by its telegram of April 24 and Fairmont claims it was not bound.

CASES	SUMMARIES
Fairmont Glassworks, continued	**HOLDING:** The court considered the language in all the parties' correspondence and concluded that, when read as a whole, the meaning of the words "for immediate acceptance" in Fairmont's April 23 letter was evidence of a present offer to sell at the stated prices. Crunden's prior letter was an inquiry for the price and terms and Fairmont's response was not a mere quote but a "definite offer to sell on the terms indicated, and could not be withdrawn after the terms had been accepted."
Lefkowitz v. Great Minneapolis Surplus Store (1957) →(CB pg. 148)	**FACTS:** A store advertised in the newspaper "SATURDAY 9 A.M. 2 BRAND NEW PASTEL MINK 3-SKIN SCARFS Selling for $89.50 Out they go Saturday. Each . . . $1.00 1 BLACK LAPIN STOLE. . . Beautiful, worth $139.50 . . . $1.00 FIRST COME FIRST SERVED." Lefkowitz was the first customer to present himself on Saturday and demanded the Lapin stole for $1.00. The store refused to sell to him because of a house rule that the offer was intended for women only.

HOLDING: The court found that the ad for the fur was an offer because it was clear, definite, and explicit, leaving nothing open to negotiation. Further, the ad contained no restriction about a "house rule" for women only and such a restriction or modification to the offer could not be imposed after acceptance.

Note: Although the court stated that the advertisement did not indicate that it was intended for women only, Lefkowitz knew about the "house rule" because this was the store's second advertisement: when Lefkowitz responded to the first ad and the Store refused to sell to him, he was told that a "house rule" intended the offer for women only. *If Lefkowitz knew of the "house rule" that the offer was not intended for men when he responded to the store's second advertisement, then how could he reasonably believe that there was an offer he could accept?*

QUESTION TO THINK ABOUT: *What is the significance of the statement in the ad, "FIRST COME FIRST SERVED"?* |

Mistakes in Offers

Concepts:

- This section of the casebook is concerned with unilateral mistakes in offers that are computational in nature and commonly arise in bids (offers) submitted by contractors or subcontractors for work on construction projects. See Chapter 9 for a full discussion of the mistake doctrine.

- In cases of mistake, the parties have reached an agreement but one or both of the parties entered that agreement on an erroneous assumption about the facts that existed at the time of contracting. A mistaken belief may be held by one party (unilateral mistake) or shared by both (mutual mistake).

- In considering the bidders' claims for relief based on mistake, courts often distinguish between "clerical" or "computational" errors ("scrivener's error) and mistakes in judgment: it is one thing to grant relief to a contractor who has made an "innocent" computational error in tallying up what is often a complex set of numbers from a contractor who may have misjudged what was needed to perform the job. Generally, courts do not favor granting relief for errors in judgment.

- If a clerical or "scrivener's" error results in a written agreement that fails to express the parties' agreement correctly, then the appropriate remedy is reformation of the writing to reflect the agreement actually reached.

CASES	SUMMARIES
Elsinore Union Elementary School District v. Kastorff (1960) → (CB Comment, pg. 153)	**FACTS:** Kastorff, a contractor, submitted a bid for additions to the Elsinore Union's school buildings. Kastorff failed to include the $9500 plumbing sub-bid in his total but mistakenly thought he had done so. This resulted in a 89,994 bid when he intended to bid $99,494. When the bids were opened, Kastorff's bid was $11,306 less than the next lowest bid. The school superintendent asked Kastorff whether he was sure his figures were correct and Kastorff stepped into the hall to check them with his clerical assistant even though he did not have the worksheets with him. He returned a few minutes later to say that the bid was correct. The board awarded him the job. The next day Kastorff checked his worksheets and found his error. The next day, Kastorff wrote a letter to the school board explaining the error and asked to withdraw his bid. The school board refused and brought suit to recover the difference between Karstorff's bid and the new bidder it hired to do the construction. Judgment was given for the school district and Karstorff appealed. **HOLDING:** On appeal, the court reversed, finding that Kastorff had committed an honest clerical error and had acted promptly to notify the school. It further found that Kastorff's right to relief from an "unfair, inequitable, and unintended bargain" should not be denied even when he had at first informed the board that the bid was correct. Since the school expected Kastorff to install the plumbing, it must have understood that he intended to charge for it. The omission of the plumbing bid was "as unexpected by the board as it was unintended by Kastorff." Further, this omission was material to the total of the bid. Note: The above quotations are taken from the actual case and do not appear in the casebook.

Section 3. The Acceptance

Concepts: The offeror is the "master of the offer."

- An offer may invite an offeree to accept (1) by a return promise or (2) by rendering a performance. If the offer is ambiguous as to whether it invites acceptance by promise or by performance, the offer, under R2d §32, invites the offeree to accept either by promising to perform what the offer requests or by rendering the performance, as the offeree chooses.

- If the offeror invites acceptance by a promise, that return promise may be manifested by words or conduct.

- If the offer invites acceptance by promise, the acceptance must be communicated unless the offer manifests a contrary intent or circumstances permit acceptance by silence. (See analysis below for acceptance by silence.)

- Mutual assent is complete when the offeree accepts the offer in the manner and on the terms required by the offer.

FRAMEWORK FOR ANALYSIS:

ASK: If there was an offer, was it accepted?

a. Did the proper party accept the offer: was it the party with the "power of acceptance"?

b. Has the offeree accepted in the manner required by the offer? (*Int'l Filter Co. v. Conroe Gin, Ice & Light Co.*)

   i. Was it an offer that called for acceptance by return promise? If so, then ask:

      • Did the offeree express an unequivocal intent to be bound?

      • Was the offeree's expression of assent unconditional?

      • Was it a "mirror-image of the terms of the offer? If the terms of the acceptance vary from the terms of the offer, then it is a counteroffer and a rejection unless the proposed transaction involves a sale of goods. (See UCC §2-207 discussion in Section 5 below.)

   ii. Was it an offer that invited acceptance by promise or performance?

   iii. Was it an offer that invited acceptance by performance only and not a promissory acceptance? If so, then the offeree can accept by performing the act the promisor is seeking or tendering a beginning of it. R2d §45(1)

   iv. Was the manner of acceptance not specified? If so, then acceptance may be given "in any manner and by any medium reasonable in the circumstances." R2d §30(2)

      • If the offeree can choose to accept either by promise or performance, the tender or beginning of the invited performance or a tender of a beginning of it is an acceptance by performance. Such an acceptance acts as a promise to render the complete performance. R2d §62(1) and (2)

v. Can acceptance be inferred from silence? Generally, silence is not acceptance unless one of the following apply. If the offeree fails to reply in the following situations, then the offeree may be bound to the offered terms. Ask:

- Has the offeree taken the benefit of services when the offeree had a reasonable opportunity to reject them and reason to know that payment was expected? R2d §69(1)(a)

- Has the offeror stated or given the offeree reason to understand that assent may be manifested by silence or inaction and the offeree in remaining silent or inactive intends to accept? R2d §69(1)(b)

- Have the parties had prior dealings so that it would be reasonable for the offeree to notify the offeror if she did not intend to accept? R2d §69(1)(c)

- Has the offeree exercised dominion over the offered goods or property by any act that is inconsistent with the offeror's ownership? If so, then the offeree is bound by the offered terms unless they are manifestly unreasonable. R2d §69(2)

  Note: Where the offeree's exercise of dominion does not comply with the terms of the offer, then the offeree is not bound to treat it as an acceptance but may pursue remedies in tort. R2d §69(2) cmt. e

c. Is the offeree required to give notice of acceptance to the offeror? (Int'l Filter Co. v. Conroe Gin, Ice & Light Co.)

ASK:

i. Is it an offer to be accepted by return promise? Unless the offer indicates otherwise, a promissory acceptance requires either that the offeree "exercise reasonable diligence to notify the offeror of acceptance or that the offeror receive the acceptance seasonably." R2d §56

ii. Is it an offer to be accepted by performance? (i.e., where the offer proposes a "unilateral" contract, inviting acceptance by means of performance and not a promise) If so, then notification is not necessary to make the acceptance effective unless one of the following is applicable. ASK:

- Does the offer request notification? If so, notification is necessary for a valid acceptance. R2d §54(1)

- Does the offeree has reason to know that the offeror will not learn of the acceptance with "reasonable promptness and certainty" without notice? If so, the offeror's contractual duty which arose when acceptance became effective will be discharged unless:

  — The offeree exercises reasonable diligence to notify the offeror, or R2d §54(2)(a)
  — The offeror learns of the performance within a reasonable time, or R2d §54(2)(b)
  — The offer indicates that notification of acceptance is not required. R2d §54(2)(c)

d. If there was an acceptance by promise, when did it become effective?

ASK:

- *Was it an instantaneous communication?* If the parties were in direct communication with each other at the time by phone, in person, or communicating by electronic means, then acceptance occurs as soon as it is manifested.

- Was the acceptance made in a manner and by a medium invited by an offer? If so, the acceptance is effective upon dispatch "without regard to whether it ever reaches the offeror." This is the "mailbox rule." R2d §63(a)

Consider the following "race to acceptance" situations:

- Has the offeree mailed a rejection and then had a change of mind and mailed an acceptance or vice versa? Since a rejection terminates the power of acceptance, you must consider the question in terms of when a rejection becomes effective. Ask:

    i. *Was the rejection sent before the acceptance?* A rejection or counteroffer does not terminate the offeree's power of acceptance until it is received, but any acceptance dispatched by the offeree after she has dispatched the rejection is not effective unless the acceptance is received by the offeror before she receives the rejection. R2d §40

    ii. *Was the acceptance sent before the rejection?* The contract is binding as soon as the acceptance is dispatched and the subsequently dispatched revocation of acceptance does not undo the acceptance, whether it is received by the offeror before or after her receipt of the acceptance.

- Did the offeror send the offeree a revocation? If so, it becomes effective upon receipt, not dispatch. R2d §§40, 42

- Was it acceptance of an option contract? Acceptance of an option is effective upon receipt by the offeror, not upon dispatch. R2d §63(b)

CASES	SUMMARIES
International Filter Co. v. Conroe Gin, Ice & Light Co. (1925) →(CB pg. 157)	**FACTS:** Filter sent a "proposal" to Conroe for the purchase of equipment which stated that it would become a contract when accepted and approved by a Filter executive officer. Conroe sent its "acceptance" and, on the same day, Filter's president endorsed the acceptance with "O.K." Filter sent Conroe its "acknowledgment" of the "order"; Conroe then "countermanded" its "order." Filter brought suit for breach of contract and Conroe claimed that there was no contract because there was no acceptance — the "O.K." did not count — and even if there was an acceptance, notice of acceptance was required by the offer and it was not given. **HOLDING:** Here, Filter's "proposal" was not the offer but a solicitation for an offer but one which contained all the terms. Conroe's response was the offer which adopted the terms from the proposal, including what was needed for it to become a contract: approval by Filter's executive officer. The court found for Filter, finding that there was no need to communicate acceptance since the terms of the offer stated what was necessary for it to become a contract: "when approved by an executive officer." The contract was complete at this moment and notice of that approval was not required for acceptance.

CASES	SUMMARIES
White v. Corlies & Tift (1871) →(CB pg. 162)	**FACTS:** Corlies gave White, a builder, specifications for renovating their offices and asked for a price. White gave an estimate and Corlies sent him a note on September 29 that stated, "[u]pon an agreement to finish the fitting up . . . you can begin at once." White did not reply to this note but immediately purchased lumber and began work on it with intent to accept. The next day, Corlies revoked the offer. White brought suit for breach of contract. **HOLDING:** The court found that Corlies' revocation was timely since White had not yet accepted the offer: White had not communicated a return promise nor had he begun a performance which would have indicated acceptance. Although White had purchased lumber, it was "stuff as fit for any other like work" and nothing in this act "indicated or set in motion an indication" to Corlies that their offer had been accepted. Consequently, Corlies could still revoke its offer.
Ever-Tite Roofing Corp. v. Green (1955) →(CB pg. 164)	**FACTS:** The Greens signed a document setting out the work to be done and the price to be paid to Ever-Tite for reroofing their home. A provision stated that the agreement would become effective upon either written acceptance by the contractor or "upon commencing performance of the work." The Greens knew it would take some time for Ever-Tite to get their credit approved. Nine days later, Ever-Tite loaded their truck with materials and sent workmen to the Greens. When the workmen arrived, they found other workmen doing the job and they were not permitted to do the work. The Greens claimed that they could revoke their offer by having other workmen perform because Ever-Tite had not yet accepted the offer by commencing performance. **HOLDING:** The court held that Ever-Tite had commenced performance within a reasonable time because of the need to verify credit and with performance commencing when the workers loaded the truck with the necessary materials and transported such materials and the workmen to the Green's home. **QUESTIONS TO THINK ABOUT:** • *Where do you draw the line?* • *Where does preparation end and commencement begin?* • *What was the performance that Ever-Tite was supposed to commence?* • *Would the court have found commencement of performance if Ever-Tite had placed the materials on its driveway but not yet loaded them on the truck?* • *Would it have been commencement of performance when the workers came to work?* • *Is there commencement of performance at some time before arrival at the property where the work is to be performed?* • *Do you think that loading the truck was commencement of reroofing the house?*

CASES	SUMMARIES
Carlill v. Carbolic Smoke Ball Co. (1893) →(CB pg. 166)	**FACTS:** A company advertised a "£100 reward" to anyone who contracted "the epidemic or other disease within a reasonable time after having used the smoke ball." When a consumer contracted influenza after buying and using the smokeball according to the directions, the company refused to pay and claimed that she had not notified it of her acceptance. **HOLDING:** The court found that notice of acceptance was not necessary where, as here, the person making the offer has impliedly dispensed with notice based on the nature of the transaction. The company could not possibly have expected all users of its product to contact them. In such advertisement cases, performance of the condition is a sufficient acceptance without further notification.
Allied Steel and Conveyors, Inc. v. Ford Motor Co. (1960) →(CB pg. 167)	**FACTS:** On August 19, 1955, Ford, a buyer, ordered machinery from Allied, a seller, on Ford's Purchase Order which provided that if Allied was to perform the work on Ford's premises, then Allied would be responsible for all damage caused by the negligence of its own employees. Attached to the Purchase Order was another form which included a broader indemnity provision requiring Allied to assume full liability for the negligence of Ford's employees in connection with Allied's work as well as being liable for its own employees. This page was marked VOID. Allied accepted this Purchase Order and the contract was performed. On July 26, 1956, Ford submitted to Allied Amendment 2 to the Purchase Order which contained the same provision and attached the same additional indemnity form but this this time was not marked VOID. It also contained additional language that "[a]cceptance should be executed on acknowledgment copy which should be returned to buyer." An Allied employee was injured in the course of performing work related to the second Purchase Order several months before the acknowledgement copy was executed. The court found that the language regarding execution and return of the acknowledgment copy was merely a suggested method of acceptance and not an exclusive one. It did not preclude Allied's acceptance by another method. **HOLDING:** The court found that Allied accepted when it began performance by installing the required machinery and Ford accepted the benefit of this performance. Further, it is well settled that acceptance by part performance is sufficient to complete the contract.

CASES	SUMMARIES
Corinthian Pharmaceutical Systems, Inc. v. Lederle Laboratories (1989) →(CB pg. 170)	**FACTS:** Corinthian, the buyer, purchased drugs and vaccines from Lederle, the seller, on a regular basis but never more than 100 vials. Lederle issued price lists to its customers. Each price list stated that all orders were subject to acceptance and prices were subject to change without notice and that changes take effect at the time of shipment. On May 19, an internal memo to Lederle's salespeople indicated that the price for the vaccine would be increased from \$51 to \$171 per vial. A letter was also sent out to customers on May 20, the day the price increase was to take effect. Somehow Corinthian found out about the letter the day before and placed an order for 1000 vials through Lederle's computer ordering system. Corinthian sent two order confirmations stating the price was \$64.32 per vial. Lederle shipped 50 vials at this price with a letter indicating that this was a partial shipment and it was made at the lower price in exception to its usual terms. Corinthian stated that the rest of the shipment would be shipped the week of June 16 and billed at \$171; if Corinthian wished to cancel, it should contact Lederle by June 13. Corinthian brought suit for specific performance for the 950 vials. **HOLDING:** The court found that Lederle's price list was only an invitation to make an offer because the price was subject to change and any order was subject to Lederle's acceptance. Corinthian's phone order of May 19 for 1000 vials was the offer; by shipping only 50 vials at the low price, Lederle's shipment was non-conforming but its letter seasonably indicated that it was meant as an accommodation. Lederle had no obligation to make the shipment at the lower price and did so as a favor to Corinthian. This shipment therefore was not an acceptance under UCC §2-206(1)(b).

Section 4. Termination of the Power of Acceptance

Concepts:

- For an acceptance to be valid, it must be made while the power of acceptance is still in effect.

- An offer is freely revocable at any time before acceptance unless the offer qualifies as an option contract or is otherwise made irrevocable.

- A revocation must be communicated to the offeree to be effective. Communication may be direct or indirect. An indirect communication of revocation occurs when the offeror takes definite action that is inconsistent with an intent to enter the contract and the offeree acquires this information through a reliable source.

FRAMEWORK FOR ANALYSIS:

ASK: Did the offeree still have the power of acceptance or was it terminated in one of the following ways?

- By lapse of the offer?
- By revocation by the offeror?
- By the offeror's death or incapacity?
- By the offeree's rejection/counter-offer?

(A) Lapse of an Offer

Concepts:

- An offer lapses after a period of time, either because the time specified in the offer for acceptance has passed or, if no time was specified, then a reasonable time has passed. What is a reasonable time depends on the circumstances.

- Where the parties are bargaining face-to-face or over the telephone, the time for acceptance ends with the conversation unless a contrary intention is indicated. (*Akers v. J.B. Sedberry, Inc.*)

(B) Revocation of Offers

Concepts:

- Revocation of a general offer made by newspaper or other general notification made to the public may be revoked

- by using the same medium in which the offer was made. R2d §46

- An offeror may revoke the offer at any time before acceptance, even if the offer says it will remain open, unless an option contract based on consideration or reliance is created or the offer is a "firm offer" under UCC §2-205 or some other statute (e.g., New York General Obligations Law §5-1109 — an offer is irrevocable without consideration for the time stated if it is in a writing signed by the party to be charged. If no time is stated, it is irrevocable for a reasonable time)

- An option contract or irrevocable offer may be created in one of the following four ways:

  1. By a promise to hold the offer open which is supported by consideration R2d §25

  2. By a "firm offer" UCC §2-205

  3. By an promise inviting acceptance by performance only and not a return promise and the offeree tenders or begins the invited performance R2d §45

  4. By reliance by the offeree R2d §87(2)

FRAMEWORK FOR ANALYSIS:

If revoked, then ask:

- Was the revocation received?
- Was it an indirect revocation?
- Was it the revocation of a general offer?

Was there an option contract?

ASK: Was there a "firm offer" under UCC §2-205 which would allow an offeree to enforce an offer which, by its terms states that it will be held open even though this promise was not supported by consideration?

1. Was there an actual offer?
2. Was it made by a "merchant" to buy or sell goods?
3. Was it in a signed writing?
4. Did it give assurances that it would be held open?

UCC

revocation

If the answer is "yes" to all of the above, then the offer is not revocable for lack of consideration during the time stated, or for a reasonable time if no time is stated, but in no event may such period of irrevocability exceed three months.

CASES	SUMMARIES
Dickinson v. Dodds (1876) →(CB pg. 181)	**FACTS:** On June 10, Dodds made a written offer to sell property to Dickinson stating that the offer would remain open until 9:00 a.m. on June 12. On the 11th, Dickinson decided to buy the property but thought he had time to tell Dodds until the next morning. That afternoon, Dickinson was informed by Mr. Berry that Dodds had offered or agreed to sell the property to another person. In the evening, Dickinson delivered his written acceptance to Dodds' mother-in-law. When Dobbs was finally reached at 7:00 a.m. the next morning, he refused Dickinson's acceptance stating that he had already sold the property. **HOLDING:** The court held that the offer was revocable by Dodds at any time before acceptance because there was no consideration to keep the promise open until 9:00 Friday morning. Absent consideration, Dobbs was free to revoke the offer any time before Dickinson accepted. The offer was effectively revoked when Dickinson learned that Dodds had sold the property to someone else. **QUESTION TO THINK ABOUT:** *Does it make a difference whether Dickinson learned that Dodds had sold the property or that he had been offering to sell it?*

CASES	SUMMARIES
Drennan v. Star Paving Co. (1958) →(CB pg. 188)	**FACTS:** Drennan was the general contractor bidding for a public school project. Star Paving phoned in a bid to Drennan to do the paving work for $7131.60, which was the lowest bid Drennan received. It was customary to rely on the bids in computing the general bid and so Drennan incorporated this bid into his own, including Star's name in the list of subcontractors as required by CA law. Drennan was awarded the bid. The next day Star's engineer told Drennan that Star had made a mistake in its bid and could not do the job for less than $15,000. Star refused to do the work and Drennan got another contractor to do it for $10,948.60. Drennan brought suit for the $3,817 difference it had to pay. **HOLDING:** The court first noted that there was "no evidence that defendant offered to make its bid irrevocable in exchange for plaintiff's use of its figures in computing his bid." Nor was there evidence to support an interpretation that Drennan's use of Star's bid constituted a promise by Drennan to award the subcontract to defendant if plaintiff won the main contract. The court found neither an option supported by consideration nor a bilateral contract which would bind both parties. However, Drennan claimed that he relied to his detriment on Star's bid. The court held that Drennan's reliance on Star's bid in computing his bid made Star's offer irrevocable. In holding Star's offer to be irrevocable, the court cited to the First Restatement §90. The court noted that Star had reason to expect that if its bid was low, it would be used by Drennan and so induced "action . . . of a definite and substantial character on the part of the promisee." The court reasoned that even though Star had made no express promise to keep its offer open, a subsidiary promise not to revoke an offer for a bilateral contract could be implied where there was "reasonable reliance resulting in a foreseeable prejudicial change in position." The purpose of the First Restatement §90 is to make a promise binding even though consideration is lacking. Reasonable reliance serves to hold the offeror in lieu of the consideration usually required to make the offer binding (a court would now rely on R2d §87(2)). Here, Star had a stake in Drennan's reliance on its bid. This interest, plus Drennan being bound by his own bid, makes it only fair that Drennan should have the chance to accept Star's bid after the general contract was awarded to him. While Star's bid was the result of mistake, it was not such a mistake that Drennan knew or should have known it was in error.

(C) Death of an Offeror

Concepts: Death or incapacity R2d §48

- The offeror's death terminates the power of acceptance — whether or not the offeree has notice of the death.

- The offeror's incapacity terminates the power of acceptance in the same manner as the offeror's death.

- Since only an offeree has the power of acceptance, when the offeree dies or is incapacitated, acceptance is no longer possible.

- The death or incapacity of the offeror does not terminate the offeree's power of acceptance under an option contract.

(D) The Consequences of Rejection

Concepts:

- Rejection of the offer by the offeree terminates the power of acceptance and the offeree can no longer accept the offer. Should the offeree subsequently attempt to accept the offer, this purported acceptance might itself be an offer.

- The acceptance must be the "mirror-image" of the offer or it is a counter-offer and terminates the offeree's power of acceptance.

(E) The "Mailbox Rule": Contracts by Correspondence

Concepts:

- When a contract is formed by correspondence, the mechanics of assent follow the mailbox rule which holds that where an offer invites acceptance by mail, the acceptance is effective upon dispatch. At this time, the offeror's power to revoke is terminated and the offeror is bound, even though the offeror does not know that the offer has been accepted. Of course the offeror, as master of the offer, can depart from the mailbox rule by providing otherwise in the offer. *Adams v. Lindsell.*

- Upon dispatch, the mailbox rule also binds the offeree to the acceptance and it is now too late for the offeree to either reject the offer or revoke the acceptance.

- It is important to note that the mailbox rule applies only to **acceptances** by mail, not revocations. A revocation is not effective until received by the offeree; hence, a revocation by mail or telegram is not effective until receipt. This means that if an offeror mails an offer and the next day mails a revocation, the offeror may still be bound if the offeree puts an acceptance in the mail after receiving the offer but before receiving the revocation.

- Acceptance under an option contract is operative only on receipt by the offeror. R2d §63.

CASES	SUMMARIES
United States Life Insurance Company v. Wilson (2011) →(CB pg. 197)	**FACTS:** Dr. Griffith's life insurance policy expired for failure to pay premiums. The insurer offered to reinstate the policy if Dr. Griffith paid the past due premium by August 14 by mailing the payment to the insurer's program administrator. On July 23, Dr. Griffith directed his online bank, Bank of America, to remit the payment to the insurer's program administrator. On July 25, Bank of America sent a check, drawn on J.P. Morgan Chase, to AMAIA which AMAIA received on July 30. In the meantime Dr. Griffith was killed in an accident on July 28. **HOLDING:** The issue on appeal was whether Dr. Griffith's life insurance policy was in effect on July 28, the date he died. The court noted that Williston "explains that the 'dispatch rule' [also referred to as "the mailbox rule" or the "postal acceptance rule"] applies equally to bilateral and unilateral contracts. If an offer for a unilateral contract calls for the performance of an act by the offeree that can be accomplished by sending money through the mail, including in the form of a check, 'as soon as the money is sent it would become the property of the offeror, and the offeror would become bound to perform its promise for which the money was the consideration.'" The court concluded that the "mailbox rule governing the time of formation of a contract by written acceptance" governs the issue of when Dr. Griffith's policy was reinstated. The court pointed out that this case "resembles a traditional acceptance by writing mailed to the offeror, in that a writing (the check) was 'sent' to AMAIA, even though its creation was directed electronically and it was created not by the offeree but by the bank . . . ." As of July 23, Dr. Griffith still had the power to reverse his instructions to the bank, but when Bank of America sent the check on July 25 to AMAIA "the permissible means for acceptance was in motion and, so far as is established by the common law mailbox rule, was beyond Dr. Griffith's power to stop. This would be true whether Bank of America sent the check through the United States Postal Service, a courier service, or otherwise." Thus Dr. Griffith's policy was reinstated as of July 25 and was in force when he died on July 28.

Section 5. Acceptance Varying Offer: Contract Formation and Contract Terms

(A) The Common Law Approach and the Mirror Image Rule Concepts

- Under the common law's "mirror-image rule," the acceptance must be on the exact terms proposed by the offer and, if it is not, it is a rejection of the offer and a counter-offer to the original offer.

- A counter-offer is distinguishable from an unqualified acceptance which is accompanied by a proposal for a modification or for a separate agreement. For example, a mere inquiry regarding the possibility of different terms, a comment upon the terms or a request for a better offer is not necessarily a counter-offer.

(B) The "Battle of the Forms"

Concepts:

- Under UCC §2-207, a contract may be formed even though a definite and seasonable expression of acceptance or a written confirmation is sent within a reasonable time states additional or different terms from the offer. The issue under UCC §2-207 in many cases is not whether a contract was formed, but what are its terms.

(C) UCC §2-207: Transcending the Mirror Image Rule

FRAMEWORK FOR ANALYSIS: "Battle of the Forms" Recap

Working through a Code provision means beginning at the top and proceeding step by step.

ASK:

1. Is there a "definite and seasonable expression of acceptance" or a written confirmation which is sent within a reasonable time?

   Section 2-207 varies the "mirror-image rule." It treats a party's definite and seasonable expression of acceptance which contains terms that are "additional to or different from" those in the other party's offer as an acceptance and not a counteroffer. However, there must be agreement on the essential "dickered terms" (such as quantity) or the purported acceptance will not be considered an "expression of acceptance" and the inquiry ends here. (*Dorton v. Collins & Aikman Corp.*)

2. If there is a definite expression of acceptance, a contract is formed *unless* acceptance is "expressly made conditional" on assent to the additional or different terms contained in the acceptance. UCC §2-207(1)

   Note: The "expressly made conditional" proviso in UCC §2-207(1) does not apply to the written confirmation situation but only to the "expression of acceptance."

   Assuming that there is an acceptance and therefore a contract was formed or there was a timely written confirmation, then as to any terms stated in the acceptance or confirmation that are additional to those offered or agreed upon, proceed to Step 3a and if the acceptance or written confirmation contains any different terms from those contained in the offer or that were agreed upon, proceed to Step 3b.

3. What is to be done with additional or different terms? UCC §2-207(2)

   a. The additional terms are considered "proposals for addition" to the contract:

      (1) if one or both of the parties are consumers, the additional terms are excluded from the contract, unless expressly agreed to.

      (2) if the parties are merchants, such terms become part of the contract unless:

         (a) the offer expressly limited acceptance to the terms of the offer;

(b) they materially alter it; (*Step-Saver Data Systems, Inc. v. Wyse Technology*); or

(c) notification of objection to them was already given or given within a reasonable time after notice of them is received.

b. There is a problem with what to do with different terms since UCC §2-207(2) speaks only of "additional" terms. (*Northrop Corp. v. Litronic Industries*)

Courts vary in their treatment of different terms in the acceptance or confirmation:

(1) One approach treats different terms the same as additional terms and applies UCC §2-207(2) to different terms;

(2) A second approach simply disregards different terms contained in the acceptance since they are not mentioned in UCC §2-207(2);

(3) A third approach applies the "knock out" rule where the conflicting terms on the parties' forms "knock each other out" and neither term becomes part of the contract. What is left are the terms on which the two writings do not conflict; the contract, therefore, consists of the terms on which the forms agree.

4. If there is no definite expression of acceptance, then there is no contract formed under UCC §2-207(1); however, there may be conduct by both parties which recognizes the existence of a contract and this is sufficient to establish one under UCC §2-207(3). (*Itoh & Co. Inc. v. Jordan Int'l Co.*) (See Step 5)

5. Conduct: UCC §2-207(3)

If no contract is formed through UCC §2-207(1), then ask: does the conduct of both parties "recognize the existence of a contract"? If the answer is "yes," then under UCC §2-207(3), a contract of sale is established. For example, the goods may have been shipped, accepted, and paid for before a dispute arises and there is no question that a contract has been formed by the parties' conduct.

If a contract is formed by conduct under UCC §2-207(3), the next question to ask is: what are the terms of the contract? Here, under UCC §2-207(3), the terms of the particular contract consist of those terms on which the writings of the parties agree together with the UCC's supplementary terms.

CASES	SUMMARIES
Dorton v. Collins & Aikman Corp. (1972) →(CB pg. 206)	**FACTS:** Dorton, d/b/a as the Carpet Mart (CM), bought carpets from Collins & Aikman (C&A) over a three year period and involving 55 transactions. CM would telephone orders to C&A and C&A would then send CM an acknowledgement form that stated that its acceptance was "subject to" the terms on the reverse side — one of which was an arbitration provision. When CM learned from customer complaints that some of the carpets were lower quality than it had paid for, it brought suit in court for damages. C&A moved for a stay of the court action, claiming that CM was bound to arbitrate its claim based on the arbitration provision in C&A's acknowledgement forms. The lower court held that there was no binding arbitration

CASES	SUMMARIES
Dorton, continued	agreement. However, it did not decide whether C&A's acknowledgment forms were acceptances of CM's oral orders or confirmations of a prior agreement between C&A and CM. Nor did the lower court decide whether CM's oral orders embodied an arbitration provision. **HOLDING:** On appeal, the Sixth Circuit discussed the changes made by UCC §2-207 to the common law mirror image rule and that "under Subsection (1), a contract is recognized notwithstanding the fact that an acceptance or confirmation contains terms additional to or different from those of the offer or prior agreement, provided that the offeree's intent to accept the offer is definitely expressed . . . and provided that the offeree's acceptance is not expressly conditioned on the offeror's assent to the additional or different terms." Assuming the acknowledgment forms were acceptances, the court noted that the words "subject to" in the acknowledgment forms were not sufficient to bring the case within the "unless" proviso of Section 2-207 (1) because the proviso "was intended to apply to an acceptance which clearly reveals that the offeree is unwilling to proceed with the transaction unless he is assured of the offeror's assent to the additional or different terms therein." (citation omitted) Thus, if the acknowledgments were acceptances and if the arbitration provision was not embodied in CM's oral orders then the arbitration provision would be an additional term to CM's oral orders and because both parties were merchants the arbitration provision would become part of the parties' agreement unless it was a material alteration. On the other hand, if the acknowledgment forms were confirmations of the parties' prior agreement — and not acceptances — a similar analysis would be required. Thus, if the acknowledgment forms were confirmations of prior agreements and the arbitration provision was not part of the parties' prior agreements then the arbitration provision would be an additional term and because both parties were merchants, the arbitration provision would become part of the parties' agreements unless it was a material alteration. In sum, on remand, whether the lower court found that the acknowledgment form was an acceptance of CM's oral orders and that such orders had no arbitration provision or a confirmation of the parties' prior oral agreement, the arbitration clause in the acknowledgment forms would be treated as an additional term which would become part of the agreements if the lower court determined that it was not a material alteration.
***C. Itoh & Co. (America) Inc. v. Jordan Int'l Co.* (1977)** →(CB pg. 210)	**FACTS:** Itoh sent Jordan a purchase order for steel coils. In return, Jordan sent back its acknowledgment form containing a clause making its acceptance "expressly conditional" on Itoh's assent to the additional or different terms in its form. One of the terms on Jordan's acknowledgment was an arbitration clause which was not on Itoh's purchase order. The form also stated that the buyer should notify the seller at once if the terms were not acceptable. Itoh never responded because of the "expressly made conditional" clause that no contract would be formed unless Itoh assented to the additional terms in Jordan's acknowledgment. **HOLDING:** The court found while the parties' exchange of forms did not result in a contract, their subsequent performance created one under UCC §2-207(3) because it consisted of conduct by both parties which recognized the existence of a contract.

CASES	SUMMARIES
C. Itoh, continued	The parties' contract would then consist of those terms on which the writings of the parties agreed, together with supplementary terms incorporated under any other UCC provisions. The question then became whether the arbitration provision would be considered one of the Code's "supplementary terms" so as to become part of the parties' agreement. The court found that the "supplementary terms" contemplated by the Code were limited to the standard "gap fillers" which do not include an arbitration provision and so the arbitration provision did not become part of the contract formed pursuant to UCC §2-207(3).
Bayway Refining Co. v. Oxygenated Marketing & Trading A.G. (2000) →(CB pg. 213)	**FACTS:** OMT offered to buy 60,000 barrels of petroleum from Bayway by fax. Bayway's acceptance contained the additional term that OMT, buyer, would pay Bayway, seller, any taxes that Bayway had to pay with respect to the goods because OMT lacked a tax exemption. OMT did not object to Bayway's acceptance or to the addition of the tax clause. Bayway delivered the 60,000 barrels and the transaction created a tax liability which Bayway paid. OMT refused to reimburse Bayway. Bayway sued and the district court held that the tax clause had become part of the parties' agreement under UCC §2-207(2). **HOLDING:** On appeal, the court held that in a "battle of the forms" case, the party opposing the inclusion of an additional term bears the burden of proof that the term was material. After considering the distinction between material and immaterial terms as well as "surprise" and "hardship," the court found that the tax clause was not a material alteration so OMT was required to pay Bayway. The court proceeded through the analysis as follows: first, under UCC §2-207(1), Bayway's acceptance was effective to form a contract even though it stated an additional term, the tax clause, because the acceptance was not conditional on OMT's acceptance of the additional term. Under UCC §2-207(2), the tax clause was a proposal for an additional term. Since both parties were merchants, the tax clause is presumed to become a contract term unless one of the enumerated exceptions applies. Since OMT claimed that the tax clause fell within §2-207(2)(b) as a material alteration and thus did not become a contract term, OMT had the burden of showing that adding the tax clause was a material alteration of the contract. A material alteration is one that would "result in surprise or hardship if incorporated without express awareness by the other party." (UCC §2-207 cmt. 4) Although there are certain terms which would be considered a material alteration as a matter of law, i.e., the addition of an arbitration clause in New York, the court did not find the tax clause to be a material alteration because the clause was limited to the tax payable on a specific sale of goods. The court also found that the clause did not result in surprise or hardship for OMT. With respect to "surprise," the court stated that there is a subjective element — the parties actual knowledge — and an objective element — what the party should have known. To prove surprise, "a party must establish that, under the circumstances, it cannot be presumed that a reasonable merchant would have consented to the additional term." Here, OMT was subjectively surprised but it failed to prove objective surprise since it introduced no evidence that the tax clause would surprise a reasonable petroleum merchant. Further, Bayway introduced evidence showing that the tax clause is the custom in the petroleum

CASES	SUMMARIES
Bayway, continued	industry. With respect to "hardship," the court questioned whether hardship was an independent ground to support a finding of material alteration and noted that some courts have held that hardship is not a criterion of material alteration. In any event, the court did not decide whether hardship is an independent ground since OMT did not raise any genuine factual issue as to hardship. Among other things, the court said that any hardship was self-inflicted because OMT could have avoided the effects of the tax clause by registering for the tax exemption which it did not do.
Northrop Corp. v. Litronic Industries (1994) →(CB pg. 218)	**FACTS:** Litronic offered to sell printed circuit boards to Northrop, a defense company. The offer contained a 90-day warranty in lieu of all other warranties. Northrop's return invoice had an unlimited warranty. After 90 days, Northrop tried to return some of the boards as defective and Litronic refused to accept them, claiming the warranty period had passed. The question was how to treat "different" terms in the acceptance when the language of UCC §2-207(2) speaks only of "additional" terms. **HOLDING:** The court identified three approaches to the problem: first, the "knock-out rule" where the conflicting terms in the offer and acceptance knock each other out and do not become part of the contract; second, where the offeree's different terms are disregarded and the terms in the offer control; and, third, where "different" terms are treated the same as "additional" terms. After reviewing these approaches, the court adopted the "knockout rule" (which is the majority approach and the one the court believed Illinois would adopt) and affirmed the lower court's judgment for Northrop. The lower court had found that the parties' conflicting warranty terms canceled each other out and were replaced by a UCC gap-filler. It then proceeded to section UCC §2-309 which provides that nonconforming goods may be rejected within a "reasonable" time and held that the six months that Northrop took to reject Litronic's boards was a reasonable time because of the complexity of the required testing.
Step-Saver Data Systems, Inc. v. Wyse Technology (1991) →(CB pg. 221)	**FACTS:** Step-Saver placed orders for software programs over the phone with The Software Link (TSL) and TSL would accept and promise to ship the goods promptly. After the phone order, Step-Saver would send a purchase order identifying the items to be purchased, their price, shipping, and payment terms. TSL would ship the order of software along with an invoice which contained similar terms as the purchase order. Neither the phone calls, purchase orders, nor the invoices mentioned a disclaimer of warranties. However, the software packages shipped by TSL contained additional terms printed on the package of each copy of the program ("box-top license"). One of these additional terms was a disclaimer of warranties. The license also stated that opening the package would indicate acceptance of the terms and if a person did not agree with them, then they could return the package unopened for a refund. Step-Saver resold the software to other companies and was sued when there were problems with the software. Step-Saver brought suit against TSL for breach of warranty and sought indemnity for costs in resolving its customers' suits.

CASES	SUMMARIES
Step-Saver, continued	**HOLDING:** The district court held that the box-top license was the final and complete expression of the parties' agreement. The Ct of Appeals disagreed and reversed and remanded the warranty claims for further consideration. It found that since the parties' performance showed the existence of a contract, the dispute was over its terms and not its existence. In applying UCC §2-207(1), the court found that the box-top license was not a conditional acceptance because TSL did not clearly express its unwillingness to proceed unless its additional terms were made part of the agreement. The court then considered whether the additional terms became part of the deal through the parties' repeated transactions. The court found that TSL's unilateral act of repeatedly sending copies of the box-top license did not establish a course of dealing that adopted the terms. Finally, the court held the box-top license to be a written confirmation with additional terms which, under UCC §2-207(2), did not become part of the agreement because, assuming that there were warranties in the parties' original agreement, the boxtop license disclaimer of warranties materially altered the agreement.
ProCD, Inc. v. Zeidenberg (1996) →(CB pg. 227)	**FACTS:** The buyer, Zeidenberg, purchased ProCD's software in a retail computer store and paid for it at the checkout counter. There was a statement on the outside of every software box that the sale was subject to license terms that were inside the box. The license limited use of the program to non-commercial purposes; this license was encoded on the CD-ROM disks, printed in the manual, and appeared on the user's screen every time the software ran. Zeidenberg ignored the license and formed a company to resell the information at a price less than ProCD was charging its commercial customers. ProCD brought suit seeking an injunction against further dissemination that exceeded the rights in the license. Zeidenberg claimed and the district court held that placing the software on the store shelf was the "offer" which the customer "accepted" by paying the price and leaving the store with the goods. Since the terms of the shrink-wrap license were inside the box, they were not known to the buyer and therefore the district court held that the purchaser did not agree to the license terms at the time of purchase. **HOLDING:** On appeal, the court speaking through Judge Easterbrook, held that Zeidenberg was bound by the shrinkwrap license included with the software when he used the software after an opportunity to read the terms and to reject them by returning the product. In reaching its decision, the court treated the license as an ordinary contract accompanying the sale of goods and governed by the common law of contracts and the UCC. It also concluded, without discussion, that UCC §2-207 was irrelevant in this case since there was "only one form" and instead relied on UCC §2-204(1). The court found that ProCD proposed a contract that a buyer would accept by using the software after having an opportunity to read the license terms and to reject them by returning the goods. Zeidenberg could have rejected the product if the license terms were unsatisfactory to him but he did not and therefore he was bound.

CASES	SUMMARIES
ProCD, Inc., continued	**QUESTIONS TO THINK ABOUT:** *Doesn't UCC §2-207 (1) speak of a "written confirmation" which is singular and Comment 1 refer to a situation where "one or both of the parties" send a confirmation?* *Can a party agree to unknown terms where the printed terms on the outside of the software box indicate that the sale was subject to license terms inside the box?*
Hill v. Gateway 2000, Inc. (1997) →(CB pg. 230)	**FACTS:** The Hills ordered a computer over the phone. The box arrived with the computer and a list of terms which were said to become part of the contract unless the customer returned the computer within 30 days. These terms had not been read to the customer over the phone. One of the terms was an arbitration clause requiring all disputes to be settled by arbitration. The Hills claimed that this clause did not stand out and that while they noticed that there was a statement of terms, they denied reading it closely enough to find the arbitration clause. They kept the computer more than 30 days before complaining about its performance. When the Hills brought suit in federal court, Gateway asked for the arbitration provision to be enforced. The judge refused and Gateway appealed. **HOLDING:** The court found that the contract was not concluded over the phone but, as in ProCD, after the customer had received the goods and had a chance to inspect them and kept them. Because the Hills kept the computer beyond the 30 days, they had accepted Gateway's offer and were bound by the arbitration provision. According to the court, why wasn't it acceptance when the Hills paid for the computer? Court says this is not the only way to form a contract. Here, the contract was not formed in the store with the payment of money or over the phone but after the customer had a chance to inspect the item and the terms. Further, the court noted that the Hills knew before ordering the computer that the shipping carton would include some important terms since Gateway's ads state that their products come with limited warranties. Since the Hills did not try to determine what these terms were in advance of delivery or within 30 days thereafter, the Hill's accepted Gateway's offer, including the arbitration clause. **QUESTION TO THINK ABOUT:** *When is the contract formed? What is the act of acceptance? Is it when you pay for the goods and walk out of the store with them? Or is it when you get them home and have time to open the box and study its contents?*

Section 6. Precontractual Liability

Concepts:

- Generally, parties have the freedom to negotiate and may break off negotiations without liability at any time for any or no reason without the risk of precontractual liability except for option contracts and firm offers. Under the basic rules of offer and acceptance, contractual liability is not incurred until a contract is formed by the acceptance of an offer.

- Liability for unbargained for promises made during precontractual negotiations may be based on a theory of promissory estoppel.

- Promissory estoppel: there are some promises which, although the promisor makes them without bargaining for anything in return, nonetheless induce the promisee to rely to her detriment. In such circumstances, recovery may be available on a reliance basis. (*Hoffman v. Red Owl Stores*)

- Requests for bids: unless the parties have agreed otherwise, where a subcontractor submits a bid to a general contractor for use by the general contractor in computing his overall bid for the award of a construction contract, the subcontractor's bid is irrevocable until the general contractor has had a reasonable opportunity to notify the subcontractor of the award and accept the subcontractor's bid. This is based on a reliance theory. (*Drennan v. Star Paving Co.*) R2d §87(2) ill. 6

FRAMEWORK FOR ANALYSIS: Is there a claim based on promissory estoppel (R2d §90)?

ASK: Are the elements for promissory estoppel satisfied?

- **Promise** — has a promise been made? Did the promisor use clear and definite language such that a reasonable person in the position of the promisee would be justified in believing a commitment had been made?

- **Foreseeability of Reliance** — did the promisor have reason to expect the promisee to rely on the promise?

- **Justified Reliance** — did the promise induce actual reliance and was the reliance justified?

- **Avoiding Injustice** — are the circumstances such that injustice can be avoided only by enforcement of the promise?

- **Recovery may be limited** — what is the appropriate form of relief? The remedy may be limited as justice requires. This means that the promisee may not receive full contractual relief which would include expectation damages but may be limited to reimbursement of the actual loss expended in reliance on the promise.

With respect to letters of intent, ask:

- Have the parties reached agreement on the material terms of the final agreement?

- Did the parties obligate themselves to negotiate in good faith?

- What did the parties intend by the letter? Did they intend to be bound or is it an "agreement to agree" which means that it is open to negotiations?

- When do the parties intend to be bound? Is it before there is a formal, signed agreement or not until the agreement is reduced to a final formal writing?

CASES	SUMMARIES
Hoffman v. Red Owl Stores (1965) →(CB pg. 236)	**FACTS:** Hoffman, a bakery owner, sought a franchise from Red Owl Stores which owned a supermarket chain. A representative of Red Owl assured Hoffman that he would be able to get a franchise if he took steps to get experience and that it would be possible with the $18,000 Hoffman had to invest was sufficient. Over the course of more than two years, Hoffman took the following actions on assurances of a franchise from a Red Owl representative: Hoffman sold his bakery business, acquired and sold a small grocery store to gain experience, put $1,000 down on a lot selected by Red Owl in Chilton, paid rent on a house in Chilton, and spent $140 to move his family to Neenah at Red Owl's suggestion that he get experience by working at a Red Owl store there. Negotiations collapsed when Hoffman refused to agree to a proposed financial statement that would show his contribution to be $34,000, including a $13,000 gift from his father-in-law. Hoffman brought suit to recover his expenses and the jury awarded him damages which the trial court confirmed, except for the $16,735 for the sale of the Wautoma grocery store as to which the trial court ordered a new trial. Red Owl appealed. **HOLDING:** On appeal, the court considered whether a cause of action for promissory estoppel required that the promise contain all the essential details of the proposed transactions so as to be the equivalent of an offer. It concluded that R2d §90 did not impose this requirement and that "injustice would result here if plaintiffs were not granted some relief because of the failure of defendants to keep their promises which induced plaintiffs to act to their detriment." The court noted that where damages are awarded in promissory estoppel, they should be limited to those "necessary to prevent injustice." The court further concluded that the trial court's award of damages was proper. With respect to the sale of the Wautoma store, justice did not require Hoffman to receive damages that exceed any actual loss as measured by the difference between the sales price and the fair market value when they sold the Wautoma grocery story at Red Owl's behest. Since the evidence did not support the large award of damages from this sale, the trial court properly ordered a new trial on this issue.
Dixon v. Wells Fargo, N.A. (2011) →(CB pg. 241)	**FACTS:** Based on the doctrine of promissory estoppel, the Dixons, homeowners, brought suit against Wells Fargo which held the mortgage on the Dixons' home, seeking to enjoin Wells Fargo from foreclosing on the mortgage. Wells Fargo moved to dismiss the complaint. From the Dixons' complaint and statements in opposition, it appeared that the Dixons alleged that Wells Fargo promised the Dixons to engage in negotiations for a modification of their mortgage loan if the Dixons stopped paying the mortgage and provided certain financial information, that the Dixons did so in reasonable reliance on Wells Fargo's promise to consider them for a loan modification, and that the bank took advantage of the Dixons' default and instituted foreclosure proceedings against them. The question was whether these allegations were sufficient to state a claim for promissory estoppel.

CASES	SUMMARIES
Dixon, continued	**HOLDING:** The court noted that in MA a promissory estoppel claim must be based on a promise that is definite and certain in its terms to the same extent as an offer. However, the court also pointed out that MA law adopted R2d §90, the promissory estoppel doctrine, which does not require the promise to meet the requirements of an offer — nowhere in the comments of R2d §90 or in R2d §2 which defines the word "promise" is there an express indication that the promise must meet the requirements of an offer. Rather, the Restatement "expressly approved" the use of promissory estoppel to protect a party's reliance on indefinite promises. The court recognized this tension in MA law between insistence that a promise be definite with its adoption of the Restatement's more relaxed standard for the word "promise"; it explained that MA case law shows that an indefinite promise during preliminary negotiations may be enforced where the promisor's words or conduct was designed to take advantage of the promisee. Here, Wells Fargo persuaded the Dixons that they had to stop mortgage payments in order to be eligible for a loan modification. By exposing the Dixons to a foreclosure proceeding, Wells Fargo gained an advantage. As a matter of fair dealing, the bank's promise to consider a loan modification if the Dixons stopped mortgage payments and submitted certain financial information, necessarily included a commitment not to foreclose. Wells Fargo's conduct in foreclosing without warning after opportunistically stringing the Dixons along, called for the application of promissory estoppel. In sum, the court held that the complaint stated a promissory estoppel claim because the complaint's allegations, if proven, would show that "Wells Fargo promised to engage in negotiating a loan modification if the Dixons defaulted on their payments and provided certain financial information, and they did so in reasonable reliance on that promise, only to learn that the bank had taken advantage of their default status by initiating foreclosure proceedings." As to the measure of recovery, the court said that the Dixons' damages would be limited "to the value of their expenditures in reliance on Wells Fargo's promise."
Cyberchron Corp. v. Calldata Systems Development, Inc. (1995) →(CB pg. 247)	**FACTS:** Cyberchron, a hardware developer, entered into negotiations with Calldata, a subsidiary of Grumman, to provide computer equipment ("Equipment") for Grumman's defense contract with the Marine Corps. After lengthy negotiations, Grumman delivered a Purchase Order dated 5/15/90 to Cyberchron which identified the disputed terms regarding the weight of the Equipment (145 lbs) and severe penalties for exceeding that weight. While Cyberchron never agreed to these terms, a Grumman representative urged Cyberchron to proceed with production as if there had been agreement on the weight and the terms of the Purchase Order would be resolved later. By letter dated 6/26/90, "Grumman 'insisted' that Cyberchron continue to perform its 'contractually binding obligations' under the Purchase Order." Cyberchron produced some of the Equipment but none was ever delivered nor was any payment made. The parties never reached agreement and Calldata requested Cyberchron to show cause within 10 days why the Purchase Order should not be terminated. Calldata rejected Cyberchron's response and terminated the Purchase Order for default.

CASES	SUMMARIES
Cyberchron, continued	**HOLDING:** The district court found that no enforceable contract had been made because the parties never reached agreement on two essential terms: the Equipment weight and the weight penalties. However, Cyberchron was entitled to recover for out-of-pocket labor and material costs under a theory of promissory estoppel. On appeal, the Second Circuit noted that in New York, promissory estoppel requires (1) a clear and unambiguous promise (2) foreseeable reliance and injury caused by the reliance. Sometimes, as the district court said, an "unconscionable injury" is required. The Second Circuit relied on the district court's assessment that Grumman's conduct of putting great pressure on Cyberchron to produce the Equipment and then abruptly terminating the transaction to purchase heavier, inferior equipment at a later date from another company was unconscionable.
	The Second Circuit affirmed the district court's judgment allowing recovery on a promissory estoppel theory but vacated the judgment and remanded for a redetermination of damages. The court rejected a promissory estoppel recovery for the period prior to mid-July-1990 when Grumman made a clear and unambiguous promise but acknowledged that recovery for reasonable overhead costs would be recoverable "when it is shown that there is a demonstrable past history of ongoing business operations, without requiring proof that a specific alternative project would have absorbed the overhead costs at issue." The court also held that shutdown costs might be recoverable even though they were incurred after termination of negotiations to the extent the costs were incurred due to reliance on Calldata's promises.
Channel Home Centers, Division of Grace Retail Corp. v. Grossman (1986) →(CB pg. 252)	**FACTS:** On 12/11/84, Channel, a home improvement store chain, executed a letter of intent to lease a store location in a mall from Grossman, a real estate broker and developer. The letter included terms that Grossman would withdraw the premises from the rental market and negotiate a final lease agreement with Channel. Grossman signed the letter of intent and claimed that Channel orally agreed to submit a draft lease within 30 days. Channel denied making such a promise. Thereafter, both parties took actions toward satisfying the lease conditions, such as: (1) Channel directed its legal department to prepare a lease, obtained measurements for renovations and construction, and developed marketing and building plans; and (2) Grossman applied for permits to erect commercial signs for Channel and other mall tenants. By 1/25/85, Grossman was showing the property to Channel's competitor. On 2/6/85, Grossman notified Channel that negotiations regarding the lease were terminated due to Channel's failure to submit a signed and mutually acceptable lease within the 30 days of the 12/11/84 letter of intent.
	HOLDING: Channel argued that the letter, together with the surrounding circumstances, formed a binding agreement to negotiate in good faith. By unilaterally terminating negotiations and entering into an agreement with Mr. Good Buys, Channel argues that Grossman acted in bad faith and breached his promise in the letter of intent to withdraw the store from the market and negotiate a lease to completion. Grossman claimed that the promise to negotiate in good faith to reach a written agreement was enforceable only if the parties had in fact reached agreement on the underlying transaction. Grossman further argued that even if the agreement

CASES	SUMMARIES
Channel Home Centers, continued	were an otherwise enforceable contract, the letter of intent was unenforceable because it lacked consideration. The court found that the "parties intended to enter into a binding agreement to negotiate in good faith." It further found that Grossman's promise to withdraw the store from the rental market and negotiate the lease to completion was sufficiently definite to be enforceable. The court also found consideration to support the agreement to negotiate a lease in good faith because execution of the letter of intent had substantial value to Grossman for obtaining financing for his purchase of the mall. **QUESTION TO THINK ABOUT:** *Should the letter of intent also be enforced under the doctrine of promissory estoppel?*

Section 7. The Requirement of Definiteness

Concepts:

- The terms of an offer must be reasonably certain in order for it to be accepted. R2d §33(1); UCC §2-204

- Terms are reasonably certain "if they provide a basis for determining the existence of a breach and for giving an appropriate remedy." R2d §33(2); UCC §2-204

- If one or more terms of a proposed agreement are left open or uncertain, it may show that a manifestation of intent to enter into an agreement is not intended. R2d §33(3); UCC §2-204

- An offer which appears to be indefinite may be given precision by usage of trade or by course of dealing between the parties. R2d §33 cmt. a

- Under UCC §2-204(3), a contract for the sale of goods does not fail for indefiniteness even if one or more terms are left open "if the parties have intended to make a contract and there is a reasonably certain basis for giving an appropriate remedy." See also R2d cmt. a

FRAMEWORK FOR ANALYSIS: Is the agreement sufficiently definite to be enforced?

ASK: Are the terms sufficiently clear and definite so that a court could determine what the parties intended and fix damages in the event of breach? In making this determination, ask:

- Does the contract contain such significant and essential terms as the parties to the contract, the subject matter of the contract, the time for performance, and the price to be paid?

■ If such essential terms are missing or vague, then the offer may fail for indefiniteness unless it can be cured. Even if some terms have been left open, it may still be possible to meet the requirement for definiteness by the time for performance arrives. Ask the following:

- Can the indefinite term be cured by the conduct of the parties through full or part performance? R2d §34
- Can the missing term(s) be implied from the usages of trade, by a prior course of dealing between the parties, or by a course of performance between them after the agreement?
- In a sale of goods, can the missing term(s) be cured by the court with a UCC "gap filler"?

CASES	SUMMARIES
Toys, Inc. v. F.M. Burlington Co. (1990) →(CB pg. 259)	**FACTS:** Burlington, a mall owner, entered into a five-year lease with Toys, Inc., a retailer. The lease gave Toys an option to renew for an additional five years if Toys gave written notice of its intent to exercise the option one year before the lease expired. The lease further provided that the "fixed minimum rental [for the renewal period] shall be renegotiated to the then prevailing rate within the mall." Toys provided timely written notice of its intent to renew; Burlington confirmed Toys exercise of the option and stated the then prevailing rate per square foot in the mall. Toys replied that it had a different understanding of the prevailing rate and a dispute arose. When negotiations over the next ten months failed to reach agreement, Burlington advised Toys that it was listing the location for rent. Toys moved out and sued for breach of contract. The trial court granted summary judgment for Toys, holding that the lease had created a binding option. Burlington appealed, claiming that the option was too indefinite. **HOLDING:** In affirming the lower court's decision, the appellate court stated that the test for determining whether an option agreement is enforceable is whether it contains "all material and essential terms to be incorporated in the subsequent agreement." However, the court noted that the option need not contain all the contract terms "as long as it contains a practicable, objective method of determining the essential terms." In this case, the language in the option agreement — "the then existing prevailing rate within the mall" — set forth a sufficiently definite means for determining the price term for the lease extension. Therefore, the option was not indefinite and thus enforceable. **QUESTIONS TO THINK ABOUT:** *What if the option provision stated that the rental for the renewal period shall in part be mutually agreed upon?* *Does such a provision at least impose on the parties an obligation to negotiate in good faith to reach an agreement?*
Oglebay Norton Co. v. Armco, Inc. (1990) →(CB pg. 266)	**FACTS:** Armco and Oglebay entered a long-term contract in 1957 requiring Oglebay to have adequate shipping capacity available and requiring Armco to use that capacity to ship its iron ore on the Great Lakes. The contract established a primary and a secondary price rate mechanism which called for the pricing to be established by the season's market rate as recognized by the leading iron ore shippers or if

CASES	SUMMARIES

Oglebay, continued

none, the parties "shall mutually agree upon a rate... taking into consideration the contract rate being charged for similar transportation by the leading independent vessel operators" in the region. The parties modified the contract four times over the next 23 years. After the fourth modification, which extended the agreement to 2010, Oglebay began a $95 million capital improvement program. After the 1984 shipping season, the parties were unable to reach agreement on a shipping rate. At this time, the iron ore business was in a downturn. In April 1986, Olgebay sought a declaratory judgment asking the court to declare the contract rate to be the correct rate or, in the absence of such rate, to declare a reasonable rate. Armco counterclaimed, asserting that the contract was unenforceable because the parties did not intend to be bound if their agreed-upon pricing mechanisms broke down. Armco argued that there was a breakdown of the primary pricing mechanism because after 1985 a new rate was not being published and there was breakdown of the secondary pricing mechanism because the information necessary to determine rates charged by leading independent vessel operators became impossible to obtain. The trial court issued a declaratory judgment which was affirmed by the court of appeals.

HOLDING: The case came before the Ohio Supreme Court and presented several issues: first, whether the parties intended to be bound, even upon the failure of the pricing mechanisms; second, if the parties did intend to be bound, whether the trial court could establish $6.25 per gross ton as a reasonable rate for the 1986 shipping season; and third, whether the trial court could continue to exercise its equitable jurisdiction over the parties and order them to use a mediator if they were unable to mutually agree on a shipping rate for each annual season.

The Ohio Supreme Court answered "yes" to all the questions. It found that the trial court recognized that the 1957 contract pricing mechanism failed. But the trial court concluded on the basis of credible evidence that the parties intended to be bound despite the failure of pricing mechanisms. The trial court relied on evidence that showed the parties had a long standing and close business relationship which included joint ventures, interlocking directorates, and Armco's ownership of Oglebay stock. The trial court also had authority to determine a reasonable rate for Oglebay's services during the 1986 shipping season because the parties intended to be bound. Finally, the trial court also had jurisdiction to order the parties to negotiate or, if negotiations failed, to proceed to mediation. Citing to R2d §362 which the court noted was similar in effect to R2d §33, the court stated that specific performance in this case was necessary because "the undisputed dramatic changes in the market prices of great lakes shipping rates and the length of the contract would make it impossible for a court to award Oglebay accurate damages due to Armco's breach of the contract."

QUESTION TO THINK ABOUT: *Is the court supplying an intent which parties might never have intended?*

■ CHAPTER 3. STATUTES OF FRAUDS

Section 1. Introduction

Concepts:

- While oral agreements may be as binding as written ones, certain classes of agreements are said to "fall within the statute of frauds"; such agreements are unenforceable unless there is a note or memorandum signed by the party to be charged or the agreement falls within an exception to the statute.

- Typically, a defense based on the statute of frauds is raised at the beginning of litigation by a motion to dismiss or later by a motion for summary judgment.

- An oral modification of a written agreement may itself fall within the statute of frauds, in which case its requirements must be met for the modification to be enforceable.

(A) What a Statute of Frauds Does and Does Not Do

FRAMEWORK FOR ANALYSIS: Is there a statute of frauds question?

The starting point for any statute of frauds analysis is determining whether there was a contract. "The statute of frauds requires that a contract be in writing to be enforceable, not to exist in the first place." →(CB pg. 274)

ASK: Was there a contract? If so, then the next question is whether the contract falls within the statute of frauds where a writing is required.

ASK: What type of contract is it?

- Is it a contract for the sale of an interest in land? (*the land contract provision*) R2d §110(1)(d)

- This provision pertains to any agreement with a promise to buy or transfer an interest in land.

- Is it a contract for the sale of goods for $500 or more? (*the sale of goods provision*) R2d §110(2)(a)

- Is it a contract that is not to be performed within a year of its making? (the one-year provision) R2d §110(1) (e). This provision refers to a contract where performance cannot possibly be completed within one year of its making; a contract of indefinite or uncertain duration does not fall within the statute of frauds. (*C.R. Klewin, Inc. v. Flagship Properties, Inc.*)

- Is it a contract to answer for the duty of another? (*the suretyship provision*) R2d §110(1)(b). This provision refers to a suretyship agreement. It covers a promise made by one who is not presently liable for the debt to a creditor to discharge the present or future obligations of a third person (the present debtor).

- Is it a contract made upon consideration of marriage? (*the marriage provision*) R2d §110(1)(c). This provision does not apply to mutual promises to marry but covers prenuptial agreements or contracts entered into in anticipation of the marriage in which some property settlement or other financial arrangement is made in consideration of the upcoming marriage.

- Is it a contract of an executor or administrator to answer for a duty of his decedent? (*the executor-administrator provision*) R2d §110(1)(a)

Note: The requirements of the statute apply separately so that if more than one requirement applies to a single contract, then all must be met.

If the answer is "yes" to any of the above, then ask:

- Is there a writing(s) that satisfies the statute of frauds? The writing(s) must meet the statutory requirements regarding form and content—unless an exception applies. See Section 3. Satisfying the Statute of Frauds.

(B) Background

(C) Why a Statute of Frauds?

Section 2. Scope

(A) Duration of Performance: The One-Year and Lifetime Clauses

Concepts:

- The one-year provision covers only those contracts whose performance cannot possibly be completed within a year.

- In measuring the one-year period, the two points of reference are the time of the making of the contract—not the time performance begins—and the time when performance is to be completed.

- The one-year provision does not apply to a contract that will be fully performed on the happening of an event that may possibly occur within the one-year period or to contracts of uncertain duration. (*C.R. Klewin, Inc. v. Flagship Properties, Inc.*) R2d §130 cmt. a

- "Lifetime Agreements" do not fall within the statute of frauds: because we may die at any time, a lifetime agreement may be performed in full within a year. For example, the one-year provision does not apply to a promise by A to work for B "for the rest of A's life," whereas the one-year provision is applicable to a promise by A to work for B for five years.

- Full performance on one side may take an agreement out of the one-year provision. R2d §130(2)

- A state may have a statute of frauds provision barring enforcement of a promise not to be performed during the promisor's lifetime. (*Monarco v. Lo Greco*).

CASES	SUMMARIES
C.R. Klewin, Inc. v. Flagship Properties, Inc. (1991) →(CB pg. 281)	**FACTS:** Flagship, a real estate developer, orally agreed to hire Klewin as the construction manager for a major project which was expected to take from three to ten years to complete. Klewin completed the first phase of the project but Flagship had become dissatisfied with Klewin's work and replaced him. Klewin sued Flagship for breach of contract. The district court granted summary judgment for Flagship, finding that the contract was unenforceable. The court reasoned that the contract was not of an indefinite duration and, as a matter of law, could not possibly have been performed within one year. Klewin appealed and the US Ct of Appeals sent certified questions to the CT Supreme Court. The issues were: (1) whether the statute of frauds one-year provision was applicable to an oral contract that failed to specify explicitly the time for performance because it was a contract of "indefinite duration" and (2) whether an oral contract falls within the statute when the contract contemplates performance over a time period exceeding one year but does not explicitly negate possible performance within a year. **HOLDING:** The Supreme Court of CT found for Klewin, holding that an oral contract for the construction of twenty industrial buildings, a hotel and convention center, and housing for hundreds of students and teachers was not within the statute where the "contract itself does not explicitly negate the possibility of performance within one year." It did not matter how long completion of performance would actually take. The Supreme Court of CT reasoned that an oral contract that does not state in express terms that performance is to have a specific duration beyond one year is, as a matter of law, equivalent to a contract of indefinite duration and therefore does not fall within the statute of frauds.

(B) Interests in Real Property

Concepts:

- The land contract provision covers contracts "to transfer to any person any interest in land" R2d §125(1) and contracts "to buy any interest in land." R2d §125(2)

- The phrase "contracts for the sale of land" covers more than just a basic contract to sell real estate: it covers all agreements that have the effect of conveying any interest in real property.

- An "interest in land" covers "any right, privilege, power or immunity, or combination thereof." R2d §127. The test of what is an interest in land is generally furnished by property law. R2d §127 cmt. a

- Some examples of "interests in land" include ownership of the land, mortgages, present and future interests, and leases. Most legislatures have carved out exceptions for short-term leases of real property, often limited to leases for residential purposes.

(C) The Suretyship Clause

Concepts:

- A suretyship contract is one in which one person is made liable for the obligations of another. The person liable for the obligations of another person is the *surety* and the person with whom the surety shares the obligation is the *principal*. Both the surety and the principal are liable to the *obligee* for the same performance. However, the obligee can get no more than one performance from the two obligors.

- A promisor who agrees to take on the debt of another is *not* a surety in the following two situations:

  1. When there is a "novation": here, the promisor takes the place of the principal instead of just guaranteeing that the principal will perform. If the obligee agrees to accept this substitution of one party for another, then the principal's duty under the contract is discharged and a novation has occurred.

  2. When " the third party directly enters into a contract with the obligee to pay for a benefit that the obligee will give to the recipient." →**(CB pg. 293)** Here, there is no agreement to pay the debt of another because the promisor's liability is original and not collateral. For example, suppose that Steve entered into a contract with Chrysler to pay for a car for Steve's nephew, Ben. Here, Steve is not agreeing to pay the debt of another but his own—Steve is the only one who ever had an obligation to Chrysler.

- An exception to the suretyship provision is the "main purpose" rule. This is where the surety's main purpose in making the promise is to benefit herself. Even where the promise is collateral ("I'll pay if X doesn't"), if it appears that the promisor's primary purpose in guaranteeing the obligation of another was to secure her own monetary or business advantage, the promise is enforceable even though it is not in writing. R2d §116 (*Central Ceilings, Inc. v. National Amusements, Inc.*)

CASES	SUMMARIES
Langman v. Alumni Association of the University of Virginia (1994) →**(CB pg. 295)**	**FACTS:** Langman, among others, gifted certain commercial property to the Alumni Association (AA). The gift was made by giving AA a deed which contained a provision whereby AA assumed payment of the existing mortgage and agreed to hold the grantors harmless from any liability on the mortgage. Although AA assumed the obligation to pay the mortgage, the mortgagor did not release the grantors from their existing obligation to pay the mortgage. When Langman was required to pay part of the mortgage debt, she sued AA for reimbursement under the deed's assumption clause. The trial court held that AA did not have a clear understanding of the deed's contents and so there was "no meeting of the minds with respect to the debt." **HOLDING:** The court reversed on appeal. It noted that a grantee who accepts a deed, as AA did, is contractually obligated to perform any promise that the deed imposes on the grantee, including a promise to assume an existing mortgage. However, AA asserted it was not liable for the mortgage under Virginia's statute of frauds' suretyship provision which provides that a promise to pay the debt of another is not enforceable unless the promise is contained in a written note or memorandum signed

CASES	SUMMARIES

Langman, continued

by the party to be held liable on the promise. Since AA did not sign any writing assuming the mortgage, it claimed it was not liable. The court held that the surety-ship provision was not applicable because AA's promise was an original promise not a collateral one. The Virginia Supreme Court explained that a grantee who assumes an existing mortgage "makes no promise to the mortgagee to pay the debt of another, but promises the grantor (here Langman) to pay the mortgagee the debt the grantee (AA) owes to the grantor (Langman). This is an original undertaking." [In other words, AA made a promise directly to Langman to pay the mortgage—this is a promise to pay its (AA's) own debt—not a collateral promise to pay the debt of another namely Langman—and AA made no promise to the mortgagee, the creditor, to pay the mortgage if Langman defaulted on the mortgage which would have been a collateral promise or more particularly a promise by AA to pay the debt of another—Langman's debt to the mortgagee.]

Central Ceilings, Inc. v. National Amusements, Inc. (2007)

→(CB pg. 296)

FACTS: National Amusements ("National") was the owner of a projected theater complex on which Old Colony was the prime contractor and Central Ceilings ("Central") was a subcontractor doing carpentry and other work. Central was worried about being paid by Old Colony and asked National for a guarantee of payment which National gave orally at a July 1st meeting among Central, National, and Old Colony. Central continued work when National promised it would pay. However, when National finished paying Old Colony, it refused to pay Central. National claimed that its oral promise to Central that it would pay Central what Old Colony owed Central on the project was at best a promise to pay the debt of another and as such, was unenforceable under the Massachusetts Statute of Frauds because the promise was not in a writing signed by National. National contended that the July 1st oral agreement would be outside the statute of frauds only if it constituted a novation, namely if the agreement had released Old Colony from its obligation to Central and National took Old Colony's place as the obligor.

HOLDING: The court, however, applied the "leading object" or "main purpose" exception to the statute. Under this rule, an oral agreement which did not meet the requirements of a novation would nonetheless be enforceable "if the facts and circumstances of the transaction show that the promise was given primarily or solely to serve the promisor's own interest. . . ." The court said that "a property owner's [oral] promise to pay subcontractors or suppliers may, in appropriate circumstances, come within the 'leading object' exception to the Statute." The court then addressed the question of whether in the present case the facts were such as to bring the case within the "leading object" exception. The court noted that there was evidence that National wanted to open the theater by the end of August to capture the Labor Day weekend business opportunities; that, as of the beginning of July when the parties met, the work would have to be completed in a "tight time frame"; that Central was a prime contractor and that Central was one of the few subcontractors in Massachusetts that could do the work in the necessary time frame. Accordingly, the court concluded that the evidence was sufficient to establish that National's promise "was given to secure Central's continued and expedited performance at the Project and that the satisfaction of any obligation on the part of Old Colony was merely incidental to that promise."

Section 3. Satisfying the Statute of Frauds

(A) The Content of a Writing

Concepts:

- While the statute of frauds requires no particular form for a writing, it must be signed by the party to be charged with its enforcement and it must reflect the oral agreement with adequate specificity.

- Under R2d §131, a writing satisfies the requirements of the statute of frauds if it does the following with reasonable certainty:

  1. Identifies the parties to the contract.

  2. Shows that those parties entered into a contract.

  3. Sets forth the subject matter of the contract.

  4. States the essential terms of the contract.

- What is essential "depends on the agreement and its context and also on the subsequent conduct of the parties, including the dispute which arises and the remedy sought." R2d §131 cmt. g

- If the contract is for the sale of goods, see Section 4.

(B) Issues of Form

Concepts:

- The statute of frauds does not require a particular form for a writing as long as it satisfies the content requirements identified in Section A, above.

- The writing need not be contained in one document but can be pieced together from several related documents.

- It is sufficient to satisfy the statute of frauds if there is some form of a writing even if it appears on a napkin, as an internal memorandum, a document written for some other purpose, a check, or a series of separate writings, which when considered together, provide evidence of the parties' agreement. (*Crabtree v. Elizabeth Arden Sales Corp.*)

CASES	SUMMARIES

*Crabtree v.
Elizabeth Arden
Sales Corp. (1953)*

→(CB pg. 303)

FACTS: Miss Elizabeth Arden, president of defendant Elizabeth Arden Sales Corp. ("Arden"), told Crabtree at an employment interview on September 26 that she was prepared to offer him a two-year contract at an annual salary of $20,000 for the first six months, $25,000 for the next six months and $30,000 for the second year. Arden's secretary made a memorandum headed "Employment Agreement with Nate Crabtree" which set forth various terms, including the salary and a notation, "(2 years to make good)." This memorandum was not signed. A few days later, Crabtree accepted the offer and when he reported to work, a payroll change card was prepared and initialed by a Crabtree officer. It noted that it was to be effective October 22 and indicated the salary payment schedule. After six months, Crabtree received the increase from $20,000 to $25,000 but the year-end increase was not paid. Arden's employees told Crabtree they would try to straighten out the matter with Miss Arden. The controller prepared and signed a "payroll change" card noting that there was to be a salary increase from $25,000 to $30,000 a year "'per contractual arrangements with Miss Arden.'" Miss Arden refused to approve it. Crabtree sued. Arden denied that it had agreed to employ Crabtree for two years and that even if it had, the statute of frauds barred enforcement of the employment agreement. The trial court held for Crabtree on both issues and the appellate division affirmed.

HOLDING: On appeal, the NY Ct of Appeals stated that the issue was whether there was a memorandum signed by Arden that satisfied NY's statute of frauds requirement for contracts which are not to be performed within a year. The court stated that the two payroll cards, one that was initialed and the other one signed, constituted a memorandum under the statute. It was irrelevant that they were not signed with intent to evidence the employment contract or that they came into existence after the contract was made. It was enough "that they were signed with intent to authenticate the information contained therein and that such information does evidence the terms of the contract." The only essential term missing from the cards was the duration term so the question was whether the employment duration could be supplied by the unsigned, September 26th office memorandum which had the notation "2 years to make good" and whether that was a sufficient statement of the length of employment. The court stated that a memorandum need not be in one document but may be pieced together from separate writings and "at least one writing, the one establishing a contractual relationship between the parties" must be signed by the party to be charged. Where some writings have been signed and others not, the writings must be connected in order to permit the unsigned papers to be considered part of the statutory memorandum. The court rejected the view in some jurisdictions that there be some reference in the signed writing to the unsigned writing; rather, it held that a sufficient connection is made if the signed and unsigned writings refer to the same subject matter or transaction and that oral testimony would be permitted to show the connection between the documents and to show that the party to be charged acquiesced in the contents of the unsigned document.

The court emphasized, however, that the contract's terms cannot be supplied by parol but must be contained in the writings. The court found that the unsigned office memo and the two payroll forms referred to the same transaction and therefore the three papers constituted a "memorandum" within the meaning of the statute. The only essential term in dispute was the employment duration. The court said that the

CASES	SUMMARIES
Crabtree, continued	trier of fact was warranted in finding that the words "two years to make good" designated the employment duration. Even if the term was ambiguous, parol evidence would be admissible to explain its meaning.

(C) The Statute of Frauds in the Digital Age

Concepts:

- Modern law recognizes advances in technology and accepts other forms of recording, including electronic recordings. As a result, the 2003 revision of Article 2 substitutes the word "record" for "writing," where "record" is defined in revised UCC §2-103(1)(m) as "information that is inscribed on a tangible medium or that is stored in an electronic or other medium and is retrievable in perceivable form." Please note, however, that no state has yet adopted revised Article 2.

- The Uniform Electronics Transactions Act ("UETA") governing electronic transactions was drafted by the Uniform Law Commissioners and is enacted in all but three states: Illinois, NY, and WA. UETA applies to most contracts governed by the common law and to contracts for the sale of goods that are governed by Article 2. UETA §3

- UETA provides that "if a law requires a record to be in writing, an electronic record satisfies the law," and that "if a law requires a signature, an electronic signature satisfies the law." UETA §§7(c) &(d)

- UETA becomes applicable only when the parties to a transaction agree to conduct that transaction electronically, as "determined from the context and surrounding circumstances, including the parties' conduct." UETA §5(b)

- The Electronic Signatures in Global and National Commerce Act, known as "E-SIGN," is the federal statute governing electronic transactions. It is very much like UETA with one important exception: it contains express consumer protections, E-SIGN §101. However, E-SIGN provides that its consumer protection section is superseded if a state enacts UETA. Since all but three states have adopted UETA—Illinois, New York, and Washington—E-SIGN's reach is limited.

Section 4. The Statute of Frauds and the Sale of Goods

Concepts:

- A contract for the sale of goods for $500 or more is unenforceable unless it is in writing and sufficient to indicate that a contract for sale has been made between the parties and signed by the party against whom enforcement is sought. UCC §2-201(1)

- Under the Code, a writing is not insufficient if it omits or states a term incorrectly, but the contract is not enforceable "beyond the quantity of goods shown in such writing." UCC §2-201(1)

Section 5. Exceptions to the Statute of Frauds

(A)(1) Part Performance Exceptions

Concepts:

- Exceptions to the statute of frauds may allow an aggrieved party a measure of recovery even when the contract is otherwise unenforceable because it fails to satisfy the writing requirement.

- There are two part performance exceptions with respect to the statute of frauds: the land contract provision (R2d §129) and the sale of goods provision (UCC §§ 2-201(3)(a) & (3)(c)).

- Full performance on one side may take an agreement out of the one-year provision. R2d §130(2) cmt. d

FRAMEWORK FOR ANALYSIS:

ASK: Is there an exception that will allow enforcement of a contract in whole or in part when it lacks a writing that satisfies the statute of frauds? If so, then ask:

Has there been part performance of the contract? If so, then part performance of the oral agreement may provide the performing party with a basis for recovery.

- **Land contract provision?** Was there part performance of a contract falling within the land contract provision? If so, a court may grant specific performance of an oral agreement to transfer an interest in land if there has been "performance 'unequivocally referable' to the agreement, performance which alone and without the aid of words of promise is unintelligible or at least extraordinary unless as an incident of ownership[.]" *Burns v. McCormick*, 132 N.E. 273 (N.Y. 1922).

- **Sale of goods provision?** Was it a contract for the sale of goods? If so, does one of the following exceptions apply?

  1. Does the contract call for specially manufactured goods for the buyer where the goods cannot be sold to others in the ordinary course of the seller's business, and the seller "has made either a substantial beginning of their manufacture or commitments for their procurement"? UCC§2-201(3) (a)

2. Has payment for any goods been made and accepted or have any goods been received and accepted? UCC §2-201(3)(c)

(A)(2) Reliance-based Exceptions

Concepts:

a. UCC §2-201: Some courts permit the use of promissory estoppel to enforce some contracts otherwise unenforceable under UCC §2-201. This is the result of the interaction between two Code provisions: UCC §§1-103(b) and 2-201(1). UCC §1-103(b) provides that "unless displaced by the particular provisions of [the Uniform Commercial Code], the principles of law and equity, including . . . the law relating to . . . estoppel . . . shall supplement its provisions." While the text of UCC §1-103(b) suggests that estoppel may be used to enforce some contracts whose enforcement would otherwise be barred by the statute of frauds, UCC §1-103(b) may be limited by the opening words of UCC §2-201(1): "Except as otherwise provided in this section . . . ."

Note: According to White and Summers, "Comment 2 to section 2-201 of Amended Article 2 (not likely to be adopted anywhere) now makes clear that Amended Article 2 would preserve the possibility that a promisor can be estopped to raise the statute of frauds defense in appropriate cases." Principles of Sales Law §3-6, 126 (West 2009).

b. R2d §139: This Section, similar to §90, finds a promise enforceable notwithstanding the Statute of Frauds when there is reliance which is foreseeable by the promisor and enforcement is necessary to avoid injustice. The remedy for breach may be limited as justice requires. *Monarco v. LoGreco*

CASES	SUMMARIES
Beaver v. Brumlow (2010) →(CB pg. 315)	**FACTS:** The Beavers (sellers) owned 24 acres and orally agreed to sell the Brumlows (buyers) a portion of the land. The parties walked the boundaries of the property that was being sold. Relying on the oral agreement, buyers took possession of the land and cashed in retirement funds to purchase a double-wide home that they moved on to the property. Buyers made other improvements including pouring concrete footers and a foundation, building a deck and installing various utility systems. Sellers signed an application that was submitted to the village to permit placing buyers' home on the property. Sellers were aware of buyers' improvements as they were being made and permitted buyers to rely on sellers' representations that they would sell. Although buyers repeatedly asked that a contract be formalized, sellers responded, "We will work it out." Three years after the oral agreement, sellers required buyers to sign an agreement calling for a monthly payment of $400 which buyers believed was payment for the land. When buyers wrote "Land Payment" on their checks, sellers stop cashing them and claimed that the agreement was for a rental. Sellers brought an ejectment action against buyers, claiming violation of a rental agreement. When buyers counterclaimed for breach of contract and other claims, sellers pleaded the statute of frauds as a defense.

CASES	SUMMARIES
Beaver, continued	**HOLDING**: The trial court concluded that sellers had committed a *prima facie* tort when they refused to honor the contract. The court further held that there was convincing evidence of a verbal contract to sell and that the parties' part performance removed the contract from the statute of frauds. The buyers were given a choice of remedies and chose specific performance, where, in accordance with the court's decision, buyers were required to pay sellers $10,000, the fair market value as determined by a professional appraiser. Judgment was entered directing buyers to tender to sellers $10,000 upon receipt of a warranty deed from sellers. On appeal, sellers argued that the statute of frauds barred the contract because the parties' part performance of the contract was not "unequivocally referable" to the oral agreement and that the oral agreement was not definite regarding the purchase price and time of performance.

The court noted that in New Mexico, equity may consider an oral contract removed from the statute of frauds if the contract has been performed to such an extent to make it inequitable to deny the contract. However, sellers argued that "the character of Buyers' performance was not sufficiently indicative of an oral agreement to sell land to qualify as partial performance." Further, sellers contended that buyers' acts were not "unequivocally referable" to the oral agreement because they were consistent with those of a person who was allowed to live on another person's property. Sellers argued that if there is an alternative explanation for a buyer's actions in reliance on the oral contract, then the doctrine of part performance is inapplicable. The court rejected sellers' argument that the "'unequivocally referable' concept means that outside of the contract, there can be no other plausible explanation for the part performance." Rather the language means "'that an outsider, knowing all of the circumstances of a case except for the claimed oral agreement, would naturally and reasonably conclude that a contract existed regarding the land, of the same general nature as that alleged by the claimant.'" In short, the performance need not relate exclusively to the oral contract but "must lead an outsider to 'naturally and reasonably' conclude that the contract alleged actually exists." The court pointed out that where a buyer (a) takes possession and (b) makes valuable, permanent, and substantial improvements, specific performance is usually the remedy granted. Here, buyers relied on the agreement in purchasing the mobile home and moving it to the property with sellers' consent. Buyers also made permanent improvements and landscaped the property with sellers' consent. These actions constituted part performance in reliance on the oral agreement and thus the agreement was removed from the statute of frauds.

Finally, the court held that although the oral agreement did not mention a purchase price, the oral agreement was nevertheless sufficient based on its interpretation of statements by the New Mexico Supreme Court, that in an action for specific performance, the court may set a reasonable price. Noting that the buyer was not at fault that a formal document had not been prepared, the court said that the trial court had equitable jurisdiction to set the purchase price at the fair market value as determined by an objective appraiser. As far as the sellers' claim that buyers had an adequate remedy at law, the court said that land is unique and damages could not be assessed accurately.

CASES	SUMMARIES
Monarco v. Lo Greco (1950) →(CB pg. 323)	**FACTS:** Natale and Carmela invested $4,000 in a half interest in an agricultural property. Carmela's daughter (Natale's stepdaughter) and son-in-law acquired the other half interest. At 18, Christie (Carmela's son and Natale's stepson) wanted to live independently of his parents. His parents promised him that if he remained at home and worked, then they would hold the family property in joint tenancy and the survivor would will it to him. Christie diligently worked in the family venture, giving up any opportunity to further his education or accumulate his own property. When he married, Natale told Christie that he should live with his wife on the property since he would receive all of it when his parents died. Shortly before Natale's death, he changed his will to leave his half to the plaintiff, his grandson. Plaintiff brought an action for partition of the property and by cross complaint, Carmela requested that plaintiff be declared a constructive trustee of the portion of the property he received as a result of Natale's breach. The trial court gave judgment for defendant and plaintiff appealed. **HOLDING:** The issue on appeal was whether plaintiff was estopped from asserting the statute of frauds as a defense, specifically, California's lifetime clause which bars enforcement of an oral contract not to be performed during the promisor's lifetime. The court said the doctrine of estoppel to assert the statute of frauds has been applied in California where a refusal to enforce the oral contract (1) would result in an unconscionable injury to a party who was induced by the other party to seriously change his position in reliance on the oral contract or (2) where unjust enrichment would result if the party receiving the benefits of the other party's performance were allowed to rely on the statute. Here both elements were present. Christie, who worked for 20 years, would be seriously prejudiced if his labor was not rewarded. In addition, Natale reaped the benefits of the contract and he and his devisees would be unjustly enriched if the statute of frauds could be invoked. The court emphasized that where either unconscionable injury or unjust enrichment would result from refusing to enforce the oral contract, estoppel has been applied regardless of whether plaintiff relied upon a promisor's representations "going to the requirements of the statute itself. . . ." Finally, the court stated that the remedy of damages for breach of contract or the quasi-contractual remedy for value of services would be inadequate as a remedy for "the breach of a contract to leave property by will in exchange for services of a peculiar nature involving the assumption or continuation of a close family relationship. . . ."

(B) UCC §2-201(2): The Sounds of Silence

Concepts:

- The sale of goods statute of frauds requirement of a signed writing is satisfied when the oral contract is between merchants and, within a reasonable time, a written confirmation of the oral contract is sent by one of the parties which would be sufficient under UCC §2-201(1) against the sender and the party receiving it has reason to know its contents and does not send a written objection within 10 days after it is received. UCC §2-201(2)

FRAMEWORK FOR ANALYSIS: Does the "merchant memorandum" exception apply? Was an oral sales contract entered into between merchants?

ASK: Did a merchant send a "writing in confirmation of the contract"

- to another merchant who had "reason to know" its contents?

- which was sent "within a reasonable time"?

- where it was in a form that would be sufficient to bind the sender under UCC §2-201(1)?

- and the recipient has not given written notice of objection within 10 days of receipt? (*St. Ansgar Mills, Inc. v. Streit*); UCC §2-201(2)

If all of the above criteria are met, then the requirement of a writing is met under UCC §2-201(2) and sufficient against both parties under UCC §2-201(1).

CASES	SUMMARIES
St. Ansgar Mills, Inc. v. Streit (2000) →(CB pg. 329)	**FACTS:** Duane Streit, the buyer (and defendant), called St. Ansgar, the seller, for a price quote on corn. Duane raised hogs and was assisted by his father, John, in operating a "hog finishing operation." Typically, if Duane accepted the price quote, then St. Ansgar would prepare a written confirmation and either mail it to Duane to sign and return, or wait for Duane or John to sign the confirmation when they came by the business; John came by regularly during the first 10 days of each month to pay the amount of the open account St. Ansgar maintained for the Streits' purchase of supplies and other materials. When St. Ansgar sent the written confirmation, it was not unusual for Duane to fail to sign the confirmation for a long period of time. He also failed to return contracts sent to him. Still, Duane had never refused delivery of grain he purchased by telephone. **HOLDING:** On July 1, 1996, John phoned St. Ansgar to place two orders for the purchase of corn. After the order was placed, St. Ansgar completed the written confirmation but set it aside for John to sign when he was expected to stop by the business to pay his open account with St. Ansgar. In this instance, John failed to follow his usual routine and did not stop by the business during July. St. Ansgar then asked a local banker who was expected to see John to have John stop by the business. When John came on August 10, St. Ansgar delivered the written confirmation to him. Duane later refused delivery of the corn—the price of corn dropped dramatically and Duane purchased corn on the open market for a much lower price. St. Ansgar filed suit for breach of contract (for damages of $152,100, which was the difference between the contract price of the corn and the market price at the time Duane refused delivery). Duane filed a motion for summary judgment, claiming that the parties' oral agreement was unenforceable under the statute of frauds and that the written confirmation that St. Ansgar delivered to him did not satisfy the statute of frauds because the confirmation was not received within a reasonable time after the alleged oral agreement. The district court found the written confirmation did not satisfy the writing requirements of the statute of frauds because the delivery of the confirmation to John Streit, as Duane Streit's agent, did not occur within a reasonable time after the oral contract.

CASES	SUMMARIES
St. Ansgar Mills, continued	The district court reasoned that the size of the order, the volatility of the grain market, and the lack of an explanation by St. Ansgar for failing to send the confirmation to Duane Streit after John Streit failed to stop by as expected made the delay between July 1 and August 10 unreasonable as a matter of law. St. Ansgar appealed, claiming that whether a written confirmation was received within a reasonable time was a question of fact for the jury.'

The Iowa Supreme Court reversed the decision of the district court and remanded for a factual determination of whether St. Ansgar's delay in delivery of the written confirmation until August 10 was reasonable. The court found evidence to infer that St. Ansgar did not suspect John's failure to follow his customary practice in July of stopping by the business to be a concern at the time. While the written confirmation exception imposes a specific ten-day requirement for a merchant to object to a written confirmation, the UCC employs a flexible standard of reasonableness to establish the time in which the confirmation must be received. It specifically defines a reasonable time for taking action in relationship to "the nature, purpose and circumstances" of the action. Course of dealings, usage of trade or course of performance are material in determining a reasonable time. The UCC relies upon course of dealings between the parties to help interpret their conduct. Therefore, all relevant circumstances, including the custom and practice of the parties, must be considered in determining what constitutes a reasonable time under UCC §2-201(2). |

(C) UCC §2-201(3)(b): The Judicial Admissions Exception

Concepts:

- It would seem anomalous, but it has been possible at common law for a breaching party to assert that she made an oral contract and still successfully assert the statute of frauds as a defense to its enforcement because there is no writing signed by the party to be charged.

- One statutory exception to this result is found in UCC §2-201(3)(b): if the party against whom enforcement of the sales contract is sought "admits in his pleading, testimony or otherwise in court that a contract for sale was made," then the contract is enforceable up to the quantity of goods admitted.

Section 6. Assessing the Statute of Frauds

(A) Ethical Practices and the Statute of Frauds

Concepts:

- "What should a lawyer do when when a client admits to making and breaching a contract that the lawyer knows is unenforceable because of the statute of frauds?" →**(CB pg. 336)** Ethical issues for the lawyer may be involved when representing a client with a statute of frauds defense. The casebook authors raise several questions regarding the implications of invoking technical defenses such as the statute of limitations and the statute of frauds. The questions raised warrant your thoughtful consideration.

(B) W(h)ither the Statute of Frauds?

Concepts:

- There have always been strong reactions, both for and against, the statute of frauds. The future does not seem to indicate that there will be much of a change.

■ CHAPTER 4. POLICING THE BARGAINING PROCESS

Section 1. Capacity

Concepts:

- A person must have capacity to incur contract liability.

- The general rule is that a contract made by a party while under a legal incapacity is voidable.

- One such incapacity is based on age where a person under the age of 18 has the capacity to incur only voidable contractual duties until the beginning of the day before the person's 18th birthday.[1]

- Another type of incapacity is one based on mental illness or defect where the party is not able to understand in a reasonable manner the nature and consequences of the transaction or he is not able to act in a reasonable manner in relation to the transaction and the other party has reason to know of his condition. R2d §15(1)(a)(b)

FRAMEWORK FOR ANALYSIS: When can a party avoid the contract based on a lack of capacity?

ASK: Was the party a minor at the time of the transaction? If so, then the contract may be voidable by the minor unless it was a contract for "necessities."

ASK:

- Is it a contract for food, shelter, clothing, or other such basic items typically found necessary for the maintenance of life? If so, then the minor may not avoid the contract. Still, in considering whether the contract was for a necessity, the court will consider the quantity, quality and reasonable value of that necessity in light of the minor's social status and situation in life.

- Has the minor engaged in conduct so as to ratify the agreement either by performing the contractual obligation or accepting the other party's performance under the contract since reaching the age of majority?

  If so, then the minor is bound by the contract. If not, then ask: has the minor disaffirmed the contract by taking any actions which can be construed as disaffirming the contract since reaching majority?

  — If the minor has taken steps to disaffirm the whole contract by words or conduct within a reasonable time upon reaching majority, then she can avoid the contract. Upon disaffirmance, the minor is not required to make restitution but is required to return only what she still has in her possession. There is no obligation to account for use, depreciation, or loss in value. Even where necessaries are involved, recovery is limited to unjust enrichment.

  — If the minor fails to disaffirm within a reasonable time after attaining majority, then such failure is a ratification of the contract and terminates the power to disaffirm.

---

1 R2d §14 (1979). Common law set the age of majority at 21; however, in almost every state this rule has been changed by statute where the usual age is 18.

ASK: Did the party lack mental capacity at the time of contract?

Note: It is recognized that there is a wide variety of types of mental incompetency, including brain damage, deterioration due to old age, and the use of drugs or alcohol, to name but a few. In these cases, the mental inability makes the contract voidable only if the other party had reason to know of the condition. R2d §15 cmt. b

- If, by reason of mental illness or defect, was the party able to understand in a reasonable manner the nature and consequences of the transaction? If not, then the party may have incurred only voidable contractual duties. R2d §15(1)(a)

- Knowledge of incapacity by the other party? If by reason of mental illness or defect, was the party unable to act in a reasonable manner in relation to the transaction and the other party had reason to know of her condition? If so, then the party has incurred only voidable contractual duties.

CASES	SUMMARIES
Douglass v. Pflueger Hawaii, Inc. (2006) → (CB pg. 342)	**FACTS:** Douglass was hired as a car lot technician four months before his 18th birthday. He received the employee handbook at the employee orientation which had a provision for arbitration of claims arising out of an employee's employment with the company. When Douglass was injured by a co-worker, he filed an action against the employer (after first filing a complaint with the Hawaii civil rights commission) claiming, among other things, a hostile and unsafe work environment. The employer's motion to compel arbitration was granted. **HOLDING:** On appeal, the court recognized the common law rule that a minor's contract is voidable and that the minor may, upon reaching majority, choose to disaffirm the contract. The court explained that the infancy law doctrine is based on the principle that laws should protect minors from adverse consequences of their youthful acts. An exception to the voidability of a minor's contract is "that a minor may not avoid a contract for goods or services necessary for his health and sustenance." None of the parties, however, contended that Douglass' employment was a necessity. However, there was another exception which applied in this case: Hawaii's child labor law permitted minors between the ages of 16 but not yet 18 to be employed at certain times during the year. Thus, the court said that the Hawaii legislature viewed 16 and 17 year-olds as competent to enter into employment contracts. The court noted that as an additional protection the legislature authorized Hawaii's labor department to revoke any certificate of employment issued to the minor if the employment was found to be detrimental to the minor. Because the statutory child labor law incorporated the protections afforded by the infancy doctrine, the general rule that a minor, on reaching majority, can disaffirm a contract was not applicable to an employment contract, including any arbitration provision in it. The court further held that Douglass was bound by his employment contract even though the record did not indicate whether Douglass had obtained an age certificate before his employment. Among other reasons, the court noted that nothing in the child labor law made employment invalid under those circumstances. Further, Douglass was only four months shy of majority at the time he was hired. In sum, the court held that Douglass was not entitled to disaffirm because of his minority status.

CASES	SUMMARIES
Ortelere v. Teachers' Retirement Bd. (1969) → (CB pg. 349)	**FACTS:** Ortelere, a 60 year-old teacher, was on leave for mental illness having suffered a nervous breakdown. She had a $70,925 retirement account that she accumulated over 40 years. Unbeknownst to her husband and although suffering from cerebral arteriosclerosis, she irrevocably elected to take maximum monthly benefits from the retirement account which would leave no benefits for her husband when she died. Under her prior election, she would have received a smaller benefit but her husband would have received any unused portion when she died. She died two months later and her husband sued to rescind her election because of mental incompetence. Her psychiatrist testified that she could not make a decision because she could not "think rationally." When the court found for Ortelere, the Retirement Board appealed. **HOLDING:** The NY Ct of Appeals rejected the cognitive test for determining contractual mental capacity, finding it too restrictive in light of present psychology. Instead, the court found that the Restatement Second stated the modern rule on competency where "(1) A person incurs only voidable contractual duties by entering into a transaction if by reason of mental illness or defect . . . (b) he is unable to act in a reasonable manner in relation to the transaction and the other party has reason to know of his condition." The court found that the Board of Education was, or should have been, aware of her condition so that the requirements for avoidance of the contract were satisfied. As a result, the court remanded for a new trial under the modern rule as opposed to the traditional rules regarding mental capacity which guided the trial court's findings and perhaps some of the testimony.
Cundick v. Broadbent (1967) → (CB pg. 352)	**FACTS:** In September 1963, Cundick, a 59 year-old sheep rancher signed a one page contract agreeing to sell all of his ranching properties to Broadbent, an individual to whom Cundick on occasion sold his land crop. Cundick's lawyer revised the contract into an 11 page document which the parties signed. A month later, with a lawyer's help, the agreement was amended to increase the purchase price and make another favorable change for Cundick. As amended, more than 2,000 acres were being sold for $40,000, which an expert later valued at $89,000, and Cundick's interest in a development company for approximately $47,000—an interest later valued at $184,000 by Cundick's witness, and at about $74,000 by a Broadbent witness. In March 1964, when the sale was almost completed, Cundick's wife, as guardian *ad litem* for him, brought an action to rescind the agreement, claiming that her husband was mentally incompetent to contract. Cundick had undergone psychiatric treatment in 1961 but nothing further prior to the lawsuit. A court-ordered examination disclosed premature arteriosclerosis. There was uncontradicted medical testimony that in September 1963 Cundick was incapable of transacting important business and was a "confused and befuddled man." Still, the trial court found that between September 1963 and the middle of February, 1964, Cundick acted like a person competent to manage his affairs and was aware of the effects of his actions.

CASES	SUMMARIES
Cundick, continued	**HOLDING:** On appeal, the court noted that the modern rule seems to be that absent knowledge by a party of the other party's asserted incapacity, the contractual act of a person claiming mental deficiency "'is not a void act but at most only voidable at the instance of the deficient party; and then only in accordance with certain equitable principles.'" Further, "mental capacity to contract depends upon whether the allegedly disabled person possessed sufficient reason to enable him to understand the nature and effect of the act in issue." The court noted that although Cundick's attitude towards business had changed during the period between his mental examination in 1961 and 1964, there was no evidence of any discussions among his family or friends in the community about his mental condition. The court thought that it was incredible that if Cudnick was incapable of transacting his business that his family would be unaware of his condition. As a result, the court upheld the trial court's findings that Broadbent did not deceive or overreach Cundick.

Dissent: In light of the undisputed medical testimony, the evidence the majority relied on was trivial; it was inconceivable that a mentally competent individual would sell his assets for less than half its value.

QUESTION TO THINK ABOUT: *When the court notes that the record is "silent concerning any discussion of [Cundick's] mental condition among his family and friends in the community where he lived and operated his ranch" do you think that that such discussion would have been reasonable to expect, even among friends and family, in the early 1960s?*

CASES	SUMMARIES
Kenai Chrysler Center, Inc. v. Denison (2007) → (CB pg. 354)	**FACTS:** David Denison, a developmentally disabled adult, was subject to his parent's legal guardianship pursuant to an "order that declared him incompetent to enter into a contract." David bought a car from Kenai Chrysler using his debit card. When his parents learned of the purchase, David's mother told Kenai that David had no legal authority to enter the contract. Her offer to return the car was rejected. She brought suit to declare the contract void and to enjoin Kenai from receiving further payment for the car. David's parents were granted summary judgment and defendant appealed. **HOLDING:** On appeal, the court rejected Kenai's view that Alaska had not held that a valid guardianship order automatically voids a ward's contract and therefore Kenai should be entitled to at least restitution. Under the Restatement Second, the court said, "the existence of a valued legal guardianship precludes the formation of a valid contract with the guardianship's ward." Further, under the Restatement, the guardianship order gives notice to the public of the ward's incapacity. Thus, even if a party has no knowledge or reason to know of the guardianship, it has constructive notice of the ward's incapacity. Since Kenai had constructive notice, it was not even entitled to restitution. Citing to its ruling in the *Pappert* case, the court stated that a party who attempts to contract with a ward would be entitled to restitution only if it did not have actual or constructive knowledge of the ward's incompetence.

Section 2. Overreaching

Concepts: Duress

- Since the process of forming a contract requires the parties' mutual assent, such assent must be freely and voluntarily given and not obtained through coercive conduct. If one party improperly pressures the other party into giving assent to a contract or a modification, then the contract or modification may be avoided.

- If a party's assent is induced by an improper threat by the other party that leaves the victim with "no reasonable alternative," the contract is voidable by the victim. R2d §175(1)

- The modern view is to recognize a much broader range of threats as being improper, including those that threaten economic harm. This is the doctrine of "economic duress" or "business compulsion," where the threatened harm to the victim's economic interests is wrongful and the victim has "no reasonable alternatives." (*Austin Instrument, Inc. v. Loral Corp.*)

FRAMEWORK FOR ANALYSIS for Duress: Was a party unfairly coerced into entering or modifying a contract?

ASK:

- Was there a threat?

- Was the threat improper or wrongful?

- Did the threat induce the victim's assent to the agreement?

- Was the threat one which left the victim with no reasonable alternative?

Concepts: Undue influence

- If a party's assent to a contract is the induced by the undue influence of the other party, then the contract is voidable by the victim. R2d §177

- Undue influence may be the result of unfair persuasion based on the parties' relationship or particular weaknesses which might make a person more likely to be susceptible to such persuasion.

- Undue influence involves two components: a stronger party (the dominant person) who uses unfair persuasion on the weaker party (servient person) to gain that party's assent. Here, the dominating person's influence overcomes the will of the servient person. (*Odorizzi v. Bloomfield School District*)

FRAMEWORK FOR ANALYSIS for Undue Influence: Did one party induce the assent of the other by improper persuasion?

ASK:

- Did a special relationship exist between the parties? Is one party highly susceptible to persuasion by the other? Examples include the relationships between parent/child, husband/wife, doctor/patient.

- Did the stronger party use unfair persuasion on the weaker party to gain that party's assent? One way to determine whether the dominant party exercised this type of persuasion is to ask:

    — Was there an imbalance in the resulting transaction?

    — Did the weaker party have the benefit of independent advice?

    — Was there time for reflection?

    — How susceptible was the weaker party to persuasion from the stronger party?

(A) Pressure in Bargaining

CASES	SUMMARIES
Alaska Packers' Ass'n v. Domenico (1902) → (CB pg. 359)	**FACTS:** Alaska Packers hired libelants "as sailors and fishermen" to sail from San Francisco to Pyramid Harbor, Alaska, for the salmon season and agreed to pay each worker $50 for the season. Upon arrival in Alaska where Alaska Packers had invested heavily in a salmon cannery, the workers demanded $100 for their services stating that if they did not receive the increased salary, they would stop work and return to San Francisco. Plaintiff's superintendent agreed to pay the $100 since it was impossible to get substitute workers. When the season ended, Alaska Packers paid the workers only $50 as originally agreed. The employees successfully sued to recover the additional $50. **HOLDING:** On appeal, the Ninth Circuit reversed. The real question, the court said, was whether the second contract—the superintendent's promise to pay the additional $50—was supported by consideration. The court held that Alaska Packers' consent to its employees' demand for the additional compensation was not supported by consideration because Alaska Packers' superintendent's consent was based solely upon the employees agreement to "render the exact services, and none other, that they were already under contract to render [for $50]."

CASES	SUMMARIES
Alaska Packers' Ass'n, continued	The court also found that Alaska Packers did not voluntary waive the breach of the original contract. The company was unaware of the breach until the expedition returned to San Francisco. Further, Alaska Packers' superintendent had informed the employees that he had no power to alter the old, or make a new, contract. The Ninth Circuit cited with approval a Minnesota Supreme Court case which observed that "the party who refuses to perform, and thereby coerces a promise from the other party to the contract to pay him an increased compensation for doing that which he is legally bound to do, takes an unjustifiable advantage of the necessities of the other party. Surely it would be a travesty on justice to hold that the party so making the promise for extra pay was estopped from asserting that the promise was without consideration. A party cannot lay the foundation of an estoppel by his own wrong, where the promise is simply a repetition of a subsisting legal promise. There can be no consideration for the promise of the other party, and there is no warrant for inferring that the parties have voluntarily rescinded or modified their contract. The promise cannot be legally enforced, although the other party has completed his contract in reliance upon it."
	QUESTIONS TO THINK ABOUT: *If a promise to do what a party is already contractually obligated to do is not consideration for a return promise, can the promisee assert a claim based on promissory estoppel? [See R2d §89(c), cmt. d]*
	Could the Alaska Packers' case have been decided on a theory that the employer's promise was unenforceable because of economic duress?
Watkins & Son v. Carrig (1941) → **(CB pg. 365)**	**FACTS:** In a written contract, plaintiff agreed to excavate defendant's cellar. After commencing work, plaintiff encountered solid rock. As a result, the parties orally agreed that plaintiff should remove the rock at a unit price about nine times greater than the unit price used to calculate the original contract price. A referee found that the oral agreement superseded the original written contract and reported a verdict in plaintiff's favor which resulted in judgment for plaintiff.
	HOLDING: On appeal, the court first found that plaintiff could not be relieved of its obligation based on mutual mistake. It noted that the parties did not understand that no rock would be found. Further, plaintiff had not checked the ground below the surface and the contract contained an unqualified promise to excavate and no provision for unexpected conditions. Second, the court interpreted the referee's finding that the parties' oral agreement superseded the original written contract to mean that the parties agreed to rescind the original written contract and enter into the oral contract as if it were the original one. Defendant contended that the facts did not support the view that there were two independent and separate transactions—that is, that there was a rescission of the written contract and the entering into of a new oral contract. Instead, defendant claimed that there was only one transaction in which defendant agreed to pay more for the excavation than the original written contract price but otherwise the written contract remained in effect.

CASES	SUMMARIES
Watkins & Son. continued	The court noted that it was not important to determine whether the contract was rescinded and a new one took its place or whether the original written contract was simply modified by the oral agreement. "In the view of a modification, the claim of a promise unsupported by consideration is as tenable as under the view of a rescission. A modification involves a partial rescission." The court recognized the basic rule that "a promise to pay for what the promisor already has a right to receive from the promise is invalid. The promisee's performance of an existing duty is no detriment to him, and hence nothing is given by him beyond what is already due the promisor." However, the court said that there is a significant difference "between a bare promise and a promise in adjustment of a contractual promise already outstanding." Contracting parties understand their contract "is subject to any mutual action they may take in its performance." Changes in contracts made to meet changes in circumstances and conditions should be valid if legal rules are to give effect to reasonable understandings in business matters.
	The court viewed this case as one where the defendant intentionally and voluntarily relinquished or waived his right to insist on the original price when he agreed to the new price. The parties mutually "agreed that the contract price was not to control. . . . [and] . . . If the totality of the transaction was a promise to pay more for less, there was in its inherent makeup a valid discharge of an obligation." This approach, the court said, was needed to meet the reasonable needs of business practices. The court conceded that plaintiff threatened not to perform because the contract was improvident but defendant did not protect and stand on his right but gave in to plaintiff's demand for a higher price. In not insisting on his rights but instead relinquishing them, the court said defendant should be held to the new arrangement.
	The court further stated that "[t]he law is a means to the end" and it is important that the law comport with "the important conduct and transactions of life." Here, the facts showed that after entering into written contract, plaintiff's obligation became burdensome and defendant granted plaintiff relief by agreeing to pay a fair price. Thus, the new oral contract was triggered by changed circumstances and resolved by a fair agreement.
Austin Instrument, Inc. v. Loral Corporation → (CB pg. 375)	**FACTS:** In July 1965, Loral was awarded a Navy contract to produce radar sets. The contract contained a liquidated damages clause for late deliveries and a cancellation clause if Loral defaulted. Loral awarded Austin a subcontract to supply 23 precision gear components of the 40 needed for the radar sets. In May 1966, Loral was awarded a second Navy contract. With respect to the 40 gear parts needed under this second Navy contract, Loral solicited bids from Austin and others. Austin told Loral that it would not deliver gear parts under the existing subcontract unless Loral ordered from Austin all 40 gear parts needed under Loral's second Navy contract and also agreed to a price increase under the existing subcontract. Loral contacted 10 other manufacturers of precision gears but found none that could meet the Navy's time requirement. Loral then consented to Austin's price increases under the first subcontract and awarded Austin the second subcontract for the 40 gear parts. Loral was able to timely produce the radar sets and after Austin's last delivery under the second subcontract, Loral notified Austin that it intended to recover the price

CASES	SUMMARIES
Austin Instrument, Inc., *continued*	increase. On September 15, 1967, Austin sued Loral to recover the monies due on the second subcontract. The next day Loral commenced an action against Austin to recover the price increase Loral paid under the first subcontract "on the ground that the evidence establishes, as a matter of law, that it [Loral] was forced to agree to an increase in price on the items in question [gears] under circumstances amounting to economic duress."

HOLDING: The NY Ct of Appeals stated that the applicable law was clear—"[a] contract is voidable on the ground of duress when it is established that the party making the claim was forced to agree to it by means of a wrongful threat precluding the exercise of his free will. . . ." To establish economic duress in cases such as Loral, it must be shown "that one party to a contract has threatened to breach the agreement by withholding [needed] goods unless the other party agrees to some further demand." But the court noted that a mere threat to breach the contract, though wrongful, does not by itself constitute economic duress. The threatened party must also show that (i) it could not obtain the required goods from another supplier and (ii) that the ordinary contract remedy for breach would not be adequate.

The court stated that "[t]here was no material disagreement concerning the facts." It found, as a matter of law, that Loral was subject to economic duress. Here, "Austin's threat—to stop deliveries unless the prices were increased—deprived Loral of its free will." Because of its production schedule, Loral needed the gears and it was concerned about being able to timely deliver the radar sets. The substantial liquidated damages for which it could be liable for delay and the threat of default leading to cancellation were genuine possibilities. Further, Loral had much government business and it feared that failing to timely deliver would jeopardize its chance for future government contracts. The court concluded that Loral had no choice but to give in to Austin's demands.

The court rejected Austin's argument that Loral was required to ask the government for an extension of its delivery date so Loral could purchase parts from another vendor. Loral was not required to do so because Loral wanted to be favorably viewed by the government and because it could not be sure that a substitute vendor would meet Loral's schedule. Loral also met its burden of showing that it could not obtain parts within a reasonable time from other sources and acted reasonably in only contacting manufacturers on its approved vendor list. Given the stringent requirements for precision military parts, it would be unreasonable to say that Loral should have sought out vendors which were unfamiliar to Loral. Loral's normal remedy to sue for damages would have been inadequate since Loral would still have been required to obtain the gears elsewhere, which under the circumstances would have subjected Loral to substantial liquidated damages and the threat of cancellation by the government. Thus, "Loral actually had no choice, when prices were raised by Austin, except to take the gears at the 'coerced' prices and then sue to get the excess back." Finally, Loral's waiting until after Austin made the last delivery on the second subcontract to disaffirm the modification was reasonable because Loral feared that notifying Austin earlier that it intended to seek a refund would result in Austin refusing to continue deliveries which again would put Loral in an untenable position. The possibility of compulsion by Austin existed until all gear parts were delivered.

CASES	SUMMARIES
Austin Instrument, Inc., continued	**Dissent**: Unlike the majority opinion, the dissent said that there were "sharp conflicts of fact" and that the lower courts resolved the facts in favor of Austin. Whether the facts shown amount to economic duress is usually a question of fact and here the lower courts resolved the question against Loral.
Odorizzi v. Bloomfield School District (1966) → **(CB pg. 380)**	**FACTS:** Odorizzi resigned as an elementary school teacher after he was told by his District Superintendent and School Principal, who had come to Odorizzi's home, that unless he resigned he would be fired and his arrest on June 10 for homosexual activities would be publicized. In July, the criminal charges against Odorizzi were dismissed and in September he sought reinstatement but the school district refused. Odorizzi then brought suit to rescind his resignation on the grounds, among others, of undue influence and duress. His complaint was dismissed for failing to state a claim. Odorizzi alleged that at the time he resigned he was incapable of rational action because he had just completed the arrest process, including police questions, bookings, etc. and had gone for 40 hours without sleep and was unable to think clearly. While in that condition, his superintendent and principal told him that they were trying to help him, and that he should immediately resign and that there was no time to consult an attorney. They also told him that if he did not resign, the district would dismiss him and publicize the arrest. Because of his confidence in the superintendent and principal, Odorizzi alleged that they were able to substitute their will for his and secure his resignation.

HOLDING: The court held that the amended complaint did not state a duress claim because the actions or threats must be unlawful and "a threat to take legal action is not unlawful unless the party making the threat knows the falsity of his claim." Here, Odorizzi's amended complaint showed that when the superintendent and principal indicated their intent to bring dismissal proceedings under the education law, they not only had a legal right to file such proceedings but a positive duty to do so. As long as the school representatives acted in good faith in performing their duties, any damage to Odorizzi's reputation from such a dismissal proceeding would be considered incidental. However, the court found that the amended complaint set forth sufficient facts to state a claim that Odorizzi's consent was attained by undue influence. Undue influence involves two components: a stronger party (the dominant person) who uses unfair persuasion on the weaker party (servient person) to gain that party's assent. In such cases, the dominating person's influence overcomes the will of the servient person. Here, Odorizzi claimed that he had just completed the arrest process and had been without sleep for 40 hours. The court found that such exhaustion and emotional turmoil may incapacitate a person so that Odorizzi had alleged sufficient facts to show such a weakness as to prevent him from applying his own judgment at the time of resignation.

While the court noted that there are various ways to characterize the nature of unfair persuasion and what constitutes the types of weaknesses which might make a person more likely to be susceptible to such persuasion, it found that "[w]hether a person of subnormal capacities has been subjected to ordinary force or a person |

CASES	SUMMARIES
Odorizzi, continued	of normal capacities subjected to extraordinary force, the match is equally out of balance. If will has been overcome against judgment, consent may be rescinded." The difficulty was in determining when forces of persuasion have become oppressive. Here the court found that over-persuasion tended to follow a pattern which was characterized by involving several of the following seven elements—the simultaneous presence of a number of these elements may render the persuasion excessive pressure as distinguished from legitimate persuasion: "(1) discussion of the transaction at an unusual or inappropriate time, (2) consummation of the transaction in an unusual place, (3) insistent demand that the business be finished at once, (4) extreme emphasis on untoward consequences of delay, (5) the use of multiple persuaders by the dominant side against a single servient party, (6) absence of third-party advisors to the servient party, (7) statements that there is no time to consult financial advisers or attorneys."
	Here, for example, had Odorizzi been called into the superintendent's office during business hours and told of the district's intention to file charges and that he was free to consult an attorney and that he was free to consider the alternatives overnight, a claim of excessive pressure could not have been made. But the complaint alleged that it happened differently. The court concluded that Odorizzi had pleaded "both subjective and objective elements entering the undue influence equation" and that the facts alleged raised the ultimate question of whether Odorizzi's judgment was merely influenced or whether his mind was so dominated that he was unable to make an independent judgment.

(B) Concealment and Misrepresentation

Concepts:

- A misrepresentation is "an assertion that is not in accord with the facts." R2d §159

- A statement may be true as to what is asserted but may fail to include material necessary to prevent an overall misleading impression. Such a half-truth may be treated as a misrepresentation because it is false. (*Kannavos v. Annino*)

- A party who makes a promise with no intention of performing it is misrepresenting a fact, that is, her state of mind and such a misrepresentation, which is also fraudulent, is actionable. R2d §171 cmt. a

FRAMEWORK FOR ANALYSIS: Was there a misrepresentation?

To determine whether a misrepresentation is actionable, all of the following **four elements** must be met.

ASK:

1. Was there a misrepresentation? There must be an assertion that is not in accord with the facts. An assertion can be oral or written or can be inferred from conduct. A misrepresentation may be made not only by an assertion, but also by creating a false impression or inference.

   - To determine whether a statement is false, ask the following:
   - **False Impression or Inference?** If part of the truth is told but another portion that the part disclosed creates an overall misleading impression, this may constitute a misrepresentation. (*Kannavos v. Annino*)
   - **Concealment?** Did one party engage in an affirmative act to keep the other party from learning a fact? If so, such conduct may be a misrepresentation.
   - **Non-disclosure?** Do one of the exceptions to the "no duty to disclose" rule apply? In certain situations, the failure to disclose a fact is seen as an assertion that the fact does not exist. Ask the following:

     — **Relation of Trust or Confidence?** Is there a relation of trust or confidence between the parties? The relationship need not be a fiduciary one but may be one between family members or between doctor and patient, among others. If so, then the one in whom the trust and confidence is placed is expected to disclose what she knows. Failure to disclose the fact is equivalent to an assertion that the fact does not exist.

     — **Need to Correct?** Is disclosure necessary to correct an earlier assertion? If a party who has made an assertion later learns something that bears on the prior assertion, then she is expected to speak up. Failure to disclose the fact is equivalent to an assertion that the fact does not exist.

     — **Mistake in Basic Assumption?** Would disclosure correct the other party's mistake as to a basic assumption on which the party is making the contract and non-disclosure of the fact amounts to a failure to act in good faith and in accordance with the standards of fair dealing? If so, then failure to disclose the fact is equivalent to an assertion that the fact does not exist.

     — **Mistake as to Writing?** Would disclosure correct the other party's mistake as to the contents or effect of the writing? If so, then failure to disclose the fact is equivalent to an assertion that the fact does not exist.

2. Was the assertion either fraudulent or material? A misrepresentation need not be fraudulent to make the contract voidable but if it is not fraudulent, then it must be material. R2d §164 cmt. b; but see Restatement, Second, Torts §538 where liability for fraudulent misrepresentation is limited to cases in which the misrepresentation is material.

   - **Fraudulent?** Did the maker of the misrepresentation

     — know or believe that the assertion was not in accord with the facts, or

     — not have confidence that what she stated or implied was true, or

     — know that she did not have the basis that she states or implied for the assertion?

If the answer is "no" to all of the above, then the misrepresentation must be material to make the contract voidable.

- **Material?** Was the misrepresentation likely to induce a reasonable person to assent or did the maker know that it was likely to induce the recipient to do so?

3. Did the misrepresentation induce the recipient to make the contract (reliance)?

4. Was the recipient's reliance on the misrepresentation justified? Typically, the most significant and difficult application of this requirement occurs in connection with assertions of opinion because opinions are not facts. A recipient is not justified in relying on statements of opinion only, unless one of the following exceptions applies. If the answer is "yes" to any of the following, reliance is justified.

ASK:

- **Confidential Relationship?** Does the recipient stand in a confidential or fiduciary relationship to the person whose opinion is asserted such that the recipient is reasonable in relying on it?

- **Special Skill or Judgment?** Does the recipient reasonably believe that the other person has special skill or judgment with respect to the subject matter? Is the other person an "expert" in the area? (*Vokes v. Arthur Murray, Inc.*)

- **Susceptibility?** Is the recipient particularly susceptible to a misrepresentation of the particular type involved for some other special reason?

CASES	SUMMARIES
Swinton v. Whitinsville Sav. Bank (1942) → (CB pg. 388)	**FACTS:** In September, 1938, Defendant Whitinsville Savings Bank sold Swinton, plaintiff, a house that was infested with termites. Defendant knew that the house had termites but did not disclose this information to Swinton. The infestation was not readily observable upon inspection and Swinton did not know about the termites at the time of purchase. Swinton learned about the termites in August, 1940 when he incurred great expense for repairing the damage to the house that they caused. Swinton brought an action alleging concealment. The issue was whether the seller of a home has a duty to disclose "any nonapparent defect known to him in the subject of the sale which materially reduces its value and which the buyer fails to discover." **HOLDING:** The court held that absent a false statement or representation or a half truth, concealment of a known defect is not actionable. Where, as here, (i) there is no allegation that the Defendant prevented Swinton from acquiring information about the condition of the house, (ii) it was a business deal made at arm's length, and (iii) the parties did not stand in a fiduciary relationship to each other or in a position of confidence or dependence, then "it is concealment in the simple sense of mere failure to reveal, with nothing to show any peculiar duty to speak." The court acknowledged that Swinton's case possessed "a certain appeal to the moral sense" but "the law cannot provide special rules for termites. . . ." [But compare with *Hill v. Jones*, which held that the homeowner seller had a duty to disclose the existence of termite damage which materially affected the value of the property. 725 P.2d 1115 (Ariz. App. 1986)]

CASES	SUMMARIES
Kannavos v. Annino (1969) → (CB pg. 391)	**FACTS:** Annino converted a one-family dwelling into a multi-family building with eight apartments. She did so without a building permit and in violation of the zoning ordinance prohibiting multi-family uses. Kannavos saw a newspaper ad placed by Annino's broker advertising the property for sale as a house converted to 8 apartments and giving the gross yearly income. Annino sold the house to Kannavos who was unaware of the zoning and building permit violations. Kannavos made no inquiry before the closing about zoning or building permits and no one said anything to him on that subject. When the city sued to abate the non-conforming use, Kannavos brought an action to rescind the purchase. **HOLDING:** At the outset, the court noted that if Annino, the seller, had said nothing about the use of the property, there would be no misrepresentation. However, the ad offered the house as an investment property and referred to the property as a single house converted to apartments. Further, the broker showed Kannavos the house and gave him income and expense information furnished by Annino. The court concluded that the seller's conduct, advertising, and statements were sufficient to remove the case from the rule of non-liability for mere non-disclosure as in Swinton. Once a party provides some information, it must disclose all relevant material facts within his knowledge. Here Annino knew that the buyer was planning on continuing to use the building for apartments. Her disclosures about the property—that it was suitable for investment and can continue to be so used—were inadequate and partial and thus, under the circumstances were intentionally fraudulent. The court also considered whether the buyer's failure to use due diligence to discover the truth about the property's zoning status should bar recovery. The court noted that Kannavos could have learned of the violations from the public records, unlike in Swinton where the buyer would have needed an expert to discover the termites. The court concluded, however, that when a party relies on a fraudulent representation, as Kannavos did, such party is not precluded from a recovery because they did not use due diligence to discover the truth.
Speakers of Sport v. ProServ (1999) → (CB pg. 398)	**FACTS:** Rodriguez, a successful Texas Rangers catcher, had entered into several one-year, terminable-at-will contracts with Speakers of Sport, plaintiff, a ballplayer's agency. Hoping to lure Rodriguez to its sports agency, ProServ promised Rodriguez that it would secure $2 to $4 million dollars of endorsements if he left Speakers and signed with ProServ. Rodriguez did so, but ProServ did not secure any significant endorsements for him and after a year Rodriguez switched to another agent. Speakers sued ProServ, claiming that ProServ's promise to Rodriguez was fraudulent. The trial court granted ProServ summary judgment and Speakers appealed. **HOLDING:** On appeal, the court addressed the issue of how to legally categorize ProServ's promise to Rodriguez. A sports agent—as does any business—has a right to solicit and take a customer from a competitor if it can be done without inducing a breach of contract between the competitor and its customer. This is called competition. But the privilege to take away business from a competitor "does not include a right to get business from a competitor by means of fraud." Thus a party may not

CASES	SUMMARIES
Speakers of Sport, continued	make a promise to a competitor's customer that he knows that he cannot fulfill because this would be competition by fraud.

The Seventh Circuit held that ProServ's promise of securing endorsements was puffing in the "sense of a sales pitch that is intended, and that a reasonable person in the position of the 'promisee' would understand, to be aspirational rather than enforceable—an expression of hope rather than a commitment." Here, the court said it was not plausible that ProServ was guaranteeing Rodriguez a minimum of $2 million dollars of endorsements; rather "[t]he only reasonable meaning to attach to ProServ's so-called promise is that ProServ would try to get as many endorsements as possible for Rodriguez and that it was optimistic that it could get him at least $2 million worth of them." In this sense, ProServ's "'promise' was not a promise at all. |
| *Vokes v. Arthur Murray, Inc. (1968)*

→ (CB pg. 400) | **FACTS:** Plaintiff, a 51 year-old widow, claimed that she was fraudulently induced by defendant to enter into 14 dance course contracts for a total of 2,302 hours of dancing lessons. From the outset, the dance instructor heaped on her a "continuous barrage of . . . false praise," assured her that she had "'grace and poise' . . . that she was 'rapidly improving and developing in her dancing skill' . . . [and] that the additional lessons would 'make her a beautiful dancer.'" Further, she was given dance aptitude tests, allegedly to determine how much instruction she needed. The complaint alleged that the defendant falsely represented to her that her dancing ability was improving, that she had excellent potential, and that their dancing instructions "were developing her into a beautiful dancer." In fact, plaintiff had no dance aptitude. The trial court dismissed the complaint for failure to state a cause of action.

HOLDING: On appeal, the court reversed. Recognizing that generally a misrepresentation can only be actionable if it is a misrepresentation of fact, not opinion, the court said that this rule was inapplicable if the parties have a fiduciary relationship or if the parties do not generally deal at arm's length or the person to whom the representation is made does not have the equal opportunity to learn whether the fact represented is true. Further, a statement from a party having "superior knowledge may be regarded as [making] a statement of fact although it would be considered as opinion if the parties were dealing on equal terms." From the allegation in the complaint, defendants should have reasonably known that the plaintiff's "slow and awkward progress" did not justify additional instruction and she would have known this fact if defendant had told her the whole truth.

The court acknowledged that a party in a contractual situation does not owe a duty to the other party to disclose facts within his knowledge or to answer inquiries respecting such facts but if he undertakes to do so, he must disclose the whole truth. The court concluded that the complaint stated a cause of action.

QUESTION TO THINK ABOUT: *Where a person expresses an opinion to another but does not believe the opinion it is giving, should the statement of the opinion be treated as a misrepresentation of the person's state of mind and therefore constitute a misrepresentation of fact, namely a misrepresentation of what the speaker actually believes?* |

■ CHAPTER 5. DETERMINING THE PARTIES' OBLIGATIONS UNDER THE CONTRACT

Section 1. The Parol Evidence Rule

Concepts:

- "Parol evidence" is any evidence other than the parties' written agreement that is offered by a party to prove contract terms that do not appear in the writing.

- The parol evidence rule does not exclude evidence to show that no enforceable agreement was reached: for example, evidence to show that the agreement is invalid, or avoidable, as the case may be, due to a lack of consideration, mistake, fraud, misrepresentation, duress, or illegality would be admissible.

- The parol evidence rule is not a rule of evidence, but is a rule of substance law. R2d §213 cmt. a

- The parol evidence rule excludes extrinsic evidence of terms agreed upon prior to or, as is sometimes said, contemporaneously with a binding, completely integrated agreement. It does not exclude evidence of subsequent agreements or modifications. See UCC §2-202; R2d §§ 214-216

- A writing is an *integration* if it is the parties' final expression with respect to the terms contained within it. When an integration contains some, but does not contain all of the terms of the parties' agreement, then the writing is a *partial integration*.

- A partial integration may be supplemented by consistent additional terms, but cannot be contradicted.

- If a writing is a final and complete expression of all the terms the parties agreed upon, then it is a *complete integration* and cannot be contradicted or supplemented by any additional terms.

- Although a merger clause is presumptive of a complete integration, it is not conclusive. R2d §209 cmt. b

The Parol Evidence Rule under the Uniform Commercial Code

- A writing that the parties intended as a final expression of the their agreement may be supplemented by consistent additional terms unless the court finds the writing to be intended as a complete and exclusive statement of the terms of the parties' agreement. However, the writing may be "explained or supplemented by course of performance, course of dealing, or usage of trade." UCC 2-202(a)

  Note: "Course of performance" would seem to be unnecessary because this is subsequent to the agreement.

- If the judge finds that the extrinsic additional term, if agreed upon by the parties, would "certainly" have been included in the writing, then evidence of such term is inadmissible.

Deciding the Integration Question: Whether a writing is an integrated agreement and, if so, whether the agreement is completely or partially integrated are preliminary questions decided by the judge. Courts follow different approaches in making these determinations.

ASK: Which type of jurisdiction is involved?

- Restatement Second and the view espoused by Professor Corbin take the position that a judge should consider all the circumstances, including evidence of the prior negotiations, to determine the question of integration, partial or complete.

  "Naturally" vs. "Certainly": Under R2d §216(2), an agreement is not completely integrated if the writing omits a consistent additional term which is agreed to for separate consideration or "such a term as in the circumstances might *naturally* be omitted from the writing." (emphasis added) Under the Code, the test for integration differs somewhat: Comment 3 to UCC 2-202 provides that, if there is a written agreement, evidence of terms not included in the writing are not admissible "[i]f the additional terms are such that, if agreed upon, they would certainly have been included in the document in the view of the court[.]" The main difference between the Code's test for integration and the common law is that under the Code, the court must find that the parties "certainly," rather than "naturally" would have included the terms in their writing in order to find the writing integrated.

- Professor Williston espoused the view that a judge should focus on the writing itself. A "four corners" approach looks to the writing and only if the contract appears on its face to be incomplete will parol evidence of additional terms be admissible.

FRAMEWORK FOR ANALYSIS: Is there a dispute regarding "the law of the contract ?

ASK: Is one party seeking to introduce evidence of a prior or contemporaneous agreement to show that the terms of the written agreement are other than as shown in the writing?

To determine the admissibility of extrinsic evidence, ask:

1. Is the written agreement integrated or unintegrated? Did the parties intend the writing to be a final embodiment of the terms contained in the agreement? If the parties had such an intention, the agreement is integrated, and the parol evidence rule bars evidence of prior agreements for at least some purposes. If the parties had no such intent, the agreement is said to be unintegrated, and the parol evidence rule does not apply.

   To determine whether the agreement is integrated or unintegrated, ask the following about the writing:

   a. **Prepared by one party?** If the document is prepared by only one party, then it is likely to be unintegrated and parol evidence is admissible. Your inquiry ends here.

   b. **Memo to file?** If it is a memo to file, then it is likely to be unintegrated and parol evidence is admissible. Your inquiry ends here.

   c. **Final as to one term?** If the writing is final as to one or more terms, then the agreement is integrated as to those terms and the parol evidence rule bars evidence of prior agreements that contradict those terms. Proceed to the next question.

2. If it is integrated, is it completely or partially integrated?

If the writing was assented to by the parties "as a complete and exclusive statement of all the terms" of their agreement, then it is completely integrated and not even evidence of a "consistent additional term" is admissible to supplement the writing. R2d §210 cmt. a; R2d §216(1). On the other hand, if the writing is only a partial integration, then extrinsic evidence of additional terms is admissible to supplement the writing but not to contradict it.

To determine whether the agreement is completely or partially integrated, ask the following:

a. **Completely Integrated?** Is the writing intended as a final and complete expression of the parties' agreement? Consider the following to determine whether the writing is a complete integration:

- **Merger Clause?** Is there a merger or integration clause in the agreement? The presence of such a clause is the best evidence of a completely integrated agreement. However, a merger clause is only presumptive of integration—it is not conclusive. Proceed to the next question.

- **Consistent Additional Terms?** An agreement is not completely integrated if the writing omits a consistent additional term which is agreed to for separate consideration or such a term as in the circumstances might "naturally" be omitted from the writing. R2d §216

b. **Partially Integrated?** Is the writing a partial integration such that it is final with respect to the terms it contains but it does not contain all the terms of the parties' agreement? If so, then ask: is the offered term consistent or contradictory to the writing?

- **Consistent?** If the offered term is supplementary to the writing, then it is admissible. Note: "The determination whether an alleged additional term is consistent or inconsistent with the integrated agreement requires interpretation of the writing in the light of all the circumstances, including the evidence of the additional term." R2d §216 cmt. a. Also, consider the "natural omission test" discussed above. R2d §216 cmt. d

- **Contradictory?** If the evidence is contradictory to a term in the writing, then it is barred by the parol evidence rule. Only additional, supplementary terms are admissible. Whether there is a contradiction depends on whether the two terms are consistent or inconsistent. Determining whether an alleged additional term is consistent or inconsistent with the integrated agreement is a matter of interpretation of the writing in view of all the circumstances, including evidence of the additional term. R2d §216 cmt. b

CASES	SUMMARIES
Gianni v. Russell & Co. (1924) →(CB pg. 407)	**FACTS:** Tenant and landlord entered into a three year lease whereby the tenant was granted use of the rented premises for the sale of food, candy, and soft drinks. The lease contained a provision prohibiting tenant from selling tobacco in any form. The tenant alleged that prior to and at the time of the lease signing, the landlord orally agreed that in consideration for the tenant's promise not to sell tobacco and to pay increased rent, the tenant would have the exclusive right to sell soft drinks in the building. Subsequently, the landlord leased a room in the building to a drug company without restricting it from selling soda, water and soft drinks. The tenant successfully sued for breach of the alleged oral contract.

CASES	SUMMARIES
Russell, continued	**HOLDING:** The court reversed on appeal. The court recognized the rule that where the parties, without fraud or mistake, have deliberately placed their agreement in writing, the writing is the only evidence of their agreement and it supersedes all prior conversations or verbal agreements and its terms cannot be added to or subtracted from by parol evidence. The tenant argued, however, that the oral agreement was an independent agreement that did not belong in the written lease but the court disagreed. The question for the court was when would an oral agreement "come within the field embraced by the written one." The court said that this was a question for the court and to make this determination, the written and oral agreement must be compared and a determination made whether the parties under the circumstances "would naturally and normally include the one in the other if it were made. If they relate to the same subject-matter, and are so interrelated that both would be executed at the same time and in the same contract, the scope of the subsidiary agreement must be taken to be covered by the writing." Applying this approach to the written agreement, the court noted that the written agreement covered the permitted uses of the storeroom. In the written agreement, the tenant promised not to sell tobacco and if, as plaintiff claimed, that promise was part of the consideration for an exclusive right to sell soft drinks, "it would be the natural thing to have included (in the written agreement) the promise of exclusive rights." The court stated that where a claim is predicated on an alleged oral understanding concerning a matter covered by the written agreement, it is assumed that the written agreement was intended as the entire agreement on that subject. The written lease covered the subject of the alleged oral contract and therefore under the parol evidence rule, evidence of that oral agreement was inadmissible.
Masterson v. Sine (1968) →(CB pg. 411)	**FACTS:** Dallas Masterson and his wife conveyed a ranch to Dallas' sister and her husband (the Sines) by a deed which contained a provision reserving to the sellers an option to repurchase the property on or before February 25, 1968. After the conveyance, Dallas became bankrupt and his wife and his trustee in bankruptcy brought a declaratory judgment action to establish their right to enforce the option. The Sines attempted to offer extrinsic evidence to establish that the option was personal to the grantors—that the parties had agreed that the option was not assignable in order to keep the property within the family—and therefore the trustee in bankruptcy could not exercise the option. The lower court held that the parol evidence rule precluded admitting the extrinsic evidence. **HOLDING:** On appeal, the court held that the extrinsic evidence offered by the Sines (defendants) was admissible and not barred by the parol evidence rule. The court stated that parol evidence cannot be used to add to or vary the terms of a written contract where the parties agreed to that contract "as an 'integration.'" The court

CASES	SUMMARIES
Masterson, continued	

defined the word "integration" as "a complete and final embodiment of the terms of the agreement." To determine whether a written agreement is an integration, the court must determine whether the parties intended it to be the exclusive statement of their agreement. Sometimes the writing itself will help to resolve the issue for example if it contains a clause stating in substance that "'there are no previous understandings or agreements not contained in the writing.'" The court said that a determination of the "integration" issue cannot be made from the written agreement itself.

The court concluded that evidence of an oral collateral agreement should be excluded only when the fact finder is likely to be misled and the rules should depend on the credibility of the evidence. It noted the standard used by the First Restatement of Contracts that permits proof of a collateral agreement if it "is such an agreement as might naturally be made as a separate agreement by parties situated as were the parties to the written contract." [See R2d §216(2)(b)] The UCC provides another standard which would exclude collateral agreements in fewer cases than the Restatement: the UCC would exclude evidence of a collateral agreement only "if the additional terms are such that, if agreed upon, they would certainly have been included in the document in the view of the court . . . ." UCC §2-202 cmt. 3

The court concluded that the alleged collateral agreement regarding the option in the deed clause might naturally have been made in a separate agreement and was not one that the parties would certainly have included in the deed. In so doing, the court observed that the option clause did not state that it embodied the complete agreement; nor did the deed say anything about assignability of the option clause. Further, the court noted that the formalized structure of a deed posed a difficulty to the insertion of collateral agreements and therefore it was less likely that all of the agreed terms were in the deed. It was possible that the option reservation clause was included in the recorded deed simply to put future purchasers on notice of the option and this could be accomplished without mentioning that the option was personal. Finally, the court addressed the trustee's argument that option agreements are presumed to be assignable absent any agreement forbidding a transfer and thus, the oral collateral agreement would contradict this presumed term. The court however, stated that a written memorandum "does not necessarily preclude parol evidence rebutting a term that the law would otherwise presume. . . ."

DISSENT: The option's unqualified and unambiguous language would be contradicted if extrinsic evidence were permitted to limit the option's assignability. Under California law, an optionee has a right to transfer his option—to allow parol evidence to show that the written option is not transferable would permit him to recapture rights which he has already transferred. It would be difficult to conceive of a clearer violation of two substantive rules—the parol evidence rule and the right to freely transfer property. As far as the formal structure of the deed, "[w]hat difficulty would have been involved here, to add the words 'this option is non-assignable?'"

CASES	SUMMARIES
Bollinger v. Central Pennsylvania Quarry Stripping and Constr. Co. (1967) →(CB pg. 416)	**FACTS:** The Bollingers entered into a written contract with defendant construction company in which defendant was given the right to deposit on plaintiffs' property construction waste from its work on the PA Turnpike near plaintiffs' property. The Bollingers claimed that they also had an understanding with defendant that prior to defendant depositing any such waste, defendant would remove the top soil of plaintiffs' property, deposit the waste and then restore the top soil so that the deposited waste was covered. This condition was not contained in the written contract. The Bollingers alleged that they signed the written agreement "without reading it because they assumed that the condition . . . had been incorporated into the writing." Initially, defendant acted in accordance with the alleged mutual understanding and sandwiched the waste between the earth and the top soil but after a while ceased doing so. When the Bollingers protested, defendant's superintendent said that he no longer had the equipment to remove and replace the top soil and, when reminded of the original understanding, he said he couldn't help it. **HOLDING:** Plaintiffs sought reformation of the written agreement claiming that the parties' oral understanding regarding the top soil had been omitted by mutual mistake and that the contract, as reformed, should be enforced. The court noted that a court of equity has the power to reform a contract because of a mistake between the parties but that such mistake must be mutual. The court stated that based on the testimony, the chancellor properly concluded that plaintiffs sustained the heavy burden to demonstrate that their understanding of the agreement was corroborated by the undisputed evidence—that when defendant put back the top soil over the waste it acted in a manner consistent with the Bollingers' understanding and had acted similarly in the case of one of the Bollingers' neighbors.

Section 2. The Use of Extrinsic Evidence of the Parties' Intent

Concepts:

- The basic principle of contract interpretation is that agreements are construed in accordance with the parties' intent. (*Greenfield v. Philles Records, Inc.*)

- Evidence which is otherwise barred by the parol evidence rule may be admissible to interpret ambiguous language.

- The general rule for admissibility of extrinsic evidence to explain the meaning of a writing is whether the offered evidence is relevant to prove a meaning to which the language is "reasonably susceptible." (*Pacific Gas & Electric Co. v. G.W. Drayage & Rigging Co.*)

- New York follows the "four corners" approach to determine whether the contract is ambiguous. Upon a finding of ambiguity, New York courts can look to the surrounding facts and circumstances to determine the intent of the parties. 67 *Wall St. Co. v. Franklin Nat. Bank*, 37 N.Y. 2d 245 (1975). California preliminarily considers all credible evidence of the parties' intent in addition to the contract language in order to determine whether the contract is ambiguous or not.

FRAMEWORK FOR ANALYSIS: Do the parties dispute the meaning of a term in their contract?

ASK: Will the court allow admission of extrinsic evidence to interpret the contract language?

- **"Plain Meaning" approach?** If the court follows a "plain meaning" approach, then contract meaning is determined from the "four corners" of the document without resort to extrinsic evidence of any kind. If the contract, read as a whole to determine its purpose and intent, seems a clear expression of the parties' full agreement, then the court will not allow the introduction of extrinsic evidence.

  Corbin approach? Under Corbin's approach, all relevant extrinsic evidence is admissible on the issue of meaning. R2d §212 follows this approach and allows consideration of all credible evidence to prove the intent of the parties. The question for the court is whether the offered evidence is relevant to prove a meaning to which the language is "reasonably susceptible." (*Pacific Gas & Electric Co. v. G.W. Drayage & Rigging Co.*)

If the court allows the admission of extrinsic evidence to resolve contractual ambiguity, it considers the following to aid in interpretation:

- Express language of the agreement? What is the express wording of the parties' agreement and the usual inferences to be drawn from the language? Can the term in dispute be read in light of the agreement as a whole so as to give it meaning?

- Can the parties' principal purpose be determined from their words and other conduct as interpreted in the light of all the following:

  - their conduct in performing the contract (course of performance)?

  - their conduct under any prior agreements with each other (course of dealing)?

  - the custom and usage in the market or industry in which they operate (usage of trade)?

If these sources are not helpful in ascertaining the meaning of the disputed terms, the court next looks to rules applicable to similar contracts and considers supplementary rules to fill the gap, such as:

  - "General rules of construction"? R2d §202, §203, §206

  - Is there a way to interpret the ambiguous term which gives effect to all of the terms of the agreement?

  - Can the term be interpreted according to an ordinary or lay meaning rather than a specialized meaning?

  - Is it a specific provision? If so, then it should be given greater weight than a general provision.

  - *Ejusdem generis* ("of the same kind")? Are general and specific words connected? If so, then the general word is limited by the specific one so that it means only things of the same kind.

— *Expressio unius, exclusio alterius* ("expression of one thing excludes another")? Is there a specific list of items without being followed by a general term? If so, then the implication is that all other things of the same kind are excluded.

CASES	SUMMARIES
Pacific Gas and Electric Co. v. G.W. Thomas Drayage & Rigging Co. (1968) → (CB pg. 421)	**FACTS:** Plaintiff and defendant entered into a contract providing for defendant to remove and replace a metal cover on plaintiff's steam turbine. Defendant agreed to indemnify plaintiff if defendant's performance caused "any injury to property." In the course of defendant's performance, the turbine cover fell and damaged the turbine's exposed rotor. Plaintiff sued defendant, claiming that the indemnification clause covered injury to plaintiff's property. Defendant offered extrinsic evidence such as admissions of plaintiff's agents and defendant's conduct under similar contracts with plaintiff to prove that the indemnity clause covered injury to third parties' property only and not to plaintiff's property. Although the trial court noted that the language of the indemnity provision was classical language for third party indemnity, it said that the plain language of the provision also required defendant to indemnify for injury to plaintiff's property. Since the contract had a plain meaning, the trial court refused to admit any extrinsic evidence that contradicted the court's interpretation. **HOLDING:** On appeal, the court rejected the concept that determination of the meaning of a written agreement is limited to its four corners when the court believes the contract to be clear and unambiguous. Thus, extrinsic evidence is admissible when offered to prove a meaning to which the language is "reasonably susceptible"—even if the written agreement appears to the court to be plain and unambiguous on its face. Only if it is "feasible to determine the meaning the parties gave to the words from the instrument alone" can extrinsic evidence be excluded. However, the court pointed out the words "do not have absolute and constant referents." The meaning of words varies with the context and surrounding circumstances and purposes in view of the linguistic education and experience of the parties. Thus, terms of a written agreement may be clear to a judge but that does not preclude the possibility that the parties chose the language they used to express different terms. Generally, extrinsic evidence is inadmissible to add to or vary the contract terms. However, before a court can determine whether extrinsic evidence is being offered for a prohibited use and therefore excluded, the court must first determine the terms of the agreement. To do so requires the court to preliminarily consider all evidence offered to prove the parties' intention. This includes evidence of the circumstances surrounding the making of the agreement so that the court will be in in the same position that the parties were in at the time the written agreement was made. After considering this evidence, the court must decide whether the language of the written agreement is fairly susceptible to the interpretations contended by the parties. If it is reasonably susceptible to a meaning contended for, then extrinsic evidence to prove such meaning is admissible.

CASES	SUMMARIES
Pacific Gas, continued	The court concluded that the trial court erroneously refused to consider extrinsic evidence to show that the contract was not intended to cover injuries to plaintiff's property. "Although that evidence was not necessary to show that the indemnity clause was reasonably susceptible of the meaning contended for by defendant, it was nevertheless relevant and admissible on that issue. Moreover, since that clause was reasonably susceptible of that meaning, the offered evidence was also admissible to prove that the clause had that meaning and did not cover injuries to plaintiff's property."
Delta Dynamics, Inc. v. Arioto (1968) → (CB pg. 424)	**FACTS:** Parties entered an exclusive five year distributorship contract under which Delta was to supply Pixey with trigger locks. Pixey agreed to sell a minimum of 50,000 units the first year and 100,000 units in each of the next four years. If Pixey did not meet the minimums, the agreement was "subject to termination." In case either party breached, the successful party in a litigation could recover reasonable attorneys' fees. During the first year, Pixey took only 10,000 trigger locks. Delta terminated the agreement and sued for damages. Pixey argued that Delta's sole remedy for Pixey's failure to meet the minimums was to terminate the contract but the trial court excluded extrinsic evidence to prove that meaning. **HOLDING:** On appeal, the court noted that the language of the agreement was reasonably susceptible to the meaning contended for by Pixey. It noted that the termination clause may have been included to clearly specify the condition on which Delta would be excused under the contract or to fix an exclusive remedy for Pixey's failure to meet the minimums, or for both purposes. Thus, the trial court erroneously excluded the extrinsic evidence that Pixey offered. Finally, Pixey's interpretation did not render the attorneys' fees provision meaningless since that provision would be applicable to other breaches of the distribution contract.
Greenfield v. Philles Records, Inc. (2002) → (CB pg. 425)	**FACTS:** In 1963, the Ronettes, a singing group, signed a five-year personal services musical recording contract with Philles Records, defendant Spector's production company. Under the contract, the Ronettes were to perform exclusively for the defendant and defendant acquired an ownership right to the recordings of their musical performances. The agreement provided for royalty payments to the Ronettes for their services. The Ronettes disbanded in 1977. Years later as a result of new recording technologies, defendant licensed the Ronettes' master recordings for use in movie and television, a process known in the entertainment business as synchronization. No royalties were paid to the Ronettes. The Ronettes brought suit, claiming that the defendants had no right under the 1963 agreement to license the recordings for synchronization and sought royalties from the sale of compilation albums. Defendant claimed that the 1963 agreement gave

CASES	SUMMARIES
Greenfield, continued	them absolute ownership right to the master recordings and permitted their use subject only to royalty rights. The lower court ruled for the Ronettes. The appellate division affirmed, concluding that the defendant had no rights to issue synchronization licenses since the 1963 agreement did not specifically transfer those rights to defendant, and further permitted plaintiffs to assert an unjust enrichment claim.

HOLDING: On appeal, the NY Ct of Appeals quoted the contract's ownership provision and noted that the contract unambiguously gave defendants unconditional ownership rights to the master recordings. However, the Ronettes argued that the agreement did not give defendants the right to exploit those recordings in new markets or mediums because the agreement was silent on those topics. Defendants argued that once a contract grants full ownership rights to a performance or composition, there are no restrictions on the owner's right to use the property unless the agreement explicitly enumerates any restriction. In holding for defendants, the court said technological innovations do not change rules of interpretation: a written agreement which is unambiguous on its face must be enforced according to the plain meaning of its terms. Therefore if the agreement on its face is only susceptible to one meaning, extrinsic evidence may not be considered to determine the parties' intent. Whether or not the agreement is ambiguous is an issue of law and to be decided by the court.

The court asked whether "the contract's silence on synchronization and domestic licensing create an ambiguity which opens the door to the admissibility of extrinsic evidence to determine the intent of the parties[.]" The court answered in the negative because there was no ambiguity in the terms of the 1963 agreement. Therefore, defendants were entitled to exercise complete ownership rights subject to royalty payment. The court also addressed the issue of whether defendants' claim that one of the plaintiffs, Greenfield, was barred from sharing royalties because of a general release she signed in connection with her divorce from defendant Spector. Here, in contrast to the "four corners rule" that New York applies, the court looked to California law because the release was executed there. California courts preliminarily consider all evidence of the parties' intent to see whether the extrinsic evidence can establish a meaning to which the written agreement is reasonably susceptible. Noting that the trial court had determined based on the extrinsic evidence that Greenfield's right to compensation was not an intended subject of the release, Greenfield was entitled to share in any damages that defendants were required to pay. |
| ***W.W.W. Associates, Inc. v. Giancontieri (1990)***

→ (CB pg. 428) | **FACTS:** The court considered the question of whether "an unambiguous reciprocal cancellation provision [in a contract to sell real property] should be read in light of extrinsic evidence, as a contingency clause for the sole benefit of the plaintiff's purchaser, subject to its unilateral waiver." The court noted plaintiff's misplaced reliance on extrinsic evidence for its analysis: analysis of a contractual provision must first look to what the parties said in their written contract and not to extrinsic evidence of what the parties meant. |

CASES	SUMMARIES
W.W.W. Associates, continued	**HOLDING:** As a rule, when the parties embody their agreement in a "clear, complete document," the writing should be enforced according to its terms. Generally, extrinsic evidence as to what the parties clearly intended but did not state is inadmissible to add to or vary the agreement. Further, extrinsic evidence may not be admitted in order to create an ambiguity in an agreement which is unambiguous on its face.
Trident Center v. Connecticut General Life Ins. Co. (1988) → **(CB pg. 430)**	**FACTS:** Trident, a partnership of sophisticated entities, obtained a fifteen year loan in 1983 for approximately $56,000,000 from Connecticut General for construction of a building complex. The promissory note provided that the maker could not prepay the principal for the first twelve years. It also provided that Connecticut General would have the option to accelerate the note and include a 10% pre-payment fee in case of default during the first twelve years. A few years later, Trident brought suit seeking a declaration that it was entitled to prepay the loan subject to a 10% pre-payment fee. **HOLDING:** The district court dismissed the complaint holding that the loan documents unambiguously precluded pre-payment for the first twelve years. On appeal, the Ninth Circuit agreed that the language of the note unambiguously provided that Trident could not unilaterally prepay for the first twelve years. Although the court concluded that the contract as written was not reasonably susceptible to Trident's interpretation, Trident argued—citing Pacific Gas & Electric—that it was nevertheless entitled to introduce extrinsic evidence to show that its interpretation reflected the parties' agreement. The Ninth Circuit recognized that "[u]nder Pacific Gas, it matters not how clearly a contract is written, nor how completely it is integrated, nor how carefully it is negotiated, nor how squarely it addresses the issue before the court: the contract cannot be rendered impervious to attack by parol evidence. If one side is willing to claim that the parties intended one thing but the agreement provides for another, the court must consider extrinsic evidence of possible ambiguity." The court therefore felt compelled to reverse and remand the case to allow extrinsic evidence to be presented as to the parties' intention in drafting the contract. The court noted the uncertainty that the Pacific Gas rule injects into all California transactions. It illustrates that no matter how large the transaction is and despite the fact that a contract is negotiated by sophisticated parties with the help of counsel which results in non-ambiguous contract language, litigation cannot be avoided if one party has a strong motive to challenge the contract.

Section 3. The Use of Extrinsic Evidence From Commercial Context

Concepts:

- Under the Code, a course of performance or course of dealing between the parties, or usage of trade in the industry in which they are engaged or of which they are or should be aware is relevant in determining the meaning of their agreement, may give "particular meaning to specific terms of the agreement," and "may supplement or qualify the terms of the agreement." Revised UCC §1-303(d)

- Course of performance prevails over both course of dealing and usage of trade, and course of dealing prevails over usage of trade when determining the meaning of the agreement. The express terms of the agreement prevail over all. UCC §1-303(e)

- A course of performance is "a sequence of conduct between the parties to a particular transaction" which "involves repeated occasions for performance by a party" where the other party, with knowledge of the performance and opportunity to object, "accepts the performance or acquiesces without objection." UCC §1-303(a)

- A course of dealing is "a sequence of conduct concerning previous transactions between the parties to a particular transaction." These prior dealings between the parties can be considered in establishing a common basis for interpreting their language and conduct. UCC §1-303(b)

- A usage of trade is "any practice or method of dealing having such regularity of observance in a place, vocation, or trade as to justify an expectation that it will be observed with respect to the transaction in question." UCC §1-303(c)

CASES	SUMMARIES
Frigaliment Importing Co. v. B.N.S. International Sales Corp. (1960) →(CB pg. 440)	**FACTS:** Plaintiff buyer and defendant seller entered into two contracts, each of which provided for the sale of "US Fresh Frozen Chicken" Grade A 2 ½ -3 lbs. and 1 ½-2 lbs. each. The initial shipment sent to buyer under the first contract was 2 ½-3 lb. birds which were not young chickens suitable for broiling or frying but were stewing chickens or fowl. Plaintiff protested. Nevertheless, seller again shipped stewing chicken under the second contract. Plaintiff brought suit for breach of warranty claiming that the chickens did not correspond to the contract description. **HOLDING:** The Second Circuit noted that standing alone the word "chicken" is ambiguous. Plaintiff claimed that the word "chicken" meant "young chicken" whereas defendant said "chicken" meant any bird of that genus which meets weight and quality contract specifications. The court concluded that plaintiff did not carry its burden of persuasion to show that the word "chicken" was used in the narrower sense—young chicken—rather than in the broader sense. The parties introduced a wide variety of evidence to support their contentions. First, a few days after meeting Bauer, defendant's secretary in New York, Stovicek, plaintiff's agent, asked Bauer if defendant was interested in exporting poultry to Switzerland. Stovicek showed Bauer a cable he received from plaintiff which stated that they

CASES	SUMMARIES
Frigaliment Importing Co., continued	"'are buyer' of 25,000 lbs. of chicken 2½-3 lbs weight . . . grade A Government inspected." After testing for the market price, Bauer accepted and Stovicek sent a confirmation. These and subsequent cables were predominantly in German but used the English word "chicken" because according to plaintiff buyer it understood "chicken" to mean "young chicken" whereas the German word (Huhn) for "chicken" included both broilers and stewing chicken. The court, however, noted that the strength of this evidence was largely negated when Bauer asked Stovicek what kind of chickens were wanted and Stovicek said any kind of chickens and when asked in German whether the cable meant "Huhn," Stovicek said yes.

Buyer also argued that "chicken" meant "young chicken" in trade usage. Since seller only began in the poultry trade in 1957, buyer had to satisfy the rule applicable to a party who is not a member of the trade. Buyer had to show either that seller actually knew of the usage or that the "usage is 'so generally known in the community that his actual individual knowledge of it may be inferred.'" Buyer relied on three witnesses to help establish the usage. One, a resident buyer for a large chain of Swiss cooperatives, testified that he understood "chicken" to mean "broiler." However, in his own dealings, the witness protected himself by using the word "broiler" when he wanted broilers and "fowl" when he wanted older birds. Since the witness did not rely on the alleged usage in his own dealings, his opinion did not carry much weight. The second witness was an officer of one of seller's chicken suppliers who said that "chicken" meant male species which could be a broiler, fryer or roaster but not a stewing chicken. But he also testified that when defendant (seller) asked about chickens, the witness asked the defendant (seller) whether it wanted fowl or frying chickens and in fact, supplied fowl although he protected himself by asking defendant (seller), shortly after buyer accepted the contracts, to change the confirmation of its order from "'chickens,'" as [defendant (seller)] had originally prepared it, to 'stewing chickens.'" Finally, an employee of a company which published a daily market report on the poultry trade gave his opinion that "chicken" was "broilers" and "fryers." In addition to this testimony, buyer relied on the fact that the provider of the daily market report, the Journal of Commerce, and Weinberg Brothers, a large poultry supplier, published quotations which distinguished between "broilers" and "fowl."

However, sellers' witnesses countered buyer's evidence. One witness who operated a chicken eviscerating plant testified that "chicken" is "everything except a goose, a duck, and a turkey." Another witness said that in the trade "chicken" encompasses all classifications. The third witness who conducted a food inspection service testified that any bird coming within the classes of "chicken" in the Dept. of Agriculture's regulations would be a chicken. The seller used other evidence such as Statistics of the Institute of American Poultry Industries which used the phrases "'Young chickens' and 'Mature chickens,' under the general heading of 'Total chickens.'" Seller also argued that the Dept. of Agriculture regulations which defined "chicken" to include broiler and stewing chickens, were incorporated into the contract by reference to the regulation. Although buyer said that the contract provision only related to grade and government inspection, the court believed there was force in seller's argument "particularly since the reference to Government grading was already in

CASES	SUMMARIES
Frigaliment Importing Co., continued	plaintiff's initial cable to Stovicek." The seller also relied on buyer's conduct after it received the first shipment, arguing that buyer should not have permitted the second shipment to have been made. The court rejected this argument since buyer had sent cables insisting on young chickens and that defendant's shipment of old ones would be at its peril. Finally, seller argued that its interpretation was correct because the price buyer offered to pay was not sufficient to cover the cost of broilers and allow seller to make a profit which was not the case if it was supplying fowl.

After reviewing the evidence, the court concluded that defendant believed it could deliver stewing chickens to satisfy the contract and that its subjective intent coincided with various objective meanings of chicken such as agricultural regulations obliquely referred to in the contract, some trade usage and other objective indications. The buyer similarly claimed that its subjective intent was to obtain broilers and that this coincided with virtually much of the evidence. The court did not determine the meaning of "chicken"; nevertheless, it dismissed the complaint. In so doing, it noted that it was not necessary to determine the issue of what the word "chicken" meant because the plaintiff had the burden of showing that "chicken" was "used in the narrower rather than in the broader sense, and this it has not sustained."

QUESTION TO THINK ABOUT: *Was Judge Friendly referring only to the objective evidence that was known to both parties and that, based upon the objective evidence that both parties knew or had reason to know, plaintiff failed to establish that the word chicken was used to mean broilers only and not to include stewing chicken?*

CASES	SUMMARIES
Hurst v. W.J. Lake & Co. (1932) →(CB pg. 446)	**FACTS:** Lake agreed to buy from Hurst 350 tons of horse meat scraps for $50 a ton containing "a minimum 50% protein." The parties further agreed that "if any of the scraps 'analyzes less than 50% of protein,'" buyer would be entitled to a $5 discount per ton. When Lake paid only $45 for 140 tons that had 49.53% to 49.96% of protein, Hurst sued to recover the $5 per ton balance claiming that both parties were members of a group of traders in horse meat scraps and that "the terms 'minimum 50% protein' and 'less than 50% protein'" required a buyer to accept any scraps containing 49.5% of protein or more. The trial court gave judgment on the pleadings for the buyer.

HOLDING: In reversing, the court stated that the dictionary language is not the only language we speak. For example, in the bricklaying trade an agreement to pay $5.25 per thousand does not mean that the worker must lay 1,000 bricks but only that he should build a wall of a certain size in order to be paid the $5.25 per thousand. The court disagreed with cases cited by defendant seller which refused to receive evidence of usage to establish the meaning of the contract language where the contract language was not ambiguous on its face. Thus, here, evidence that the "term less than 50% protein" included scraps that contained 49.5% of protein or more even though "the term less than 50% protein" was not ambiguous on its face.

Section 4. The Use of Extrinsic Evidence to Supplement or Qualify the Agreement: Course of Dealing, Usage of Trade and Course of Performance

CASES	SUMMARIES
Nanakuli Paving & Rock Co. v. Shell Oil Co. (1981) →(CB pg. 448)	**FACTS:** In 1969, Nanakuli, a large asphaltic paving contractor in Hawaii, entered into a long term supply contract with Shell for asphalt. The contract provided that the price would be "Shell's Posted Price at time of delivery." In 1974 when Shell increased its asphalt price $32, Nanakuli claimed that based on trade usage, it was entitled to price protection for the asphalt that it had already included in price bids it submitted for paving contracts it was seeking or had obtained from the government and private contractors. The court rejected Shell's argument that for purposes of trade usage the "trade" should be defined as the sale and purchase of asphalt in Hawaii, the only product Shell supplied to asphaltic paving contractors. The trial court held that the applicable trade should be the asphaltic paving trade which would include the suppliers of "aggregate" as well as the suppliers of asphalt, the two major components of asphaltic paving. Suppliers of aggregate to asphaltic paving contractors such as Nanakuli routinely gave price protection to their customers. **HOLDING:** On appeal, the Ninth Circuit found that the trial court's ruling that the applicable trade was the asphaltic paving trade in Hawaii was neither an abuse of discretion nor a misreading of the Code. The court stated that "under the unusual facts of this case it was not unreasonable for the judge to extend trade usages to include practices of other material suppliers toward Shell's primary and perhaps only customer on Oahu." It noted that a party is held to trade usage not only if he is a member of the trade but also a party who should know of the trade usage, which would include a person who regularly deals with members of the relevant trade (UCC §1-205(3)). Thus, Shell was held "to routine practices in Hawaii by the suppliers of the two major ingredients of asphaltic paving, that is, asphalt and aggregate. Those usages were only practiced towards two major pavers. It was not unreasonable to expect Shell to be knowledgeable about so small a market." [See UCC §1-205(2)] Shell also claimed that the price protection practice "was not sufficiently regular to reach the level of a usage. . . ." Under the UCC, the trade usage must be "proved as facts." It must have "such regularity of observance in a place, vocation or trade as to justify an expectation that it will be observed with respect to the transaction in question." UCC §1-205(2) The court rejected Shell's position, stating that Nanakuli not only showed a "regular observance" but that "price protection was probably a universal practice by suppliers to the asphaltic paving trade in 1969." The court also addressed the issue of Shell's alleged course of performance. Between 1969 and 1974, Shell raised prices for asphalt only twice and on each occasion it price-protected Nanakuli after announcing the increase. Shell claimed that its conduct on those two occasions constituted as a matter of law only a waiver of the "Posted Price" provision in the 1969 contract. If its conduct on those two occasions constituted only a waiver, Shell would be entitled to raise its price without giving Nanakuli price protection. However, the jury found that the two instances of price protection amounted to a course of performance of the 1969 contract and not simply

CASES	SUMMARIES
Nanakuli, continued	a waiver. [See UCC §2-208(1)] The court noted "a course of performance of the contract, in contrast to a waiver demonstrates how the parties understand the terms of their agreement." Thus absent any other impediment, Shell was bound by its course of performance and was required to price protect Nanakuli in 1974 when it raised the price of asphalt. UCC §2-208 comment 4 indicates that a single occasion of conduct does not constitute a course of performance. However, the comment does not say how many times constitutes a course of performance. The court held that the two instances where Shell price-protected Nanakuli was sufficient to show a course of performance since "they constituted the only occasions before 1974 that would call for such conduct." In so holding, the court also rejected Shell's argument that comment 3 favors a preference for interpreting an act as a waiver rather than a course of performance. It noted that the waiver preference only applies to ambiguous acts. Whether Shell's conduct on the two occasions was ambiguous and if not, whether the conduct constituted a waiver or a course of performance was for the jury to determine. And the jury determined Shell's conduct to be a course of performance.

The court also found that the express price term—"Shell's posted price at time of delivery"—did not preclude Nanakuli's showing of trade usage. Although express terms control over trade usage, nevertheless, trade usage is admissible if the usage can reasonably be construed as consistent with the express term. Under UCC §2-208(2) express terms and trade usage must "be construed whenever reasonable as consistent with each other" and only if "such construction is unreasonable" do express terms control over trade usage. Here a total negation of "Shell's Posted Price" term would be if the buyer claimed it was entitled to fix the price. A claim of price protection is not a complete negation of "Shell's Posted Price" but simply a claim "that an unstated exception exists at times of price increases." Thus, the jury could have found that price protection was reasonably consistent with the expressed price term—"Shell's Posted Price at the time of delivery."

Finally, the court held that Shell breached its duty of good faith in connection with the 1974 price increase. Section UCC §2-305(2) provides that "a price to be fixed by the seller . . . means a price for him to fix in good faith." Thus Shell had to observe "reasonable commercial standards of fair dealing in the trade" when it increased its price. [UCC §2-103(1)(b)] Although normally a posted price would satisfy the good faith requirement, here the dispute was not over the amount but the manner in which the increase was implemented. Nanakuli showed that when Chevron raised its price, it gave six weeks advance notice "in accord with the long time usage of the asphaltic paving trade." Shell, however, gave no notice. It simply sent a letter dated December 31st which Nanakuli received on January 4th notifying Nanakuli of a $32 price increase effective January 1st. The jury therefore could have found that Shell did not conform to good faith dealings in Hawaii by failing to give advanced notice and price protection for prices it already included in bids to secure paving contracts. |

CASES	SUMMARIES

Columbia Nitrogen Corp. v. Royster Co. (1971)

→(CB pg. 456)

FACTS: Royster, a manufacturer and seller of fertilizer, had for several years purchased nitrogen from Columbia. In 1966 Royster built a phosphate factory and Columbia agreed to buy from Royster a minimum of 31,000 tons of phosphate per year for 3 years. The contract had a price escalation clause and set minimum quantities per year that Royster was to sell to Columbia. During the first year, phosphate prices plunged and Columbia ordered significantly less than one tenth of the minimum tonnage. Royster sold the unbought tonnage and sued Columbia for damages. Columbia sought to show through witnesses' testimony that because of uncertain crop and weather conditions, it was trade practice that price and quantity terms in the mixed fertilizer industry were only projections, adjustable according to changes in the market. Columbia also offered evidence to show a course of dealing—that when Royster bought nitrogen from Columbia there were repeated deviations from the stated price. The district court excluded the evidence, stating that custom and usage or course of dealing is inadmissible when it contradicts the express terms of the agreement.

HOLDING: On appeal, the Fourth Circuit noted that the UCC states the well-established rule "that evidence of usage of trade and course of dealing should be excluded whenever it cannot be reasonably construed as consistent with the terms of the contract." However, the court rejected Royster's argument that because the contract contained detailed provisions concerning the price and quantity, the course of dealing and trade usage should be excluded. Under UCC §2-202(a), course of dealing and trade usage consistent with the express terms would be admissible even if the contract on its face appears complete. The court gave several reasons why the evidence of course of dealing and trade usage could reasonably be construed as consistent with the express terms, including the fact that the contract was silent about price and quantity adjustments in a declining market—neither permitting nor prohibiting them. Finally, Royster's argument that the evidence should be excluded under a clause that "[n]o verbal understanding will be recognized by either party hereto; this contract expresses all the terms and conditions of the agreement. . . ." was rejected because "[c]ourse of dealing and trade usage are not synonymous with verbal understandings, terms and conditions." The court noted that UCC §2-202 distinguishes between supplementing a written contract by course of dealing or usage of trade—which is permissible even if the writing is found to be a complete and exclusive statement of the parties' agreement [UCC §2-202(1)(a)]—and supplementing it by additional terms which would not be allowed if the court finds the writing to be a complete and exclusive statement of the parties agreement [UCC §2-202 (1)(b)].

Section 5. Objective Interpretation and Its Limits

Concepts:

- In order for a contract to be formed, both parties must agree to the same deal. However, it may happen that although both parties think they are agreeing to the same terms, each may have a different subjective understanding as to one or more terms.

- Where the parties express assent to the same words or terms, but attach materially different meanings to what they have said, their misunderstanding may prevent a contract from being formed. Thus, while each person may say the same thing, each means something completely different. Consequently, if neither party has reason to know of the meaning attached by the other, there is no mutual assent and hence, no contract is formed.

CASES	SUMMARIES
Raffles v. Wichelhaus (1864) →(CB pg. 459)	**FACTS:** Plaintiff agreed to sell defendants bales of cotton arriving "ex Peerless from Bombay." It turned out that there were two ships named Peerless that were sailing from Bombay. Defendant buyers claimed that the word "Peerless" meant the Peerless ship that sailed from Bombay in October and that plaintiffs did not offer to deliver to defendants any cotton that arrived on that ship. Plaintiff seller offered to deliver to defendants the cotton that arrived on the Peerless ship that sailed from Bombay in December but defendants refused to accept or pay for it. Defendants argued that there was a latent ambiguity and that parol evidence was admissible to show that defendants meant Peerless October and plaintiff meant Peerless December. **HOLDING:** In granting judgment for defendants, the court rendered an opinion consisting of only one sentence: "There must be judgment for the defendants." Note: The general principle from this case is found in R2d §20 which states that where parties attach "materially different meanings" to their "manifestations" and neither party has reason to know of the meaning attached by the other, there is no "manifestation of mutual assent."
Oswald v. Allen (1969) →(CB pg. 462)	**FACTS:** Defendant Allen had two coin collections: one known as the "Swiss Coin Collection" and the other known as the "Rarity Coin Collection." Oswald, a coin collector, examined all of the "Swiss Coin Collection" and was then shown some Swiss coins from the "Rarity Coin Collection." Oswald, who hardly spoke English, arranged to purchase from Allen what he thought was all of Allen's Swiss coins and what Allen believed was only the "Swiss Coin Collection." Allen refused to go through with the deal and Oswald sued for specific performance. **HOLDING:** In affirming the lower court's judgment dismissing the complaint after trial, the Second Circuit applied the *Raffles* rule that under the particular facts no contract existed. Although the parties' mental assent is not a requirement for contract formation, nevertheless, "the facts found by the trial judge clearly place this case within the small group of exceptional cases in which there is 'no sensible basis for choosing between conflicting understandings.'"

CASES	SUMMARIES
Colfax Envelope Corp. v. Local No. 458-3M (1994) →(CB pg. 463)	**FACTS:** Colfax, an envelope manufacturer, also does some printing of them. In 1991, it had two printing presses: one printed 78-inch-wide sheets in four colors and the other printed 78-inch-wide sheets in five colors. The industry collective bargaining agreement set minimum staffing levels: it required four men for a four-color press which printed sheets wider than 50 inches and three men for a four-color press which printed sheets between 45 to 50 inches wide. When the union and the Chicago Lithograph Association (CLA) negotiated a collective bargaining agreement, the union sent Colfax a summary of any changes to the existing agreement and Colfax would sign and return the summary if it agreed to the terms. Sometime in 1991, the union sent Colfax a summary of newly negotiated changes to the collective bargaining agreement providing for manning requirements of "4C 60 Press-3 Men." Colfax understood—in part because of information it received from union members—that this meant that all four color presses would now require only three men instead of four. Colfax accepted the union summary but when Colfax received a copy of the actual agreement, it indicated that color presses which printed sheets between 45 and 60 inches would require three men and four color presses over 60 inches would require four men. Colfax instituted a declaratory judgment action asserting that it had no collective bargaining agreement with the union because there was no agreement on an essential term regarding manning requirements. The collective bargaining agreement contained an arbitration clause. In granting judgment for the union, the district court said that the summary of changes that Colfax had accepted unambiguously referred to 60 inch presses and did not apply to Colfax's 78 inch presses. **HOLDING:** On appeal, the court affirmed. It described the dispute as one over the meaning of the term "4C 60 Press-3 Men" with Colfax believing it applied to 60 inch presses and over, and the union believing that it applied to four-color presses, 60 inches and under. Normally the arbitrators would resolve an interpretation dispute. However, when the differences as to the meaning attached to a word are "so deep," the court said it cannot be said that the parties ever agreed and thus they have no contract for anyone to interpret. Thus, the court said that in cases like *Raffles* and *Oswald*, a contract should be terminable without liability when "there is 'no sensible basis for choosing between conflicting understandings' of the contractual language. . . ." This approach should be followed when neither party is responsible for the mistake, as in *Raffles* and *Oswald*, and where both parties are equally blameable, as in *Balistreri*. This case, however, is different from these cited cases [*Raffles*, *Oswald* and *Balistreri*] and Colfax should have realized that the contract was unclear because the phrase, "4C 60 Press-3 Men" does not address the manning requirement of a 4C 78 Press. The union's interpretation that the phrase merely extended the upper bound of the old range for three-man four color presses from 50 to 60 inches may or may not have been correct. But whether the union's interpretation was correct, the court noted that Colfax had reason to believe from reading the language in the summary that the union's interpretation was plausible. The court addressed the question of when a court will resolve the dispute over a patently ambiguous term by interpretation and when will it resolve the dispute by

CASES	SUMMARIES
Colfax, continued	allowing rescission on grounds of mutual misunderstanding. The court said that "[w]hen parties agree to a patently ambiguous term, they submit to have any dispute over it resolved by interpretation. That is what courts and arbitrators are for in contract cases—to resolve interpretative questions founded on ambiguity. It is when parties agree to terms that reasonably appear to each of them to be unequivocal but are not, cases like that of the ship Peerless where the ambiguity is buried, that the possibility of rescission on grounds of mutual misunderstanding, or, the term we prefer, latent ambiguity, arises. A reasonable person in Colfax's position, however, would have realized that its interpretation of the term '4C 60 Press-3 Men' might not coincide with that of the other party or of the tribunal to which a dispute over the meaning of the term would be submitted." Thus Colfax gambled on a favorable interpretation and lost.

Section 6. Supplementing the Agreement with Terms Supplied by Law: Gap Fillers, Warranties, and Mandatory Terms

(A) Filling Contractual Gaps—Generally

(B) Filling Common Contractual Gaps by Statute

(C) Gap Filling With Respect to Product Quality—Implied Warranties in Article 2

Concepts:

- Express warranties often define the quality and character of the parties' performance obligations: "the whole purpose of the law of warranty is to determine what it is that the seller has in essence agreed to sell[.]" UCC §2- 313 cmt. 4 [more material on express warranties is contained in subsection (D)].

- To the extent that affirmations of quality become part of the agreement, they constitute a standard of quality—a warranty—to which the goods must conform at the time of delivery.

- Where the parties' agreement is silent as to any warranties of quality, the UCC provides two implied warranties regarding the quality of the goods, the implied warranty of merchantability, which arises when a merchant with respect to the goods being sold, sells those goods to a buyer and the implied warranty of fitness for a particular purpose, which arises when a seller having reason to know of the buyer's particular purpose for which the goods are needed and that the buyer is relying on the seller's skill and judgment to supply them.

- It is important to note that basically warranties are cumulative: it is often possible on one set of facts for a buyer to claim that the goods failed to meet the requirements for more than one type of warranty.

FRAMEWORK FOR ANALYSIS: Warranties of quality

ASK: Did one of the implied warranties of quality arise?

■ Implied warranty of merchantability? Did an implied warranty arise that the goods sold would be merchantable, for example, would be fit to use for their ordinary purpose?

This depends on whether the seller is a merchant with respect to the goods being sold. If the seller is a merchant with respect to the goods being sold, then the implied warranty of merchantability arose. (*Koken v. Black & Veatch Construction, Inc.*)

■ Implied warranty of fitness for a particular purpose? Did the warranty arise that the goods sold would be fit for a particular purpose? (*Lewis v. Mobil Oil Corp*).

The answer to all of the following questions must be "yes" for the implied warranty of fitness for a particular purpose to arise:

1. Did the seller at the time of contracting have reason to know of the buyer's particular purpose?

2. Did the seller know or have reason to know that the buyer is relying on the seller's skill to furnish suitable goods?

3. Did the buyer rely on the seller's skill or judgment to select the goods?

Assuming one of the implied warranties arose, was it disclaimed? The implied warranties can be disclaimed if done in conformity with UCC §2-316(2) and (3):

■ Warranty of merchantability? **ASK:**

Has the seller excluded or modified the implied warranty of merchantability by using language which mentions the word "merchantability" and, if the disclaimer is in writing, is it conspicuous?

If so, then the disclaimer is valid. If the warranty is disclaimed orally, then it must mention the word "merchantability" to be valid. If the word "merchantability" is not used in the disclaimer, either oral or written, then the disclaimer is not valid.

■ Warranty of fitness for a particular purpose? **ASK:**

Has the seller excluded or modified the implied warranty of fitness for a particular purpose by a writing which is conspicuous?

- To disclaim the warranty, it is sufficient if the writing states that "There are no warranties which extend beyond the description on the face hereof." UCC 2-316(2).
- If the disclaimer is not in writing or if it is in writing but not conspicuous, then it is not a valid disclaimer of the implied warranty of fitness.

Are the circumstances surrounding the transaction sufficient to alert the buyer's attention to the fact that no implied warranties are made or that one is being excluded?

■ **Language?** Has the seller used such language as "with all faults" or "as is"? If so, then all implied warranties are excluded. Some jurisdictions may require such language to be conspicuous.

- **Examination of the goods?** Has the buyer before contracting examined the goods (sample or model) fully or has refused to do so? If so, then there is no implied warranty with respect to defects which an examination would have revealed.

- **Course of dealing, course of performance, usage of trade?** Was any implied warranty excluded or modified by the parties' course of dealing, course of performance, or a usage of trade?

Limitation of remedies? Is there a clause in the parties' agreement limiting the buyer's available remedies upon breach? **ASK:**

- **Exclusive remedy?** Does the agreement provide for any remedy and if it does, was such remedy "expressly agreed to be exclusive?" UCC 2-719(1)(b) If so, it is "the sole remedy" unless it fails of its essential purpose.

- **Essential Purpose?** Did the "circumstances cause an exclusive or limited remedy to fail of its essential purpose?" UCC 2-719(2) To determine whether an exclusive or limited remedy fails of its essential purpose, ask whether the seller is unwilling or unable to repair the defective goods within a reasonable time or the seller is willing and able to repair but repairs cannot be done, perhaps because the goods have been destroyed. If so, then the buyer may turn to the remedies available under the Code. If not, then the limitation is enforceable.

CASES	SUMMARIES
Koken v. Black & Veatch Construction, Inc. (2005) →(CB pg. 471)	**FACTS:** During a construction project, a fire blanket was used to protect the area beneath a torch cutting operation. A fire occurred during that operation. Although the fire was put out with a fire extinguisher, the extinguisher's chemicals damaged a generator. Plaintiffs brought an action for breach of warranty against Auburn, the fire blanket's manufacturer, and Impro, its distributor, claiming that there was a breach of an implied warranty of merchantability. Under UCC §2-314(1), a warranty of merchantability is implied in a contract for the sale of goods if the seller is a merchant with respect to goods of that kind. Auburn and Impro concedingly were merchants of fire blankets. However, there was a question as to whether the goods were merchantable. To be so, the court said the goods must be "fit for the ordinary purposes for which they are used" (UCC §2-314(2)(c)) and plaintiff has the burden of proving the ordinary purpose of the goods. **HOLDING:** The court noted that there was no evidence that the fire blanket was inappropriate or appropriate for cutting operations. Auburn and Impro, however, waived the issue in the lower court when they said that they "'do not contend that the wrong blanket was used for the application described by Perry Austin.'" [Austin was the person who used the blanket.] The court said it must therefore address the issue of whether plaintiffs met their burden of showing that the blanket was not fit for its ordinary purpose. What is the test for determining whether goods are fit for their ordinary purpose? The court answered that a product is fit for its ordinary purpose if it performs in accordance with "the reasonable expectation of an ordinary user or purchaser." Here plaintiffs did not introduce evidence of the expectations of ordinary users except for the subjective views of one individual so plaintiffs did not establish that the ordinary user would

CASES	SUMMARIES
Koken, continued	reasonably expect a fire blanket to prevent the type of damage that occurred. As a result, summary judgment on the breach of warranty claim was properly granted.
Lewis v. Mobil Oil Corp. (1971) →(CB pg. 474)	**FACTS:** Lewis, a sawmill operator, converted his power equipment to a hydraulic system which he purchased from a competitor. Lewis asked Rowe, the local Mobil oil dealer, to get him the proper hydraulic fluid to operate the machinery. Rowe asked Lewis what type of system he had and Lewis said that the machinery was operated by a gear-type pump—that "it was a Commercial pump type." Rowe knew that Lewis knew nothing more about any specific requirements. Rowe did not ask for any further information; he did not know what the proper lubricant was but told Lewis he would find out. Rowe did some checking and sold Lewis Mobil's Ambrex 810, a mineral oil with no chemical additives. Lewis experienced difficulty with the hydraulic system operation, with the oil changing color, foaming, and getting hot. He changed the oil several times but nothing improved. In April, 1965 approximately six months after the hydraulic system began operation, the system broke down and a new one was installed. Lewis had problems with the system for about two years and had to change the pumps six times. He was using a Commercial pump recommended by the hydraulic system designer. For oil filtration, the pump used a metal strainer which was cleaned daily in accordance with the equipment instructions. In April 1967, Lewis installed a Tyrone pump which used a disposable filter in addition to the metal strainer filtration. Mobil recommended Ambrex 810 oil for use with this pump. After three weeks the pump broke down. A new pump was installed and Mobil's representative recommended a new oil containing certain chemical additives, principally a defoamant. Lewis's system worked satisfactorily after that. Lewis sued, asserting that Mobil breached an implied warranty of merchantability and an implied of fitness for a particular purpose. **HOLDING:** The court did not address the question of the existence of a merchantability warranty but concluded that there was an implied warranty of fitness for a particular purpose. Under UCC §2-315 a warranty of fitness for a particular purpose is implied if the seller has "reason to know" of the use for which the buyer is purchasing the goods and if the buyer relies on the seller's expertise to supply the proper product. (Seller must also have reason to know that buyer is relying on seller's skill or judgment to select the goods) The court noted—citing to UCC §2-315 comment 1—that the buyer does not have to make sure the seller knows of the particular purpose or of buyer's reliance, as long as "the circumstances are such that the seller has reason to realize the purpose intended or that the reliance exists." Here, Lewis showed that Ambrex 810 was purchased for the specific hydraulic system that he was using—and not just for a hydraulic system in general. Mobil knew of this specific purpose and the evidence was clear that Lewis relied on Mobil to supply the proper oil. Mobil claimed that Lewis did not give Mobil enough information to determine whether an additive was needed. The court, however, said that if Mobil needed any further information it was incumbent on Mobil to get the information before making any recommendation. Finally, Mobil argued that Lewis' system had a few abnormal features, namely an inadequate filtration system and a capacity to entrain excessive air. The court pointed out that these contentions go to

CASES	SUMMARIES
Lewis , *continued*	the question of causation and not to whether an implied warranty exists. Second, even if plaintiffs' system had these abnormal features, the whole point of an implied warranty of fitness for a particular purpose is that the product being supplied will be suitable for the specific purpose and if not, the seller should not supply it.

South Carolina Electric and Gas Co. v. Combustion Engineering, Inc. (1984)

→(CB pg. 478)

FACTS: South Carolina Electric (SCE) entered into a contract with Combustion pursuant to which SCE purchased a boiler unit and its ancillary equipment from Combustion. The contract had an item headed "WARRANTY" that contained an express warranty that the equipment would be free from defects for a one year period. A flexible metal hose ruptured resulting in a fire from the heated fuel oil that escaped. SCE brought an action against Combustion claiming, among other things, breach of an implied warranty of merchantability, despite the fact that the contract provision labeled "WARRANTY" also contained a sentence that stated "[t]here are no other warranties, whether expressed or implied, other than title."

HOLDING: The Ct of Appeals agreed with SCE in finding that the disclaimer did not meet the requirements of UCC §2-316. For a disclaimer of an implied warranty of merchantability to be valid, it must mention the word "merchantability" and must be "conspicuous." Here the disclaimer neither mentioned the word "merchantability" nor was it conspicuous. To be conspicuous, a clause must be "'so written that a reasonable person against whom it is to operate ought to have noticed it'" such as "'if it is in larger or other contrasting type or color.'" Here the contract was twenty-two typewritten pages, mostly single-spaced and the disclaimer was contained on page 17 in the last sentence of a two paragraph item. It was therefore "indistinctive both as to color and as to type." In addition, the disclaimer was in a paragraph headed "WARRANTY" which is misleading because it suggests that the paragraph only contains language granting a warranty, not disclaiming it. In short, the disclaimer in the contract was not conspicuous as required by UCC §2-316(2).

The court, nevertheless, found that the disclaimer was effective under UCC §3-316(3)(a) which provides for the exclusion of implied warranties by "language which in common understanding calls the buyer's attention to the exclusion of warranties and makes plain that there is no implied warranty." Although the court did not quote this language of the Section, it quoted comment 6 to find that "the circumstances surrounding the transaction are in themselves sufficient to call the buyer's attention to the fact that no implied warranties are made or that a certain implied warranty is excluded." Here the parties exchanged several documents over a period of many months which showed that the parties specifically discussed the implied warranty of fitness with SCE stating that Combustion must agree to the warranties implied by the laws of South Carolina and Combustion telling SCE that it could not accept SCE's condition; ultimately SCE indicated that any warranties would be limited to what was included in the original proposal.

The court made it clear that it found the language of the disclaimer clear and unambiguous and was not using the parties' correspondence to clear up any ambiguity.

CASES	SUMMARIES
South Carolina Electric, continued	Rather the correspondence showed that as a matter of law "the language [of the disclaimer] was bargained for and expected." Thus any implied warranties were properly disclaimed. Note: The court did not discuss the question—and the parties might not have raised it—whether an exclusion under UCC §2-316(3)(a) must be conspicuous and whether actual knowledge of an exclusion is sufficient to satisfy the conspicuous requirement.
Henningsen v. Bloomfield Motors, Inc. (1960) →(CB pg. 482)	**FACTS:** Claus Henningsen bought a new Chrysler car from Bloomfield. Shortly after the car had been delivered, his wife was injured when the car's steering mechanism failed. Henningsen sued Bloomfield Motors and Chrysler for breach of an implied warranty of merchantability under the Uniform Sales Act. Defendants relied on a disclaimer provision contained among 8 ½ inches of fine print on the back of the purchase contract which limited the buyer's remedy for any breach of warranty to replacement of defective parts. Above the signature lines on the front, in six point type, (as distinguished from twelve point type for most of the language on the front) was a statement to the effect that the front and the back contained the entire purchase agreement and that the buyer had read and agreed to the terms on the back. From a judgment for Henningsen, defendants appealed. **HOLDING:** The court noted that the warranty was the standardized form of the American Manufacturers Association (AMA) which included as members General Motors, Ford, Chrysler, and others. Thus, if a consumer wants to buy an automobile, he must accept the standardized form without any bargaining. In the area of express warranty, therefore, there was no competition among car makers and a buyer could not go to another dealer to negotiate better protection. In the car industry, the court stated there was a gross inequality in the parties' bargaining positions. It was undisputed that the dealer did not call Henningsen's attention to the warranty on the back of the purchase order and that the word "warranty" or the word "limited warranty" did not appear in the fine print above the space of the signature. The court noted, however, that even if the fine print on the front had directed the buyer's attention to the warranty on the reverse side, "can it be said that an ordinary layman would realize what he was relinquishing in return for what he was being granted?" The warranty provided in part, that Chrysler's obligation under the warranty was "limited to making good at its factory any part or parts thereof." A reasonable layman, reading this language, might conclude that Chrysler was agreeing to replace defective parts but that he would not be entitled to a new car. "It is not unreasonable to believe that the entire scheme being conveyed was a proposed remedy for physical deficiencies in the car." However, in the context of the warranty, the court said, one would have to abandon all sense of justice to hold "as a matter of law" that the phrase "its obligation under this warranty being limited to making good at its factory any part or parts thereof" would signify to a reasonable person that he was giving up any personal injury claim that might arise from the defective car's use.

CASES	SUMMARIES
Henningsen, continued	The court noted that the automobile industry is unique in the sense that there are few manufacturers and they have a strong bargaining position. As far as warranties are concerned, the AMA has created a united front and a purchaser has no arms' length negotiation power on the subject of warranties. "Public policy is a term not easily defined." Although parties should not be unnecessarily restricted in their freedom to contract, a court will not "hesitate to declare void as against public policy contractual provisions which clearly tend to the injury of the public in some way. . . ."

(D) Express Warranties

Concepts:

- An express warranty relating to the goods is created by a seller when the seller makes an "affirmation of fact or promise" which relates to the goods and becomes part of the "basis of the bargain." UCC §2-313(1)

- Express warranty cases raise distinct questions: one is whether the seller's statement was an "affirmation of fact or promise" or only the seller's opinion or "puffery"; another is whether the seller's promise or affirmation became part of the "basis of the bargain." (*Bayliner Marine Corp. v. Crow*, CB pg. 4)

- Express warranties can be created by "any description of the goods which is made part of the basis of the bargain." UCC §2-313(b); express warranties can also be created by "any sample or model which is made part of the basis of the bargain." UCC §2-313(c)

FRAMEWORK FOR ANALYSIS: Express warranty

ASK: Did the seller's statements or acts create an express warranty?

- Affirmation of fact or promise? Did the seller make some statement of fact about the goods which became part of the basis of the bargain? If so, then an express warranty has been created. However, if the seller's words lack specificity or are equivocal or are "merely the seller's opinion or commendation of the goods," then an express warranty has not been created. UCC §2-313(2)

- Description of the goods? Did the seller provide a description of the goods which became part of the basis of the bargain? If so, an express warranty has been created.

- Sample or Model? Did the seller make reference to a sample or model of the goods which became part of the basis of the bargain such that the whole of the goods shall conform to the sample or model? If so, an express warranty has been created.

(E) Supplementing the Contract With Mandatory Terms—Good Faith

Concepts:

- The obligation of good faith is well-recognized in general contract law as an implied term in every contract.

- Both the common law and the UCC impose upon each party to a contract the duty of good faith and fair dealing in its performance and enforcement. R2d §205: "Every contract imposes upon each party a duty of good faith and fair dealing in its performance and its enforcement." Revised UCC §1-304: "Every contract or duty within [the Uniform Commercial Code] imposes an obligation of good faith in its performance and enforcement."

- This duty is based on fundamental notions of fairness and its scope varies according to the nature of the agreement. Some conduct, such as subterfuge and evasion, clearly violates the duty, even if the actor believes his conduct to be justified. R2d §205 cmt.d

- Under the Code, good faith is deemed so important to the essence of the bargain relationship that parties are specifically prohibited from disclaiming "the obligations of good faith, diligence, reasonableness and care prescribed by [the Uniform Commercial Code] . . . ." UCC §1-302(b)

See also Chapter 6, Section 4. Performing in Good Faith

■ CHAPTER 6. LIMITS ON THE BARGAIN AND ITS PERFORMANCE

Section 1. Unfairness

Concepts:

- While there is no additional requirement of "equivalence in the values exchanged" (R2d §79(b)) if the primary requirement of consideration is met, courts have developed a variety of measures or "conventional controls" in order to "limit certain bargains marked by an inequality of exchange." →**(CB. PG. 489)** (*McKinnon v. Benedict*)

- Restrictions on the use of land "are not favored in the law." (*Mueller v. Schier*)

CASES	SUMMARIES
McKinnon v. Benedict (1968) → **(CB pg. 491)**	**FACTS:** In 1960, McKinnon assisted the Benedicts in buying an 80 acre resort camp which in part was enclosed by a 1,000 acre property owned by McKinnon. McKinnon promised the Benedicts some help in getting business and also made a $5,000 loan to them which they used as a down payment for the purchase of the resort. In exchange, the Benedicts agreed to a 25-year restriction not to cut any trees between the camp and McKinnon's property and not to make any improvements closer to McKinnon's property than the present camp's buildings. Within seven months, the Benedicts repaid the loan but did not have much success with the resort business. In 1964, the Benedicts began improving the camp and in the summer, 1965, when McKinnon returned from Arizona where he spent the winter, he instituted suit against Benedicts seeking to enjoin construction of the improvements. The trial court issued the injunction. **HOLDING:** On appeal, the court noted that equity will not enforce oppressive contracts and that public policy did not favor restriction on the use of land. The court found that the contract imposed great hardship on the Benedicts with the Benedicts receiving very little value for the promised restriction. The value of the $5,000 loan was only approximately $145.00 and McKinnon's promise to generate business resulted in one group occupying the camp for less than one week and McKinnon made only one attempt to resolve the occupancy of one of the cottages which had a 50-year lease at a $5.00 per year rental. Although McKinnon argued that without the loan the Benedicts could not have bought the property, the court took this as evidence that the Benedicts could not deal at arm's length with McKinnon and that they were willing to enter into a contract that was inequitable. The court found the inadequacy of consideration was unconscionable and thus McKinnon was not entitled to invoke the court's equitable powers. The court also looked to the benefit the contract afforded McKinnon to see whether oppressive terms outweighed the benefits McKinnon derived from the contract. Although McKinnon only used the property in the summer, it was important that there be no disruption of the quiet and pleasant enjoyment from the trailer camp. However, the McKinnon's home apparently was shielded from the resort during the summer when the leaves were on the trees. Thus the detriment to McKinnon, which was an appropriate item to consider, was minimal as compared to the hardship on the Benedicts.

CASES	SUMMARIES
McKinnon, continued	In short, given the inadequate consideration, the minor benefit McKinnon derived from the contract, and the oppressive condition imposed on the Benedicts, the contract failed to meet "test of reasonableness" necessary for enforcement in equity. Citing to Corbin, the court noted that this type of contract may be enforceable at law to recover damages but in a court of equity, a harsh and oppressive contract will not be enforced.
Tuckwiller v. Tuckwiller (1967) → (CB pg. 494)	**FACTS:** Mrs. Tuckwiller lived on a family farm half owned by Mrs. Morrison. When she was about 70, Mrs. Morrison contracted Parkinson's Disease which she knew was a progressive disease where the victim would ultimately depend entirely upon outside care. She left New York and returned to the farm. Mrs. Morrison wanted Mrs. Tuckwiller to quit her job and care for her. In a writing she drafted shortly before Mrs. Morrison's death—and signed by Mrs. Morrison—Mrs. Tuckwiller said she would take care of Mrs. Morrison for her lifetime in exchange for which Mrs. Morrison would will her the farm. Mrs. Tuckwiller gave up her job and Mrs. Morrison made an appointment to change her will. However, in early May, on the day Mrs. Morrison made the appointment she fell ill, was taken to the hospital, and except for 4 days, was in the hospital until she died on June 14 at the age of 73. Mrs. Tuckwiller spent time at the hospital assisting as she could. Mrs. Tuckwiller brought an action to specifically enforce her contract with Mrs. Morrison and was granted judgment.

HOLDING: On appeal, the court said that whether a contract is so unfair or inequitable or is unconscionable must be determined by viewing the contract prospectively. Here, Mrs. Tuckwiller gave up her employment to undertake an obligation of unknown and uncertain duration which involved duties that would be increasingly difficult in light of the usual course of Parkinson's. From Mrs. Morrison's standpoint, the contract was not unfair. Mrs. Tuckwiller had given her care and attention before the contract was signed which Mrs. Morrison appreciated and, knowing that she had no immediate family and aware of her future, she was thankful for Mrs. Tuckwiller's attention and personal care and was concerned over impersonal care in a nursing home or other institution. Defendant argued that in light of the brief duration of Mrs. Tuckwiller's services and the disparity of their value in comparison with the farm's value, Mrs. Tuckwiller should only be entitled to the reasonable value of her services. However, the court said once a contract is deemed fair and adequate consideration is found, then the contract which was one for real estate, should as a matter of course be specifically enforced. |
| *Black Industries, Inc. v. Bush (1953)* → (CB pg. 496) | **FACTS:** Black Industries, a manufacturer of machine parts, was asked to bid on contracts with The Hoover Company ("Hoover") and Standby Products to supply anvils for $8.10 per thousand, holder primers for $16.00 per thousand, and plunger supports for $21.20 per thousand, which Hoover and Standby would use to fulfill government contracts during the Korean War. In turn, Black entered into a contract with Bush to buy those items which Bush agreed to manufacture in accordance with government |

CASES	SUMMARIES
Black Industries, continued	specifications: anvils for $4.40 per thousand, holder primers for $11.50 per thousand, and plunger supports for $12.00 per thousand. Under the Black-Bush contract, Hoover was to issue a purchase order directly to Bush who would deliver the merchandise to Hoover but Black would have the right to bill Hoover. Black would retain as compensation the difference between Bush's price to Black and Black's price to Hoover. Black and Standby had a similar contract. Bush started but failed to complete the order; Black sued for damages. Bush moved for summary judgment, claiming that the contract was void as against public policy because Black's profits were excessive (e.g. 84.09% on anvils) and were passed on to the government in the form of increased prices. In support of its position, Bush cited two federal laws which were intended to prevent excessive profits on war contracts. **HOLDING:** At the outset, the court stated that recognized legal principles must be invoked to declare a contract void as against public policy. It noted that the Bush/Black contract could not be held void based on the precedents Bush relied on: the contract did not contemplate bribing a government official or doing an illegal act nor did it involve collusive bidding on a public contract. Black might be receiving too high a profit because Hoover agreed to pay too much or Bush might have quoted too low a price. But even if Black were making more than Bush for a smaller contribution, it is irrelevant because a contract negotiated at arm's length is not affected by the relative values of the consideration. Finally, the court noted that the fact the government was the ultimate purchaser of the products using Bush's parts was not a reason to hold the contract against public policy. If it were, then it would require either holding all contracts which compensate middlemen such as Black to be void if the product was sold to the government, or deciding case by case whether the middleman's compensation was reasonable. In the latter case, the court would become a price regulator. The court noted that its function is not to interfere in determining contract validity between ordinary businessmen on the basis of its belief as to the adequacy of its consideration. There are procedures in place, the court said, that are more effective to make sure the government pays a reasonable price for supplies.

Section 2. Standard Form and Adhesion Contracts

Concepts:

- Standard form contracts: industry-drafted contracts.

- Adhesion contracts: a contract where the terms are offered on a "take-it-or-leave-it" basis and are often oppressively one-sided. (*Graham v. Scissor-Tail, Inc.*)

CASES	SUMMARIES

O'Callaghan v. Waller & Beckwith Realty Co. (1958)

→ (CB pg. 503)

FACTS: The tenant, Mrs. O'Callaghan, sued defendant for negligence in maintaining and operating its large apartment building which resulted in her injury when she fell while crossing a defectively paved courtyard. Her lease contained an exculpatory clause relieving the landlord from liability to the tenant for personal injuries caused by the landlord's negligence. The tenant claimed that such a clause in a residential lease was invalid as contrary to public policy. The jury returned a verdict for Mrs. O'Callaghan and defendant appealed.

HOLDING: On appeal, the court noted that such exculpatory provisions are generally enforced "'unless (1) it would be against the settled public policy of the State to do so, or (2) there is something in the social relationship of the parties militating against upholding the agreement.'" The court noted that in the absence of a statute it knew of no court of last resort (other than a New Hampshire case), that had held clauses in residential as well as commercial leases which exculpated landlords for negligence, to be invalid. The court rejected plaintiff's argument that a housing shortage gave the landlord an unconscionable advantage over the tenant. It noted that Mrs. O'Callaghan made no showing at trial that she was concerned about the exculpatory clause or that she tried to negotiate its modification or elimination or that she tried to rent elsewhere. The court recognized that there was a housing shortage but noted that there were legislative responses to it including rent controls setting a maximum that landlords could charge for rent. The court noted that any further response should come from the legislature rather than through judicial action. A housing shortage at one time or place does not mean that there will be future shortages or indicate that shortages have always and everywhere existed. The court pointed out that "[j]udicial determinations of public policy cannot readily take account of sporadic and transitory circumstances."

DISSENT: The form lease with its exculpatory clause was entered into in 1947 when there were waiting lists for housing and that any element of competition was purely theoretical. The dissent realized that there was no precise definition of public policy or rule to test whether a contract is contrary to public policy. Each case must be determined on its own particular circumstances. However, there is a recognized policy of protecting people "in need of goods or services from being overreached by those with power to drive unconscionable bargains." Citing to Williston, the court stated that in determining whether exculpatory clauses are void, the "courts have weighed such factors as the importance which the subject has for the physical and economic well-being of the group agreeing to the release; their bargaining power; the amount of free choice actually exercised in agreeing to the exemption; and the existence of competition among the group to be exempted." Applying this criteria to the exculpatory clause which relates to shelter, an indispensable necessity for a tenant's well-being, the dissent stated that the tenants had no free choice or equality of bargaining power in agreeing to the exculpatory clause and that "every material ground for voiding the exculpatory clause exists in the lease involved in the instant case. . . ."

CASES	SUMMARIES
Graham v. Scissor-Tail, Inc. (1981) → (CB pg. 508)	**FACTS:** Graham, an experienced musical concert producer, entered into four identical form contracts with Scissor-Tail which represented the recording artist, Leon Russell. The form contract, known in the industry as the "American Federation of Musicians Form B Contract," provided that any disputes would be arbitrated by the union's national executive board. A dispute arose as to whether losses on one contract could be offset by profits on another. Graham sued for breach and Scissor-Tail successfully moved to compel arbitration. Graham appealed from a judgment confirming an arbitrator's award in favor of Scissor-Tail. Graham claimed that the contract was unenforceable because it was an adhesion contract and that the arbitration provision was unconscionable. **HOLDING:** On appeal, the court explained that the term "contract of adhesion" refers to "'a standardized contract, which, imposed and drafted by the party of superior bargaining strength, relegates to the subscribing party only the opportunity to adhere to the contract or reject it.'" In this case, the court found the contract to be one of adhesion despite Graham's prominence and success in promoting musical concerts. The court noted that basically all prominent concert artists are American Federation members and under its rules are prohibited from signing any contract other than the union's form contract. Thus the reality of Graham's business—a concert promoter—required him to sign the form contract with any concert artist with whom he wanted to do business. The court stated that a contract of adhesion does not mean that the contract is unenforceable. Such a contract is enforceable subject to two judicially imposed limitations: (1) that the contract falls within the reasonable expectations of the weaker party or (2) that even if the contract is consistent with the parties' reasonable expectations, it will not be enforced if, "considered in its context, it is unduly oppressive or 'unconscionable.'" The court concluded that the form contract met Graham's reasonable expectations. Among other things, the court noted that Graham was a party to literally thousands of American Federation contracts containing similar arbitration provisions, including contracts with Scissor-Tail. However, as to the second judicially imposed limitation, the court found that since the American Federation arbitration provision "designates an arbitrator who, by reason of its status and identity, is presumptively biased in favor of one party" the arbitration provision was unconscionable.
Doe v. Great Expectations (2005) → (CB pg. 518)	**FACTS:** Two claimants entered into similar contracts with defendant in which defendant offered to expand the client's social horizon mostly by an internet posting of the client's video which other clients could see and decide whether to pursue social interaction. A boilerplate printed form had standard terms that did not promise any social referrals. The court held that the contract was subject to New York's "Dating Services Law" which regulates "social referral services" that fall within the scope of NY's General Business Obligations Law §394-c (Gen. Bus. §394-c[1][a]). **HOLDING:** The court found (1) that the contract was not statutorily compliant because the client was not assured a specified number of social referrals per month and thus the defendant could not charge more than the statutory fee of $25.00 and (2) that defendant's form contract violated the Dating Service Law in every respect

CASES	SUMMARIES
Doe, continued	except one. On the issue of damages, claimants were entitled to recover actual damages which included the difference between the contract price ($1,000 paid by one claimant and $3,790 by the other) and the maximum $25 fee permitted under the Dating Services Law for these contracts. However, defendant also had an obligation to make sure that each dating service client knew its statutory rights. Thus, it was required to give them a copy of the "Dating Service Consumer Bill of Rights" which it did not do. Since each claimant would not have signed the contract containing terms violating the law had they known of their rights, the claimants were also entitled to a refund of the $25 balance. Finally, the court considered whether it should report the violations to the appropriate governmental agencies. After considering various factors, the court decided to forward a copy of its decision in the case to the appropriate public officials.

Section 3. Unconscionability

Concepts:

- An unconscionable contract is one that is manifestly unfair or oppressive – a contract which no one in her right senses and not under a delusion would make.

- The contract must be unconscionable at the time of its making.

- In determining whether a contract is unconscionable, the court looks to see whether it is procedurally and substantively unconscionable.

FRAMEWORK FOR ANALYSIS: Is the contract manifestly unfair or oppressive?

In determining whether a contract is unconscionable, look for an overall imbalance based on the following considerations at the time of contract:

a. Procedural Unconscionability—was the bargaining process characterized by any of the following:
  - An absence of meaningful choice?
  - Unequal bargaining power?
  - A lack of opportunity to study the contract and inquire about the terms?
  - Non-negotiable terms?

b. Substantive Unconscionability—were the terms of the contract unfairly one-sided?
  - Is there a large disparity between the prevailing market price and the contract price? (*Jones v. Star Credit Corp.*)

CASES	SUMMARIES
Williams v. Walker-Thomas Furniture Co. (1965) → **(CB pg. 525)**	**FACTS:** Williams and Thorn each purchased items from defendant Walker-Thomas during the period from 1957 to 1962. Each of the printed form contracts provided that Walker-Thomas would retain title until all monthly payments equaled the value of the items listed in the contract. Default in payment of any monthly installment entitled Walker-Thomas to repossess the item. Further, the preprinted contracts contained a clause that provided that all payments would be credited pro-rata on all outstanding accounts at the time each payment was made. This meant that until the balance due on all items were paid, each new item purchased became subject to a security interest for all of the prior dealings. In 1962, Williams bought a stereo on which she defaulted and Walker-Thomas sought to replevin all items Williams purchased since December 1957. Similarly, Walker-Thomas sought to replevin all items Thorn purchased since 1958 when he defaulted on his monthly payments for three tables and two lamps purchased in May, 1962. The lower courts [both the trial and appellate courts] rejected plaintiffs' argument that the contracts were unconscionable and found for Walker-Thomas. **HOLDING:** On appeal, the court held as a matter of first impression that if the contract is unconscionable it should not be enforced and that this rule was the District of Columbia's common law. It noted that after the contracts here were entered into, Congress enacted the UCC which permits a court under Section 2-302 to refuse to enforce a contract or any provision that it finds unconscionable at the time the contract was made. The court stated that unconscionability includes "an absence of meaningful choice on the part of one of the parties together with contract terms which are unreasonably favorable to the other party." Whether there is meaningful choice must be decided by examining all surrounding circumstances such as the manner in which the contract was entered into, the parties' education, whether each party had a reasonable opportunity to understand the terms and whether important terms were buried in fine print and minimized by deceptive practices. Although a party assumes the risk of not reading a contract, the court explained that where there is "little bargaining power, and hence little real choice," the signing of a "commercially unreasonable contract with little or no knowledge of its terms" means that it is unlikely "that his consent, or even an objective manifestation of his consent, was ever given to all the terms." Under these circumstances, the usual rule that contract terms are not questioned should be abandoned and the unfair contract not enforced. **DISSENT:** Agreed with the lower court's view that while the situation was an unhappy one, it was Congress that should undertake any corrective action.
Jones v. Star Credit Corp. (1969) → **(CB pg. 532)**	**FACTS:** Plaintiffs, welfare recipients, agreed to purchase a $900 home freezer unit at a total cost of $1234.80 which included purchase price, time credit charges, credit life insurance and credit property insurance. Although plaintiffs had paid $619.88 toward the purchase, defendant claimed that with added credit charges, plaintiffs still owed $819.81. When purchased, the freezer unit had a maximum retail value of about $300. UCC §2-302 permits a court to find a contract unconscionable and this Section, the court said, extends to the price term of an agreement. The court found that under these circumstances, the contract was unconscionable as matter of law, noting that "deciding the issue is substantially easier than explaining it."

CASES	SUMMARIES
Jones, continued	**HOLDING:** The court reasoned that in many cases the lack of credit would deprive many, including welfare recipients, of basic conveniences. However, in this instance the sale of the freezer for $900 was exorbitant on its face given that the retail value was $300 and that presumably includes a reasonable profit margin. The credit charges alone exceeded by more than $100 the retail value of the freezer. The court warned against reducing "the import of Section 2-302 solely to a mathematical ratio formula. It may, at times, be that; yet it may also be much more." The purchaser's very limited financial resources, known to the sellers at the time of the sale, should be considered. Indeed, "the value disparity itself leads inevitably to the felt conclusion that knowing advantage was taken of the plaintiffs. In addition, the meaningfulness of choice essential to the making of a contract, can be negated by a gross inequality of bargaining power." (citing *Williams v. Walker*) The court held in accordance with UCC §2-302 that the contract's payment provision should be limited to the $600 plaintiffs already paid.
Scott v. Cingular Wireless (2007) → **(CB pg. 540)**	**FACTS:** Plaintiffs' cellular phone calling plans agreement with defendant, Cingular, contained a clause requiring mandatory arbitration and that clause contained a provision prohibiting class actions and class arbitrations, i.e., a "class action waiver." Plaintiffs brought a class action claiming they were improperly billed for certain services resulting in individuals being overcharged about $45 a month. Cingular moved to compel each plaintiff to individually arbitrate. Plaintiffs claimed that the class action waiver was unenforceable because it was substantially and procedurally unconscionable. Although concluding that it was an adhesion contract, the trial court nevertheless granted Cingular's motion because the agreement was not sufficiently complex or misleading to be considered procedurally unconscionable nor did the court find any substantive unconscionability. On appeal, plaintiffs argued that the class action waiver clause was unconscionable because it denied consumers a meaningful opportunity to prove their case and undermined the protections of Washington's CPA [Consumer Protection Act]. **HOLDING:** The Washington Supreme Court took direct review and concluded that the class action waiver was unconscionable because it effectively denied large numbers of consumers the protection of Washington's Consumer Protection Act (CPA) and because it exculpated Cingular from liability for a whole class of wrongful conduct. The court further found that since the arbitration clause provided that if any part of it was found unenforceable, then the entire clause was void, there was no basis to compel arbitration. Accordingly, the court vacated the order compelling arbitration and remanded the case to the trial court for further proceedings consistent with its opinion. In its analysis, the court noted that an agreement that was against the public good or injurious to the public violated public policy. The court explained that consumer actions under Washington's CPA vindicated not only individual rights but the public interest by allowing plaintiffs to seek injunctive relief to deter future wrongful conduct, thus benefiting the public. Class actions are a critical aspect of enforcing consumer protection law because absent a class action, many meritorious claims would not be asserted because the dollar damage to any individual consumer would be

CASES	SUMMARIES
Scott, continued	

small. The court concluded that the class action waiver was "an unconscionable violation" of the State's policy "to protect the public and foster fair and honest competition" because it seriously diminished the ability to vindicate consumer rights. Because the waiver clause prevented CPA cases from being brought, the clause was substantively unconscionable. In a footnote, the court added that since the waiver clause was substantially unconscionable, it was unnecessary to consider whether it was procedurally unconscionable.

Note: This court's analysis departs from the usual unconscionability analysis which considers both procedural and substantive unconscionability in a determination of whether a contract provision, on the whole, would be sufficiently objectionable to be found "unconscionable."

Next, the court discussed whether the clause was also unconscionable because it effectively exculpated Cingular from liability for a large class of wrongful conduct. Here the waiver clause insulated Cingular against legal liability for any wrong where the cost of pursuing a claim outweighed the potential recovery. However, redress for a small injury is often only possible as a class action. In fact, in many cases, a class action informs many consumers that they have a claim. Apparently, claims as small as those in this case would be impractical to pursue individually "even in small claims court, and particularly in arbitration." Plaintiffs introduced evidence that prohibitive cost prevents claims and indeed, no individual customers brought arbitrations against Cingular for six years prior to the present case. Finally, the court noted that Cingular's promise to pay attorney fees only applied if the plaintiffs recovered 100%—not 99.9%—of their demand and even then, the arbitrator could consider the amount in dispute in deciding attorney fees. As a practical matter, attorneys generally will not take an individual arbitration involving trivial amounts. Finally, since the waiver provided that if it was found to be unenforceable then the entire arbitration clause would be void, there was no basis to compel arbitration.

DISSENT: If there was to be a state policy prohibiting class action waivers in consumer agreements, then the legislature should make that public policy. Further, unconscionability should be determined on a case by case basis and, under the Federal Arbitration Act, an arbitration agreement should be presumed valid.

Section 4. Performing in Good Faith

Concepts:

- "Every contract imposes upon each party a duty of good faith and fair dealing in its performance and its enforcement." R2d §205

- In general, "good faith performance or enforcement of a contract emphasizes faithfulness to an agreed common purpose and consistency with the justified expectations of the other party; it excludes a variety of types of conduct characterized as involving 'bad faith' because they violate community standards of decency, fairness or reasonableness." R2d §205 cmt. a

- While a complete listing of types of bad faith is impossible, R2d §205 comment d identifies the following types of behavior as illustrative of bad faith behavior: evasion of the spirit of the bargain, lack of diligence and slacking off, willful rendering of imperfect performance, abuse of a power to specify terms, and interference or failure to cooperate in the other party's performance.

CASES	SUMMARIES
Dalton v. Educational Testing Service (1995) → (CB pg. 550)	**FACTS:** Dalton took the SAT in May and again in November. Because his combined score increased 410 points, it fell within the defendant Educational Testing Service's (ETS) category of "discrepant scores." This required ETS to review his tests. The handwriting on the two tests seemed different and a document examiner said that the writing was from two different individuals. ETS decided that there was enough evidence to cancel Dalton's November score. When he registered for the November SAT, Dalton had accepted ETS' standardized form agreement which provided that if a test score's validity was questioned, Dalton would have five options, the first of which was "the opportunity to provide additional information." Dalton submitted additional information, including evidence that he was suffering from mononucleosis at the May test, diagnostic test results from a prep course he had taken before the November test which were consistent with his November test score (he had not taken a similar course prior to the May SAT), statements from an ETS proctor and from two students who said that Dalton was present in November, and a document examiner's report that Dalton wrote both tests. After Dalton submitted this information, ETS did no more than to submit handwriting samples to another examiner who also came to the conclusion that the tests were not written by the same person. ETS believed that the only issue was the disparity in handwriting and that evidence of Dalton's health or his presence at the exam was irrelevant. The trial court concluded that ETS had not acted in good faith and directed ETS to release Dalton's November score; the appellate division affirmed. **HOLDING:** On appeal, the NY Ct of Appeals stated that there is an obligation of good faith in every contract and this includes a pledge not to do anything which would injure the other party's right to receive the contract's benefits and that "[w]here the contract contemplates the exercise of discretion, this pledge includes a promise not to act arbitrarily or irrationally in exercising that discretion." The court emphasized, however, that the duty of good faith has limits and "no obligation can be implied that 'would be inconsistent with other terms of the contractual relation-

CASES	SUMMARIES
Dalton, continued	ship.'" After noting that ETS "was under no duty, express or implied, to initiate an external investigation into a questioned score" the court said that ETS was required to consider any relevant material that Dalton furnished ETS. ETS argued that the information Dalton provided was irrelevant except for the handwriting examiner's report. However, the court said, "ETS expressly framed the dispositive question as one of suspected impersonation" so the statements of evidence of his presence as well as his health and the diagnostic test were all relevant on the issue of whether Dalton or someone else took the November exam. Here ETS refused to even consider relevant material Dalton submitted and therefore it breached its contractual obligation to comply in good faith with its test security procedures. The court pointed out that it would not interfere with any discretionary determination by ETS unless that determination was done arbitrarily or irrationally. The court agreed with the lower courts that specific performance of the contract was the appropriate remedy; however, this remedy entitled Dalton to a good faith consideration of the material he gave ETS and not as the lower courts said, to the release of the November score as if it were valid.
De La Concha of Hartford, Inc. v. Aetna Life Insurance Company (2004) → (CB pg. 559)	**FACTS:** In 1975, the plaintiff, De La Concha, rented space in defendant's Hartford Civic Center, an enclosed mall, to sell tobacco products. Consumers who came to the mall to buy from one retailer often bought from others so mall traffic was important to all of them. The Civic Center never found an anchor tenant and even when fully occupied, the mall lost money. In 1995, the Civic Center's new manager determined that the mall had lost more than $50 million since 1975 and its losses continued because of high expenses and low rental income. The manager considered several options, including closing the mall or finding a partner who could run it profitably. The manager believed a sale was most likely so to make it most saleable, he adopted a policy of granting short term leases, basically stopped promoting the mall, and cut its promotion budget. In 1999, defendant agreed to sell the Civic Center for development of a high rise residential complex. In 2000, plaintiff sought to exercise its option to renew its lease for five years. Defendant refused to renew because plaintiff was behind in its rent and had not maintained annual minimum sales of $262,500 as its lease required. Plaintiff claimed that defendant breached an implied obligation of good faith and fair dealing by changing its policy on leasing and promotions and refusing to renew plaintiff's lease. The trial court entered judgment for defendant. **HOLDING:** On appeal, the court stated that there is an implied duty in every contract that neither party should "do anything that will injure the right of the other to receive the benefits of the agreement." A party breaches the good faith obligation when it acts in bad faith to impede the other party's right to receive the reasonably expected contract benefits. Generally, bad faith "'implies both actual or constructive fraud, or a design to mislead or deceive another, or a neglect or refusal to fulfill some duty or some contractual obligation, not prompted by an honest mistake as to one's rights or duties, but by some interested or sinister motive. . . . Bad faith . . . involves a dishonest purpose.'" Applying these principles to defendant's conduct, the court agreed with the trial court in finding that defendant had not breached any express term of the lease nor the implied obligation of good faith. While plaintiff claimed that defendant had acted to "starve out" the tenants to make it more saleable once it had decided to sell the Civil Center, the court found that defendant's actions were

CASES	SUMMARIES
De La Concha, continued	undertaken for the purpose of unloading an unsuccessful business venture that had resulted in losses of $50 million over 20 years. Further, defendant had gone to great lengths to retain existing tenants and attract new ones by offering certain tenants rent reductions to induce lease renewals. The court found that defendant's elimination of promotional activity expenditures did not materially bear on plaintiff's gross sales: the reduction of plaintiff's gross sales from 1998-2000 resulted from the economy and the end of the cigar boom and not from defendant's management policies. The court noted that defendant had the right to take action to reduce the losses it had suffered and was not obligated to ensure plaintiff's economic well-being. The court upheld the trial court's decision and concluded that since defendant was not responsible either for plaintiff's non-payment of rent or for its not having gross annual revenues of at least $262,500, it was entitled to refuse to renew the lease: defendant's actions were motivated by legitimate business interests and not by some improper purpose.
Market Street Associates v. Frey **(1991)** → **(CB pg. 564)**	**FACTS:** J.C. Penney sold to, and leased back from, General Electric Pension Trust ("Trust") certain property. Under paragraph 34 of the lease, the Trust agreed that if Penney asked for financing to make improvements, the Trust would consider it; if, among other things, the negotiations over financing were unsuccessful, Penney had the option to repurchase the property. After twenty years, Market Street Associates (Market Street succeeded Penney under the lease) wanted to repurchase the property at a favorable price computed by the formula in paragraph 34. Mr. Orenstein of Market Street sent two letters to the Trust, requesting $4 million in financing but without mentioning paragraph 34. In response to the first letter, Erb of the Trust responded that the Trust had a $7 million minimum for financing. Orenstein testified in his deposition that Erb might not have known about paragraph 34 but that was unlikely because someone at the Trust would probably have checked the file. About a month later, Orenstein wrote Erb exercising Market Street's option to repurchase the property but the Trust refused to sell. Market sued for specific performance. The trial court granted the Trust summary judgment, holding that Market Street breached its duty of good faith. **HOLDING:** On appeal, Judge Posner noted that in contract formation a person, without violating any duty of good faith, can take advantage of the other party's ignorance such as buying something you know the seller has undervalued. And even after contract formation when dealing with contract performance, a party is not obligated to bail out the other party who has trouble performing his side of the bargain. However, Judge Posner stressed that "[i]t is another thing to say that you can take deliberate advantage of an oversight by your contract partner concerning his rights under the contract. Such taking advantage is not the exploitation of superior knowledge or the avoidance of unbargained-for expense; it is sharp dealing.. . ." The Seventh Court reversed and remanded for the trial court to determine what Orenstein believed. The court said that "[i]f Orenstein believed that Erb knew or would surely find out about paragraph 34, it was not dishonest or opportunistic to fail to flag that paragraph, or even to fail to mention the lease, in his correspondence and (rare) conversations with Erb, especially given the uninterest in dealing with Market Street Associates that Erb fairly radiated."

CASES	SUMMARIES
Market Street Associates, continued	Note 1 following the case indicates that the district court on remand found that Market Street breached its duty of good faith in dealing with the Trust: although Orenstein initially assumed that the Trust would check the lease "he subsequently realized that the Trust was not operating under paragraph 34." But Orenstein did not call the Trust's attention to paragraph 34 and acted in a way that would enable Market Street to exercise the purchase option and obtain the property at a low price.
Bloor v. Falstaff Brewing Corp. (1979) → (CB pg. 567)	**FACTS:** Bloor, the bankruptcy trustee for Balco, formerly named Ballantine, sued Falstaff claiming it breached a "best efforts" clause. The clause which was contained in a March 1972 contract pursuant to which Falstaff purchased the Ballantine label and other property, provided that Falstaff would use "its best efforts to promote and maintain a high volume of sales . . . ." Falstaff was also to pay \$.50 a barrel for six years but if during that period Falstaff "substantially discontinues the distribution of beer under the brand name 'Ballantine,'" it was required to make a liquidated damage payment to the seller. Bloor argued that Falstaff breached the best efforts clause and that such breach amounted to a substantial discontinuance of the distribution of Ballantine beer, obligating Falstaff to make the liquidated damage payment. The trial court held that Falstaff breached its best efforts obligation but dismissed the claim that there was a substantial discontinuance triggering the liquidated damage payment. **HOLDING:** On appeal, the Second Circuit did not specify what the best efforts clause required Falstaff to do but stated that the trial court did not consider the best efforts clause as requiring Falstaff to go bankrupt in promoting Ballantine "or even to sell those products at a substantial loss." However, the trial court did say that the best efforts obligation was not fulfilled by a policy that Kalmanovitz summarized by saying "We sell beer and you pay for it" and "We sell beer . . . You come and get it." While this might have been a sensible policy for Falstaff's other products, it was insufficient given Ballentine's drastic reduction in sales. The Second Circuit noted that once the possibility of Falstaff's insolvency had passed, Falstaff was required at minimum to see what it could do to stop or lessen the rate of decline of Ballantine's sales by steps which did not involve substantial losses. The trial court pointed out that instead Falstaff took steps which contributed to the "catastrophic drop in Ballantine's sales" including Falstaff's choice of distributors that owned competing brands, not treating Ballantine's products on a par with Falstaff's, and discontinuing setting goals for salesmen by the Kalmanovitz policy of stressing profit at the expense of volume. The trial court concluded that even considering Falstaff's right to give reasonable consideration to its own interests, Falstaff had breached its best efforts duty as stated in Van Valkenburgh, 330 N.Y.S.2d at 334. The Second Circuit said that the district court correctly concluded that Falstaff breached its best efforts clause. It noted that Falstaff was required to do more than treat Ballantine's brands as well as its own. As to its own brands, Falstaff could use its business judgment on how to make the most profit even if it meant a loss in volume. However, Falstaff's obligations to pay a \$.50 royalty on Ballantine sales required Falstaff to make a good faith effort to have substantial Ballantine sales unless it substantially discontinued distribution which would require it to pay liquidated damages. The Second Circuit agreed that the best efforts clause did not require

CASES	SUMMARIES
Bloor, continued	Falstaff to bankrupt itself in promoting sales, but "it did prevent the application to them of Kalmanovitz' philosophy of emphasizing profit" over everything else to show what steps Falstaff could reasonably have taken to maintain a high volume of Ballantine sales. Plaintiff met its burden by showing that Falstaff didn't care about Ballantine's volume and that it was content to permit the Ballantine sales to drop as long as that was best for Falstaff's overall profit picture. Falstaff then had the burden to prove that no significant steps could have been taken to promote Ballantine sales that would not have been financially disastrous.

Section 5. Public Policy

Concepts:

- If either the consideration or the object of the contract is illegal, the bargain is treated as an illegal contract.

- Some contracts are illegal because they are expressly prohibited by statute (for example, gambling agreements or promises for usurious interest) whereas others are classified as illegal because they violate public policy (for example, contracts in restraint of trade or contracts to impair family relations).

(A) Illegal Contracts

CASES	SUMMARIES
Bovard v. American Horse Enterprises, Inc. (1988) → (CB pg. 577)	**FACTS:** In 1978, Ralph agreed to buy American Horse Enterprises—a company which manufactured jewelry and drug paraphernalia used to smoke marijuana—from Bovard. When Ralph stopped payments to Bovard on the purchase price, Bovard sued. Although manufacturing drug paraphernalia did not become illegal in California until 1983, the trial court held as a matter of law that implicit in the state statute making "possession, use, and transfer of marijuana unlawful" was a public policy against the manufacturer of drug paraphernalia. The trial court found that the consideration for the contract was against public policy and therefore, the contract was illegal. **HOLDING:** On appeal, the court noted that a court must refrain from entertaining an action to enforce an illegal contract and should not permit the settlement of a claim based on such a contract. Whether a contract is contrary to public policy is

CASES	SUMMARIES
Bovard, continued	a question of law which must be determined based on the particular facts of the case. The court stated that only in cases free from doubt should a court declare a contract void as against public policy. Applying the test set out in the R2d §178, the court concluded that the interest in enforcing the contract was slim. No one could reasonably have expected that the state would not eventually outlaw the manufacturer of paraphernalia for illegal drug use. Furthermore, Bovard through "self-help" recovered the machinery used to manufacture jewelry and any forfeiture in not enforcing the sales contract was at best negligible. In contrast, the Restatement factors favoring a public policy against enforcement were powerful. Public policy against manufacturing drug paraphernalia was strongly implied in the statutory prohibition against using marijuana and non-enforcement would put all manufacturers of drug paraphernalia on notice that that they could not turn to the courts to advance their business interests. The court said that "the trial court correctly declared the contract contrary to the policy of express law" and therefore illegal.
X.L.O. Concrete Corp. v. Rivergate Corp. (1994) → (CB pg. 580)	**FACTS:** X.L.O., a subcontractor, agreed with Rivergate, a general contractor to construct the concrete superstructure for a project in Manhattan. After X.L.O. fully performed, Rivergate refused to pay X.L.O., claiming that the contract was related to an antitrust conspiracy known as the "Club"—an arrangement between the "Commission" of La Cosa Nostra and certain concrete construction companies (including X.L.O.) and labor unions. The Commission decided which concrete company would get a construction job worth in excess of $2 million and required the contractor to pay the Commission a 2% fee for labor peace. Through bid rigging, the Commission ensured that the designated concrete company would be the low bidder. Rivergate knew of the Club and its rules when it entered into the contract with X.L.O. When X.L.O. brought its action for breach of contract, the trial court granted the defendant's motion for summary judgment dismissing the complaint and the Appellate Division reinstated the complaint. **HOLDING:** The NY Ct of Appeals affirmed the Appellative Division's order, stating that antitrust defenses in contract actions were disfavored because if such a defense were allowed a party could enrich itself by reaping the contract benefits and then avoiding its burdens through that defense. However, the court pointed out that an antitrust defense would be recognized in cases where a judgment would result in enforcing the very conduct which the law makes unlawful. The court said that "the critical question is whether the contract is so integrally related to the agreement, arrangement or combination in restraint of competition that its enforcement would result in compelling performance of the precise conduct made unlawful by the antitrust laws." Answering that question, the court said, requires factual development at trial. Thus, whether the contract price in this case did not reflect fair market value because of unlawful attempts to stifle competition needed to be factually developed. Relevant to this is whether a party can recover based on *quantum meruit* if the court declares a contract void for illegality. In assessing the availability of unjust enrichment, the court should take into account "the relative culpability, bargaining power, and knowledge of the parties to the contract."

(B) Judicially Created Public Policy

Concepts:

- The vast majority of American workers are subject to the employment-at-will doctrine which grants employers absolute freedom to discharge an employee without notice or cause where the hiring is for an indefinite term. The only limitation on the employer's right is that the termination cannot violate a state or federal employment statute. (*Sheets v. Teddy's Frosted Foods*)

    — Non-compete agreements are generally disfavored as imposing an undue restraint on trade but may be enforced if the agreement is reasonable in geographic scope, reasonable in duration, and protects a legitimate interest of the employer. (*Hopper v. All Pet Animal Clinic*)

    In determining whether a non-compete agreement protects a legitimate interest of the employer, a court considers whether the employee subject to the restriction was special, unique or extraordinary in some way so that the employee would be competing unfairly against his former employer. In making this assessment, several factors are considered including, but not limited to the following:

    — Whether the employee possessed confidential information or trade secrets

    — Whether the agreement seeks to eliminate competition which would be unfair to the employer or simply seeks to eliminate general business competition

    — Whether the agreement presents a bar to the employee's sole means of support

    — Whether the agreement seeks to stifle the employee's inherent skill and experience

    — Whether the employee's skill or talent which the employer seeks to suppress was developed while working for the employer

CASES	SUMMARIES
Hopper v. All Pet Animal Clinic (1993) → (CB pg. 589)	**FACTS:** Hopper, a newly minted veterinarian, was employed by All Pet Animal Clinic ("All Pet") in March 1989. She signed a non-compete clause ("Covenant") in which she agreed not to practice small animal medicine within a certain geographical area for three years from the date of termination of the agreement. Hopper was fired and in July 1991 opened a practice in which half of her gross income was earned from small animal practice with a substantial overlap of clientele with her former employer. All Pet, located in the city of Laramie, lost 187 clients to Hopper. In November, All Pet sued, seeking to enjoin Hopper and to recover damages. The case was tried more than two years after Hopper was discharged. All Pet did not seek a temporary injunction. The trial court enjoined Hopper but denied her damages because they were too speculative. **HOLDING:** On appeal, the court noted that an employer must prove that a covenant not to compete is reasonable and that the covenant was necessary for protection of its business interest. An employer may protect itself against improper and unfair competition by a former employee but is not entitled to protection against ordinary competition. The court said that Wyoming had adopted a rule of reason inquiry

CASES	SUMMARIES
Hopper, continued	from the First Restatement of Contracts and that the present formulation of the rule is found in R2d §188. The court noted that All Pet had introduced Hopper to pricing policies and practice development techniques—skills that she did not have before her employment. Her exposure to all of All Pet's clients and the knowledge of clinical operations that All Pet gave her had a monetary value for which All Pet had a right to reasonable protection from irreparable harm. Stating that the determination of the reasonableness of a covenant not to compete is a question of law, the court noted that the Covenant imposed a practice restriction only for small animals; without relocating, Harper could have practiced large animal medicine which was a significant area of practice in Wyoming. The court concluded that the Covenant's restriction on the type of veterinary activity Hopper could engage in was such as to avoid undue hardship to Hopper while protecting All Pet's special interests. As to the Covenant's geographical limit—a five mile radius within the corporate limits of Laramie—the court found it reasonable since All Pet's clients were located throughout the county and Hopper could open a practice at other locations within the county that did not run afoul of the five mile limit. Finally, the court believed that a one-year duration for the Covenant and not the three years as the Covenant provided was sufficient to protect All Pet's pricing policies and practice development information since pricing policies would change yearly and practice development information lost its value quickly as technological changes occurred. The court remanded to have the injunction against Hopper limited to a duration of one year from the date of termination since the court held, as a matter of law, that the Covenant's three year term imposed a partially unreasonable restraint of trade.

With respect to damages for Hopper's breach of the Covenant, the court noted that All Pet's damage calculations were based on "gross profits" and that the lower court's finding that the amount of damages suffered was speculative and had not been proven by a preponderance of the evidence was not clearly erroneous. Dissent: The dissent opined that Hopper had "beaten the system." The dissent noted that the majority concluded, as a matter of law, that a one year restriction was reasonable and a longer period was not. The dissent would have enjoined Hopper for one year from the date that the trial court entered a modified judgment on remand.

QUESTION TO THINK ABOUT: *Was not the court's remand meaningless when the one year from the date of termination had already run?* |
| *Sheets v. Teddy's Frosted Foods (1980)*

→ (CB pg. 595) | **FACTS:** From November 1973 to November 1977, defendant Teddy's Frosted Foods, a producer of frozen food products, employed plaintiff as its quality control director and at some point also its operation manager. In May 1997, plaintiff informed defendant that some of defendant's vegetables were substandard and some meat components were underweight which meant that defendant's labeling was misleading and violated Connecticut's Uniform Food, Drug and Cosmetic Act ("Act"). In November 1977, defendant terminated plaintiff's employment—which defendant claimed was for unsatisfactory performance—but was really in retaliation for his insistence that defendant comply with labeling laws. Plaintiff sued claiming, among other things, a violation of public policy. The trial court struck the complaint as legally insufficient. |

CASES	SUMMARIES
Sheets, continued	**HOLDING:** On appeal, the Connecticut Supreme Court reversed. The issue was whether the court should "recognize an exception to the traditional rules governing employment at will so as to permit a cause of action for wrongful discharge where the discharge contravenes a clear mandate of public policy." The court made it clear that "[t]he plaintiff does not challenge the general proposition that contracts of permanent employment, or for an indefinite term, are terminable at will" and does not "argue that contracts terminable at will permit termination only upon a showing of just cause for dismissal." Cases from other jurisdictions, the court noted, established at minimum "the principle that public policy imposes some limits on unbridled discretion to terminate the employment of someone hired at will." The problem was deciding "where and how to draw the line between claims that genuinely involve the mandates of public policy and are actionable, and ordinary disputes between employee and employer that are not." Plaintiff's complaint alleges that he was fired for insisting that defendant comply with the Act. As defendant's quality control director, plaintiff could have been exposed to criminal prosecution under the Act for defendant's mislabeling. The court concluded that the complaint stated a tort claim for intentionally tortious conduct. It noted that it did not have to decide whether it was necessary to show a violation of the state statute to claim that an employment discharge violated public policy: "For today, it is enough to decide that an employee should not be put to an election whether to risk criminal sanction or to jeopardize his continued employment."

DISSENT: Creating a cause of action for retaliatory discharge as an exception to the rule of at-will employment on the facts of this case created an overly broad cause of action whose "nuisance value alone may impair employers' ability to hire and retain employees who are best suited to their requirements." Plaintiff could have protected the consumer by anonymously communicating to the commissioner of consumer affairs regarding defendant's violation. Plaintiff could have complied with Connecticut's public policy, avoided the remote possibility of criminal sanction, and never jeopardized his continued employment. |
| *Balla v. Gambro, Inc. (1991)*

→ **(CB pg. 601)** | **FACTS:** Balla was in-house counsel at Gambro, a kidney dialysis equipment distributor. Balla's duties included legal matters and non-legal duties as "manager of regulatory affairs." When Gambro ignored Balla's warning to reject a shipment of dialyzers that did not comply with FDA regulations, Balla informed Gambro's President that he would take action to stop the sale of the dialyzers which Gambro was going to sell to "a customer who buys only on price." On learning about this, Balla told the president that he would do whatever was required to stop their sale. Gambro fired Balla who then reported the shipment to the FDA and the dialyzers were seized. Balla brought suit in tort for retaliatory discharge. The trial court granted Gambro summary judgment stating that Gambro had an absolute right to discharge its attorney.

HOLDING: On appeal, the court noted that the tort of retaliatory discharge "is a limited and narrow exception to the general rule of at will employment" and that in the instant case the public could be protected without giving Balla this cause of action. Under the Illinois Code of Professional Responsibility, a lawyer has an obligation to reveal client information necessary to prevent the client from acting in a way |

CASES	SUMMARIES
Balla, continued	that would result in death or serious bodily injury. Balla was under a duty to report the sale of the dialyzers. The court rejected the idea that if house counsel is not permitted to sue in tort, house counsel would be forced to choose between (a) complying with the client/employer wishes and risk the loss of his law license and exposure to criminal sanctions or (b) refusing to comply and risk the loss of employment. The court said that house counsel have no choice but to follow their ethical obligations and may not comply with illegal or unethical client demands. Therefore, Balla was required to report Gambro's intent to sell the dialyzers and protect public policy of safeguarding the lives and property of citizens. Further, the court stated that generally a client can discharge an attorney—whether house counsel or outside counsel. To grant house counsel a right to sue for retaliatory discharge may inhibit clients from being candid with their house counsel when seeking advice regarding questionable corporate conduct knowing that such information could be used in a retaliatory discharge action. Given this possible chilling effect on communications between employer and house counsel, the court believed it better not to grant house counsel the right to sue in tort. Furthermore, the court thought that it would be inappropriate for the employer to bear the cost of house counsel's adherence to its ethical obligation. Attorneys should know that at some point they have to forgo economic gains to protect the profession's integrity. Finally, the court rejected Balla's claim that he acted in his capacity as manager of regulatory affairs and that as a mere "employee" he should be entitled to sue for retaliatory discharge. The court stated that the discharge resulted from information Balla learned in his capacity as general counsel.
Simeone v. Simeone (1990) → (CB pg. 604)	**FACTS:** On the night of their wedding in 1975, Catherine Walsh, an unemployed nurse, was presented with a pre-nuptial agreement ("Agreement") which provided for a $25,000 maximum payment by her fiancé, Frederick Simeone, a neurosurgeon, in the event of separation or divorce. Catherine signed the agreement without consulting an attorney. The parties separated in 1982 and divorce proceedings started in 1984. Between 1982 and 1984 Frederick made payments to Catherine that met the $25,000 limit of the Agreement. Catherine requested alimony pending the proceedings but the master upheld the Agreement. **HOLDING:** On appeal, the court stated that "the law has advanced to recognize the equal status of men and women in our society." Pre-nuptial agreements are contracts and therefore the same criteria applicable to other types of contracts should be applied to pre-nuptials. Since contracting parties are bound even if they did not read or fully understand the agreement and whether or not the bargain was reasonable, the Agreement was binding even if Catherine did not fully understand it. The court rejected Catherine's argument that parties entering into a pre-nuptial agreement must obtain independent legal counsel. The court pointed out that to do so would be contrary to contract principles and would interfere with parties' freedom to enter contracts. Further, the court said that it would not inquire into the Agreement's reasonableness, since by signing the Agreement the parties recognized its reasonableness. Indeed the Agreement stated that the parties considered the Agreement to be fair and reasonable.

CASES	SUMMARIES
Simeone, continued	The court however, required that there be full and fair disclosure of the parties' financial condition. Since parties to a pre-nuptial agreement stand in a relationship of mutual confidence, the parties have a duty to fully and fairly disclose their financial positions. The duty of disclosure, the court said, is consistent with traditional principles of contract law and the failure to disclose would allow a party to claim a material misrepresentation in the inducement for entering into the agreement.
	DISSENT: (Papadakos): Pre-nuptial agreements are contracts of adhesion and the law protects the subservient party, without regard to the party's sex, in order to assure equality under the law.
	DISSENT: (McDermott): Given the state's paramount interest in the preservation of marriage and the family relationship, a spouse should be able to avoid a pre-nuptial agreement if the spouse can show by clear and convincing evidence that despite fair and full disclosure, the agreement is nonetheless inequitable and unfair.
In the Matter of Baby M (1988) → (CB pg. 608)	**FACTS:** William Stern and Mary Beth Whitehead entered into an agreement in which, for $10,000, Whitehead agreed to be inseminated with Stern's sperm and that any resulting baby would be given to Stern and Whitehead's parental rights would be terminated. Whitehead delivered a baby girl and refused to turn her over to Stern. The trial court granted Stern specific performance and terminated Whitehead's parental rights. On appeal, the court granted custody to Stern because it was in the best interest of the infant but voided the termination of Whitehead's parental rights and the adoption of the baby by Stern's wife. The court remanded to determine Whitehead's visitation rights.
	HOLDING: At the outset the court noted that a woman who voluntarily and without payment agrees to act as a "surrogate" mother is valid so long as there is no agreement to surrender her child. Here the court said the $10,000 payment was made "to obtain an adoption" and not for Mary Beth Whitehead's personal services. The court found the Stern/Whitehead "surrogacy contract" invalid because it directly conflicted with state statutes prohibiting the use of money in connection with an adoption; laws which required proof that a parent was unfit before parental rights would be terminated or an adoption granted; and laws making consent to adoption revocable in private placement adoptions.
	The court also found the "surrogacy contract" invalid because the contract contravened New Jersey's public policy. The court noted that the surrogacy contract's premise that natural parents can decide before birth who is to have custody has no relationship to the laws' requirement that the child's best interest determines custody. The "surrogacy contract" in this case totally disregarded the child's best interest since there was no indication that any determination would be made as to whether the Sterns were fit to be custodial or adoptive parents or of the effect on the child of not living with its natural mother. The court noted that virtually every evil that prohibits the payment of money for adoptions was present in this case and the fact that Whitehead agreed was irrelevant. The court concluded that "[t]he surrogacy contract is based on, principles that are directly contrary to the objective of our

CASES	SUMMARIES
In the Matter of Baby M, continued	laws. It guarantees the separation of a child from its mother; it looks to adoption regardless of suitability; it totally ignores the child; it takes the child from the mother regardless of her wishes and her maternal fitness; and it does all of this, it accomplishes all of its goals, through the use of money." While the court concluded that the Stern/Whitehead "surrogacy contract" was invalid, it stressed again that the court did not "find any legal prohibition against surrogacy when the surrogate mother volunteers, without any payment, to act as a surrogate and is given the right to change her mind and to assert her parental rights."

■ CHAPTER 7. REMEDIES FOR BREACH

Section 1. Specific Relief

Concepts:

- Sometimes the award of money damages will not be adequate to protect the injured party's expectation interest—that is, to compensate the aggrieved party for its loss.

- Where money damages are not adequate to make the plaintiff whole—for example, due to the difficulty of proving damages with reasonable certainty or the difficulty of obtaining a suitable substitute performance (i.e., because of the uniqueness of the item or promised performance), the court has discretion to grant specific performance of the contract.

FRAMEWORK FOR ANALYSIS:

ASK: Will the award of money damages not compensate the aggrieved party for its loss? If so, the following may be available:

Specific Performance? Is the plaintiff entitled to a court order directing the defendant to perform the contract as promised? If so, then the court will grant plaintiff a mandatory injunction. In answering this question, consider the following:

— **Is a Substitute Available?** If the contract is for something unique such as the purchase of land or where the subject of the contract involves matters of taste or heirlooms, then a damage award is not adequate because no substitute is available to compensate the aggrieved party and specific performance is the only way to do so. (*Campbell Soup Co. v. Wentz*)

—**Are the Contract Terms Definite and Certain?** The terms of the contract must be sufficiently definite to allow the court to determine with certainty what it must order each party to do to carry out the agreement.

—**Is Enforcement Feasible?** Specific performance will not be granted where the burdens on enforcement or supervision of the order would not be feasible. For example, the difficulty of judging the quality of a performance or supervising a performance over an extended period of time. (*Northern Delaware Industrial Development Corp. v. E.W. Bliss Co.*)

—**Is it a Personal Service Contract?** A court will not grant an order requiring a service that is personal in nature due to difficulties in enforcement, supervision and evaluation. If specific performance is denied, a court may, in its discretion, enjoin the defendant from performing the service for a third party.

—**Prohibitory Injunction?** Is the plaintiff entitled to prohibit the defendant from performing a specified act? If an injunction would provide substantial protection to the injured party without offending the policies against requiring specific performance, then the court will order a "negative injunction." For example, this would be the remedy in the case of a restrictive covenant where the employee possesses unique skills or trade secrets—the employee would be "enjoined" from working for the competitor.

CASES	SUMMARIES
Campbell Soup Co. v. Wentz (1948) → (CB pg. 618) *Specific Performance granted - no substitute available*	**FACTS:** Campbell Soup entered into a contract with the Wentzes (farmers) in which the Wentzes agreed to deliver to Campbell all of the "Chantenay red cored carrots" to be grown in the 1947 season on the Wentz farm. In early 1948, the Wentzes told Campbell that they would not deliver at the contract price of $30/ton. At the time the market price was $90 per ton and Chantenay red cored carrots were virtually unavailable. Campbell sued to compel specific performance and to enjoin the sale of the carrots to others. The lower court denied the equitable relief of specific performance. **HOLDING:** On appeal, the Third Circuit said that "[a] party may have specific performance of a contract for the sale of chattels if the legal remedy is inadequate." The court found that here the legal remedy of damages was inadequate because the Chantenay carrot, which Campbell used in large quantities, was virtually unobtainable on the open market. Although the Chantenay carrot was not more nutritional than other carrots, its shape made it easier to handle in processing and its color and texture differed from other varieties. Plaintiff used carrots in 15 of its 21 soups and it also appeared that "it uses these Chantenay carrots diced in some of them and that the appearance is uniform. The preservation of uniformity in appearance in a food article marketed throughout the country and sold under the manufacturer's name is a matter of considerable commercial significance and one which is properly considered in determining whether a substitute ingredient is just as good as the original." In holding that specific performance was appropriate, the court said that Campbell had built a reputation in which uniform appearance of its products was important and that the contract carrots were unavailable on the open market. The court further observed that that specific performance could be granted without court supervision. [Writers' Note: While it is not clear from the edited version of the case, the court affirmed the lower court instead of reversing with an order for specific performance even though the court found that the case was a "proper one for equitable relief." It did so because of the terms of the contract itself. The court stated that "[w]e think it is too hard a bargain and too one-sided an agreement to entitle the plaintiff to relief in a court of conscience." The court stated specifically that it was not suggesting that the contract was illegal nor was it suggesting any excuse for the grower who breached its agreement with Campbell. Rather, as the court stated: "We do think, however, that a party who has offered and succeeded in getting an agreement as tough as this one is, should not come to a chancellor and ask court help in the enforcement of its terms."]

CASES	SUMMARIES

Klein v. PepsiCo, Inc. (1988)

→ (CB pg. 621)

There is a BoK, but money damage are adequate b/ these are comparable substitutes

FACTS: On March 31, 1986, Uniform Jet Sales (UJS) President telexed Pepsico offering to buy its Gulfstream G-II corporate jet for $4.4 million, subject to a satisfactory factory inspection and a "definitive contract." Pepsi countered on April 1 with a $4.7 million asking price and after some negotiations, UJS President sent a telex on April 3 accepting Pepsico's offer to sell the jet for $4.6 million. UJS intended to resell the jet to Klein for $4.7 million dollars. A pre-purchase inspection revealed certain cracks on the turbine blades and Pepsico agreed to pay for their repair. Before the April 1 scheduled closing, Pepsico withdrew the jet from the market. Pepsico argued that no contract had been formed because "the March 31 and April 1 telexes explicitly stated that no contract would exist until a written agreement was executed." Although UJS had sent Pepsico a sales agreement, Pepsico never signed it. In a conclusion of law, the trial court held that "the intent to memorialize the contract in writing was not necessarily a condition to the existence of the contract itself." Pepsico gave no reasons to show that the trial court's findings were clearly erroneous. Its disagreement with the trial court's characterization of the facts did not mean that a mistake was made. As to Pepsico's argument that no contract was formed because the inspection condition did not occur, the trial court ruled that the condition was satisfied because Pepsico agreed to make the necessary repairs and that in any event, the condition was excused because Pepsico refused to tender the jet so that the buyer could express his dissatisfaction. Pepsico did not suggest that the trial court committed any error other than to urge its own version of the facts.

HOLDING: In reversing the trial court's grant of specific performance, the Fourth Circuit noted that Virginia's adoption of the UCC "does not abrogate the maxim that specific performance is inappropriate where damages are recoverable and adequate." The court noted that the trial court repeatedly indicated that Klein could be compensated with money damages and that Klein himself argued that he wanted the plane to resell at a profit. As to the trial court's finding—with which the Fourth Circuit disagreed—that the jet was unique because there were only three comparable aircrafts on the market, the court noted that there were 21 G-II's on the market, three of which were comparable. It further noted that Klein had made bids on two other G-II's after Pepsico reneged. The trial court held that Klein's inability to cover is not "other proper circumstances" under UCC §2-716. In fact, Klein testified that he didn't purchase any G-II's because prices had started to rise.

Morris v. Sparrow (1956)

→ (CB pg. 626)

FACTS: Sparrow, a cowboy, entered into an agreement with Morris, a cattle rancher, to do certain work in return for $400 and a brown horse called Keno that Morris owned. Morris refused to deliver the horse claiming that delivery of the horse was conditioned on Sparrow doing a good job which he did not do. The court said that although ordinarily a court of equity will not enforce a contract for the sale of chattels, "it will do so where special and peculiar reasons exist which render it impossible for the injured party to obtain relief by way of damages in an action at law." Sparrow had turned Keno, a green unbroken pony, into a roping horse which, the court noted would have peculiar and unique value. The court held that Sparrow was entitled to the horse and not simply its market value in dollars.

Laclede Gas Co. v. Amoco Oil Co. (1975)

→ (CB pg. 630)

Propane is not a 'unique' good w/o a substitute, but SP was ordered b/c it was in the interest of public policy.

SP is only granted (maybe) when the *seller* breaches... Can't make a buyer buy something... money damages will suffice.

FACTS: Laclede Gas (Laclede) entered into a long term supply contract dated 9/21/70 with Amoco. Amoco would supply Laclede with commercial propane gas which Laclede in turn would supply to its customers. The agreement was to provide central propane gas distribution systems to certain residential developments in Jefferson County until natural gas was available in these areas. As individual developments were planned, developers would apply to Laclede for central propane systems and in turn Laclede would request Amoco to supply the propane to that development. This request would be made in the form of a supplemental form letter which Amoco would sign if it decided to supply the propane. The September 21 agreement was to be in effect for one year from Amoco's first delivery of gas and would automatically renew for additional one year periods unless Laclede canceled by giving 30 days' notice to Amoco prior to the expiration of the initial one year period or any subsequent one year renewal. Laclede was to pay Amoco "the Wood River Area Posted Price" for propane plus an additional four cents." By letter dated 5/14/73, Amoco terminated their September 21 agreement claiming a lack of mutuality. The trial court held for Amoco, concluding that the contract was void for lack of mutuality because Laclede alone had the right to arbitrarily cancel the agreement.

HOLDING: On appeal, the court held that Laclede's power to terminate did not make Laclede's promise illusory and the contract for Laclede's requirements for the subdivision was enforceable. As to whether Laclede was entitled to specific performance—an issue not considered by the trial court—the Eighth Circuit said that whether to grant specific performance "lies within the sound discretion of the trial court." This discretion however is limited because when certain equitable rules are met "and the contract is fair and plain 'specific performance goes as a matter of right.'" At the outset, the court noted that a party is entitled to specific performance even if the other party would not be entitled to it—there need not be mutuality of remedy in order to grant an equitable relief to one party. Further, while a court may refuse to grant specific performance where constant court supervision would be required, this is a discretionary rule which the court noted "is frequently ignored when the public interest is involved." Here, providing retail customers with gas is in the public interest and any supervision would not be difficult. The court recognized that the parties disagreed over the meaning of the price term and that the agreement lacked a duration term but pointed out that the trial court could resolve these issues.

The court stated that specific performance involving personal property will be granted unless the remedy at law is "'as certain, prompt, complete, and efficient to attain the ends of justice as a decree of specific performance.'" Here the court found that Laclede had no such remedy at law. Although Laclede had two other contracts with suppliers, those contracts were for short periods of time with no assurance that Laclede could obtain propane after they expired. Further, it was unclear whether Laclede could use the propane under those contracts to supply the Jefferson County subdivisions. The September 21 contract, however, was a long term supply contract and there was testimony that Laclede probably could not find a substitute supplier to enter into a long term supply contract given the uncertainty of worldwide energy supplies. Further, even if Laclede could negotiate a new

CASES	SUMMARIES
Laclede Gas Co., continued	long term supply contract with another supplier, "it would still face considerable expense and trouble which cannot be estimated in advance in making arrangements for its distribution to the subdivisions."
Northern Delaware Industrial Development Corp. v. E.W. Bliss Co. (1968) → (CB pg. 635) *SP not enforced on a service contract...* *Court cannot oversee that 300 more men will be at work.*	**FACTS:** Bliss agreed to modernize Phoenix's steel plant for $27,500,000. When the work did not progress as fast as contemplated, Phoenix sought a court order—which the court denied—to direct Bliss to hire 300 more workers, as the contract required, to make up a second shift during the time that one of Phoenix's mills had to be closed because of the work. **HOLDING:** The Court of Chancery recognized that a court of equity has jurisdiction to direct completion of "an expressly designed and largely completed construction contract." However, a court should not do so where it would be impractical to implement the order, unless there were special circumstances or the public interest was directly involved. The court concluded that Phoenix's request for specific performance was not appropriate because the contract provision relied on was imprecise and the impracticability of a court effectively enforcing a "mandatory order designed to keep a specific number of men on the job at the site of a steel mill which is undergoing extensive modernization and expansion." On re-argument Phoenix said that it was only seeking to direct Bliss to do a ministerial act of hiring more workers. The court rejected the argument saying that "'performance of a contract for personal services, even of a unique nature, will not be affirmatively and directly enforced.'"
Walgreen Co. v. Sara Creek Property Co. (1992) → (CB pg. 636)	**FACTS:** Walgreen operated a pharmacy in space that it leased from Sara Creek in a mall under a lease which provided that Sara Creek would not lease space in the mall to a store operating a pharmacy. In 1990, Sara Creek told Walgreen that it was going to lease space which was within a couple of hundred feet from Walgreen to Phar-Mor, a discount chain that would have a pharmacy. The trial court granted an injunction against Sara Creek until Walgreen's lease expired. On appeal, Sara Creek argued that calculating Walgreen's business losses due to any increased pharmacy competition involved a routine calculation exercise—determining damages representing the present value of Walgreen's lost future profits or any diminution in Walgreen's leasehold value. The court discussed the benefits and costs of substituting the remedy of injunction for the remedy of money damages which is the norm in breach of contract cases. As far as the benefits, an injunction would shift the burden of determining the cost of defendant's breach from the courts to the parties. Assuming that Walgreen's loss would be greater than Sara Creek's gain from leasing to a second pharmacy, "then there must be a price for dissolving the injunction that will make both parties better off." Thus if the injunction is sustained, the parties would engage in the less costly process of private negotiation rather than the costly process of a court determination of Walgreen's loss. Further, the injunction eliminates a court battle of experts to determine Walgreen's loss which would not be as reliable as direct negotiations between the parties to determine the amount which Walgreen would find adequate to compensate it for having to face the competition.

CASES	SUMMARIES
Walgreen co., continued Legal Remedy ($) always the first option, but the court must weigh pros & cons of granting injunctive relief.	**HOLDING:** The court noted that the cost of granting an injunction includes costly continued court supervision as well as third parties costs. "A more subtle cost of injunction relief arises from the situation that an economist call 'bilateral monopoly,' in which two parties can deal only with each other: the situation that an injunction creates. . . ." Thus Walgreen can sell its injunction rights only to Sara Creek and Sara Creek can buy such rights only from Walgreen. This lack of alternatives creates a bargaining range where the costs of negotiating to a point within that range might be high. But the damages remedy, the court noted, also has its costs and benefits. While awarding money damages avoids the cost of continuing supervision and third-party effects and the cost of bilateral monopoly, it imposes other costs: diminished accuracy in a court's determination of the diminished value of Walgreen's lease, litigation costs, and the court's time to evaluate the evidence. When asked to grant a permanent injunction, a court should weigh all the costs and benefits of an injunction and damages, but it need not explain in detail its analysis— which the trial court did not do in this case—as long as the trial court's approach "is broadly consistent with a proper analysis we shall affirm." The Seventh Circuit noted that here "[t]he determination of Walgreen's damages would have been costly in forensic resources and inescapably inaccurate. . . ." Since Walgreen's lease had 10 years remaining, Walgreen would have had to project sales and costs over the ten year period and then project the impact of Phar-Mor's competition on those figures, all of which would have involved uncertainty in the determination of the damages Walgreen would suffer from Sara Creek's leasing to Phar-Mor.

Section 2. Measuring Expectation

CONCEPTS:

- Contract damages are usually based on the injured party's expectation interest and are intended to give her the "benefit of her bargain" by awarding a sum of money that will, to the extent possible, put her in as good a position as she would have been in had the contract been fully performed.

- A party will seek to recover expectation damages because they represent the greatest measure of recovery. They compensate the injured party for the benefit of the bargain—the benefit she would have received had the contract been fully performed which may include lost profits.

 - There are several limitations on a party's ability to recover expectation damages. First, a party must show causation—that the breach of contract was the cause in fact of its loss. Second, a party's loss must be foreseeable and proved with reasonable certainty. Third, a party has a duty after the defendant's breach to make reasonable efforts to avoid loss.

- The measure of recovery *in quantum meruit* is the reasonable value of the performance—and such recovery is not diminished by any loss which would have been incurred by complete performance. (*United States v. Algernon Blair, Inc.*)

Framework for Analysis: What is the measure of a party's expectation interest?

ASK: Was the breach the cause-in-fact of the party's loss? If so, then she is entitled to recover expectation damages subject to certain limitations.

There are various ways to measure a party's expectation damages. Ask:

1. Has a party breached by failing to perform and the aggrieved party has withheld her own performance? If so, then one of the following formulations may be appropriate in calculating damages:

    a. **Substitute Performance/Transaction?** Has the aggrieved party entered into a reasonable substitute or "cover" performance? If so, then she is entitled to sue for loss based on the difference between the contract price and the cost of cover. (*Laredo Hides Co., Inc. v. H & H Meat Products Co., Inc.*: cover damages under UCC §2-712)

    b. **Lost Income?** Has the breach resulted in lost income? If so, then ask the following:

        i. **Substitute Performance Impossible?** If the contract was for plaintiff's services and there was no cost to the plaintiff other than her services and she was not able to secure work, then she will have lost her entire expectation interest in the event of breach. She would be entitled to recover the full amount due under the contract.

        ii. **Lost Income but also Cost Savings?** If the breach resulted in lost income but also saved the plaintiff costs in not having to perform, then damages are measured by deducting the savings from the expected earnings. With respect to what is deductible, consider: (Expected Earnings — $ saved by not performing)

            • **Direct or Variable Costs?** Did plaintiff incur costs solely for the purpose of performing the contract? If so, then they would be saved by the breach and should be deducted from gains to measure the true expectation interest. However, there are exceptions. Ask:

            —Has the plaintiff entered into another contract in reliance on the contract with the defendant which cannot be canceled without liability? If so, then such costs incurred as a result of the defendant's breach would not be deducted.

            —Fixed or Overhead Costs? Does plaintiff have costs or expenditures (i.e., rent) which have to be paid whether or not she performed this contract? These are fixed costs of doing business and are not saved by virtue of the breach. They are not deducted from the amount of damages. (*Vitex Manufacturing Corp. v. Caribtex Corp.*)

2. Incomplete or defective performance? Has a party breached by rendering an incomplete or defective performance? If so, ask whether there has been:

a. **Substantial Performance?** Has there been only a trivial and innocent breach such that the cost of redoing the defective or incomplete performance would be disproportionate to the actual loss suffered by the promisee and impose an unfair forfeiture on the breaching party? If so, then the proper measure of damages is the diminution in value which is the "difference in value" between what was promised and what was received (*Plante v. Jacobs*). If not, proceed to next question.

b. **Cost of Completion or Repair?** Has there been a breach resulting in defective or unfinished construction and the loss in value is not proved with reasonable certainty? If so, then the owner is not limited to the diminution in value but may, alternatively, recover the reasonable cost to repair the defective performance or to complete the unfinished construction unless such damages would be considered "economic waste." Economic waste occurs when the cost to remedy the defective performance would be disproportionate to the probable loss in value to the injured party.

c. **Delay in Use of Property?** Has there been a breach that delayed the use of property and the loss in value to the injured party is not proved with reasonable certainty? If so, the injured party may recover damages based on the rental value of the property or on interest on the value of the property.

3. **Are there limitations on recovery?** Recovery of expectation damages is subject to certain limitations. Ask:

a. **Foreseeability?** Were the losses caused by the breach reasonably foreseeable at the time of contract by the party in breach? R2d §351

b. **Avoidability/Mitigation?** Did the non-breaching party make reasonable efforts after the breach to avoid loss? The injured party is not entitled to any damages which she could have reasonably avoided. R2d §350

c. **Certainty?** Can the non-breaching party establish the amount of the loss with "reasonable certainty"? If losses cannot be calculated with reasonable certainty, they are not recoverable. R2d §352

CASES	SUMMARIES
Vitex Manufacturing Corp. v. Caribtex Corp. (1967) → (CB pg. 643) *Overhead (fixed) costs are not deducted from damages*	**FACTS:** Vitex, which was in the business of chemically showerproofing imported cloth, agreed to process 125,000 yards of wool for Caribtex. To do this, Vitex reopened its Virgin Island plant, and did everything necessary, including recalling employees, to perform the Caribtex contract. Caribtex never delivered the wool that was to be processed and Vitex brought suit to recover its lost profits which the trial court determined without taking into account Vitex's overhead expenses. **HOLDING:** On appeal, the court rejected Caribtex's argument that overhead expenses should not have been disregarded in determining the amount of Vitex's lost profits. The court stated that "[i]n general, overhead '…may be said to include broadly continuous expenses of the business, irrespective of the outlay on a particular contract'" which would include such expenses as "executive and clerical salaries, property taxes, general administration expenses, etc." Although the court noted that there is contrary authority, the court thought that in determining lost profits the better approach was to treat overhead "as a part of gross profits and recoverable as damages, and should not be considered as part of the seller's costs." This is because

CASES	SUMMARIES
Vitex, continued	overhead is fixed and since generally non-performance of a particular contract does not result in overhead cost savings, overhead should not be subtracted from gross profits in computing a seller's lost profits. Here, Vitex's costs on the Caribtex contract would have been the direct costs of labor and chemicals necessary to process the wool as well as the expense of reopening its plant. But as far as overhead, it would have been the same with or without the Caribtex contract. Since Vitex's overhead was constant, no part of it should properly be considered a cost of Vitex's performance to be deducted from the gross proceeds of the Caribtex's contract in computing Vitex's lost profits on that contract. The court recognized that in determining the price to be charged for a service or goods, businessmen would include in the price a prorated portion of fixed overhead. However, such an allocation is not a relevant factor in computing loss profits on any individual transaction. The court further noted that even if it would recognize the overhead allocation as proper, then Vitex should be entitled to an award of overhead expenses as a "loss incurred." This is so because if overhead were not awarded, a company would have to allocate its overhead to all its transactions—less the instant one where the buyer breached—thus reducing the profitability.
Laredo Hides Co., Inc. v. H & H Meat Products Co., Inc. (1974) → (CB pg. 647)	**FACTS:** Laredo, buyer, agreed to buy H&H's entire cattle hide output during the period March through December 1972. After H&H, seller, made two deliveries, Laredo mailed a check for the second shipment which was delayed in arriving. H&H demanded payment within a few hours and when Laredo did not comply, H&H notified Laredo on March 30, 1972 that it was canceling the contract. Because Laredo had contracted on March 3 to resell the hides it expected to buy from H&H, Laredo purchased hides on the open market in substitution for the hides H&H was supposed to deliver. The trial court entered judgment that Laredo should recover nothing from H&H. On appeal, the court held that H&H breached by repudiation and that Laredo was excused from any further performance. **HOLDING:** Under UCC §2-712 when a seller repudiates, a buyer may cover by making a good faith reasonable purchase without unreasonable delay in substitution for the goods due from the seller. Buyer's damage recovery is measured by the difference between the cost of cover and the contract price plus any incidental or consequential damages. Alternatively, a buyer may recover under UCC §2-713 where damages are measured by the difference between the contract price and the market price when buyer learned of the breach. Here, Laredo elected to recover under UCC §2-712 and the evidence showed that it brought "itself within the purview of the 'cover' provisions." A cover purchase such as Laredo's is presumed proper if a buyer complies with UCC §2-712 and the burden then shifts to the seller to show that cover was not properly implemented. Since H&H did not negate the presumption, Laredo was entitled to recover the difference between cover price and contract price plus its incidental damages, which included increased transportation costs and increased handling charges.

UCC 2-712   (Cover Price — Original Contract Price) + incidental damages

UCC 2-713   (Contract Price - Market Price)

CASES	SUMMARIES

R.E. Davis Chemical Corp. v. Diasonics, Inc. (1987)

→ (CB pg. 652)

Once the buyer has breached:

Lost volume seller should be able to sell the product to someone else and recover damages from breaching party.

(2x profit)

FACTS: Davis agreed to purchase certain medical diagnostic equipment from Diasonics. Prior to the Davis—Diasonics contract, Davis had agreed with third parties to establish a medical facility where the equipment would be used. The third parties breached their contract with Davis and in turn Davis refused to take delivery of the medical equipment. Diasonics resold the equipment for the same price it was going to sell to Davis. Davis sued to recover its $300,000 down payment. Diasonics did not deny that under UCC §2-718(2)(b), Davis was entitled to the $300,000 less $500. However, Diasonics claimed that it was a lost volume seller and therefore it was entitled to recover its lost profit under the Davis contract pursuant to UCC §2-708(2) [Seller's Damages for Non-acceptance or Repudiation] and to offset that amount against the $300,000 under UCC §2-718(3). The trial court held that Diasonics was entitled to recover only under §2-706(1) [Seller's Resale] and thus could only recover the difference between the resale price and the contract price plus incidental damages.

HOLDING: On appeal, the court concluded that the Illinois Supreme Court would allow a lost volume seller to recover its lost profit under UCC §2-708(2). Section 2-703 [Seller's Remedies in General] catalogs the seller's remedies but does not provide a hierarchy. The court therefore asked whether a seller may recover under §2-708 only if §2-706 or §2-709 [Action for the Price] was inapplicable; it concluded that the Illinois Supreme Court would hold that a lost volume seller reselling is entitled to reject the damage formula in §2-706 and opt to recover under §2-708.

However, the court noted that §2-708 has two subdivisions: §2-708(2) is applied only if §2-708(1) would be inadequate to put the seller in as good a position as the seller would have been had the contract been performed. Diasonics argued that §2-708(1) is not an adequate measure when it comes to a lost volume seller because it measures damages by the difference between contract price and market price which means that the lost volume seller would generally recover nothing on the breached contract—even in cases where the seller could have made both the sale under the breached contract had it not been breached as well as the resale. The court agreed "that, under some circumstances, the measure of damages provided under 2-708(1) will not put a reselling seller in as good a position as it would have been in had the buyer performed because the breach resulted in the seller losing sales volume." The court defined a lost volume seller—slightly different from other courts—as being a seller who had the capacity to supply the breached unit in addition to what it actually sold and who could profitably have supplied both units. Further, the seller must show that "it probably would have made the second sale absent the breach." The court further addressed the problem posed by the language of §2-708(2) which provides that in determining the seller's profit there should be "due credit for payments or proceeds of resale." Applied literally, the lost volume seller such as Diasonics would receive only nominal damages. Some cases have circumvented the problem by saying that the "due credit" language only applies to proceeds from the resale of uncompleted goods for scrap. Although neither the text nor the comments limit the language to the resale of goods for scrap, the court said that there was some evidence that the drafters had this limited application in mind. It concluded that the Illinois Supreme Court would adopt the most restrictive interpretation thus making the "due credit" language irrelevant to this case.

CASES	SUMMARIES
R.E. Davis Chemical Corp., continued	The court reversed and remanded to give Diasonics the opportunity to establish that it was a lost volume seller—that it had the capacity to make both the Davis sale and resale, that both sales would have been profitable and that it would have made the second sale but for Davis' breach thus entitling it to the profit it would have made on the Davis sale without any offset of profits on the resale it made after Davis breached.

United States v. Algernon Blair, Inc. (1973)

→ (CB pg. 658)

Quantum Meruit (Restitution) Allows Coastal to recover for what they had already done in the project.

Coastal didn't seek Expectation damage bc/ they would have <u>lost</u> $ had they finished the contract

FACTS: Blair had a contract with the United States to construct a naval hospital. Subsequently, Blair entered into a contract with Coastal whereby Coastal was to perform certain steel work on the project. Coastal started performing using its own cranes to put the steel in place. When Blair refused to pay for Coastal's crane rental, Coastal stopped performing and sued Blair. Although Coastal would have been entitled to recover approximately $37,000—the contract price less the amount Blair had already paid under the contract—the trial court denied Coastal recovery because it found that Coastal would have lost more than $37,000 had it completed performance.

HOLDING: On appeal, the court held that Coastal was entitled to recover in quantum meruit for the benefits of the labor and material that Coastal furnished Blair. In quantum meruit, the promisee is entitled to recover the reasonable value of its performance without taking into account any loss that would have occurred if the performance was completed. The court noted that "[w]hile the contract price may be evidence of reasonable value of the services, it does not measure the value of the performance or limit recovery." Reasonable value is measured by "the amount for which such services could have been purchased from one in the plaintiff's position at the time and place the services were rendered." The court reversed and remanded for the district court to determine the reasonable value of the material and services that Coastal furnished.

Jacob & Youngs v. Kent (1921)

→ (CB pg. 661)

Would be gross & unfair prejudice to force builder to tear down the house for a trivial matter... builder recovers the $ owed him less the trivial value difference

FACTS: Plaintiff built a house for defendant pursuant to a contract which specified that all wrought iron pipes for plumbing should be of Reading manufacture. When defendant learned that plaintiff used pipe of another manufacturer, the architect directed plaintiff to replace it. At that point, however, almost all the plumbing was enclosed by the walls. To replace the pipe would have required demolishing substantial portions of the house. Plaintiff did not replace the pipe and the architect refused to issue a certificate that final payment was due. Plaintiff sued to recover the balance on the contract of $3,483.46. The trial court gave judgment for the defendant and refused to permit the builder to introduce evidence that the brand installed was of the same quality and appearance and value as Reading pipe.

HOLDING: On appeal, the court held that the builder was entitled to recover the balance of the purchase price less any damages which resulted from its failure to use Reading pipe. The court stated that the appropriate measure of damages was the difference between the value of the house as built and its value if it had been constructed using Reading pipe—and not the cost of replacement. In most cases, the court said "[t]he owner is entitled to the money which will permit him to complete, unless the cost of completion is grossly and unfairly out of proportion to the good to be obtained. When that is true, the measure is the difference in value."

CASES	SUMMARIES
Jacob, continued	Thus, in cases such as here, where the builder has substantially performed, the builder will be entitled to recover the contract price less an amount to compensate the owner "for defects of trivial or inappreciable importance."

Plante v. Jacobs (1960)

→ (CB pg. 664)

If π has substantially performed, they can recover (contract price – damages for incompletion)

FACTS: Plante agreed to build a house for the Jacobs on Jacobs' lot in accordance with plans and specifications for $26,765. When Jacobs refused to continue payments after having paid $20,000, Plante did not complete the house. Jacobs claimed that Plante had not substantially performed, especially stressing that he had misplaced the wall between the living room and kitchen which reduced the living room by one foot. The cost to demolish and rebuild the wall where it belonged was approximately $4,000 but retail experts testified that the smaller living room did not affect the house's market value. Plante sued and the trial court found that he had substantially performed.

HOLDING: On appeal, the court noted that where a plaintiff has substantially performed, plaintiff should recover the contract price less damages for the incomplete performance. For faulty construction amounting to such incomplete performance, damages should be measured by the difference between the house's value with the faulty and incomplete construction and its value had it been properly built. Cost of repair or replacement, while not the measure of damages, is a factor to consider in determining value under the circumstances. The court stated that "[w]hether a defect should fall under the cost-of-replacement rule or be considered under the diminished-value rule depends upon the nature and magnitude of the defect." Although the court noted that under the cost of repair rule it had not allowed items of such magnitude as did the trial court, nevertheless "[v]iewing the construction of the house as a whole and its cost" the court could not say that the trial court erred in allowing the cost of (1) repairing ceiling plaster cracks, (2) mud jacking and repairing the patio floor and (3) reconstructing the non-weight bearing and non-structural patio wall. None of this involved unreasonable economic waste. As to the misplaced living room wall, the court said that it clearly came "under the diminished-value rule." The Jacobs had not demanded replacement during the construction and to do so now would involve substantial destruction of the work done as well as damage to walls and ceilings of two other rooms. The court said that such economic waste is unreasonable and unjustified. The misplaced wall did not affect the market price of the house. Although the defendants' desire for a specified room was not realized, the trial correctly found that the Jacobs "suffered no legal damage."

Groves v. John Wunder Co. (1939)

→ (CB pg. 666)

FACTS: Groves owned a 24-acre tract of land zoned as heavy industrial property on which it had a plant for excavating and screening the sand and gravel that was deposited on the land. Groves entered into a contract with Wunder whereby Wunder leased Grove's property for seven years and Wunder agreed to remove the sand and gravel and leave the property at a uniform grade, "substantially the same as the grade now existing at the roadway." Wunder removed only the best gravel and surrendered the property but not at the grade required nor at a uniform grade. The

CASES	SUMMARIES

Groves, continued

Where a party <u>willfully</u> breaches in a construction contract...

they are liable for the cost of completing the required work ($60K) even though it only adds $12K in value

reasonable cost for Wunder to comply with the contract was $60,000. The property would have had a value of $12,160 if it was left at uniform grade level. The trial court measured plaintiff's damages by the difference in the market value of Groves' land when the lease was made and what it would have been if Wunder had performed the remedial work of restoring the land it had agreed to do.

HOLDING: On appeal, the court noted that defendant willfully breached and therefore was not entitled to the benefit of the doctrine of substantial performance. But even in a case of substantial performance and good faith, the court said that where the defects are remediable, the cost of remedying the defects is the proper measure and not the difference in value between the land improvement as it is and as it would have been had it been constructed in accordance with the contract terms. The value of the land has no role in measuring damages for willful breach of a building contract. An owner has an unfettered right to improve the owner's property, including building structures which will reduce the property's value. The contractor who does not perform has no right to claim that the performance desired by the owner would be of no benefit to the owner. In this case, the important objective was the improvement of the land. The loss resulting from Wunder's breach of the construction portion of the contract was the promised alteration. Groves will not be unconscionably enriched because little or no value would be added to his land. The court stated that "there can be no unconscionable enrichment, no advantage upon which the law will frown, when the result is but to give one party to a contract only what the other has promised; particularly where, as here, the delinquent has had full payment for the promise performance." The court noted that economic waste is only that which comes from destroying a completed structure. Here no such economic waste is involved and absent economic waste, Groves is entitled to the reasonable cost of what Wunder promised to do.

DISSENT: Two dissenting justices would apply the diminished value rule unless the desired product "was to satisfy the personal taste of the promisee" and that willfulness of the breach should have no effect on the measure of damages.

Peevyhouse v. Garland Coal & Mining Co. (1963)

→ (CB pg. 671)

FACTS: Garland leased a farm from Willie and Lucille Peevyhouse to strip mine coal. Garland agreed to perform certain remedial work when the lease was over but failed to do so. The cost of the remedial work would have been about $29,000 but it would have increased the farm's market price by only $300. Both parties appealed from the trial court's judgment for $5,000. The issue was whether the measure of damages should be the cost of the remedial work that Garland did not do or whether damages should be limited to the difference in market value between the land in its present condition and the land in the condition it would have been had Garland done the remedial work it had agreed to do.

HOLDING: The court noted that Groves, "a substantially similar situation" on which plaintiffs relied, was the only case of which the court was aware that awarded the cost of performance—$60,000—even though it greatly exceeded the diminution in value resulting from the breach. The court rejected any analogy to a building and

CASES	SUMMARIES
Peevyhouse, continued	construction contract or to a grading and excavation contract stating that here the lease provisions "pertaining to remedial work were incidental to the main objective involved"—the mining of coal from the lease property. Even in building and construction contracts, the court said, the cases were not in agreement as to what factors should be considered in determining whether to apply the cost of performance or the diminution in value rule. It noted that the First Restatement's prime consideration was economic waste. Cost of performance is the appropriate measure when it does not involve unreasonable economic waste which, according to the Restatement, "consists of the destruction of a substantially completed building or other structure." But if it does, diminution in value is the proper measure. On the other hand, other authorities seem to stress the relative economic benefit between the expense involved and the end to be obtained; if reconstruction costs are disproportionate to the end to be attained, diminution in value is the rule.
[handwritten: Difference in Groves (lost cost) & this one = Merely incidental]	The court held that in a coal mining lease where a party does not do the remedial work that it agreed to do, the measure of damages ordinarily should be the reasonable cost of performing that work. But "where the contract provision breached was merely incidental to the main purpose in view, and where the economic benefit which would result to lessor by full performance of the work is grossly disproportionate to the cost of performance, the damages which lessor may recover are limited to the diminution in value resulting to the premises because of the non-performance." The court (4-3) reduced the judgment to $300.
	Dissent: Garland admitted that the Peevyhouses would not have agreed to the coal mining lease unless the remedial work provisions were included. Unless the cost of performance is the measure of damages, the dissent noted, the express contract provisions would be meaningless and that it "would be taking from the plaintiffs the benefit of the contract and placing those benefits in defendant which has failed to perform its obligations." In essence under any other measure, Garland's obligation under the contract would be rescinded to plaintiff's detriment and Garland's benefit: in effect a new contract would be made.

Section 3. Limitation on Damages

(A) Avoidability

Concepts:

- The non-breaching party must make reasonable efforts after the breach to avoid the loss. If the non-breaching party does not, the injured party is not entitled to any damages which she could have reasonably avoided. This is also referred to as the "duty to mitigate." (*Rockingham County v. Luten Bridge Co.*)

CASES	SUMMARIES
Rockingham County v. Luten Bridge Co. (1929) → (CB pg. 675) *Duty to mitigate (minimize) damages* *After a repudiation, you cannot complete the contract just to run the damages up*	**FACTS:** Plaintiff and defendant entered into a contract on January 7, 1924 whereby plaintiff was to build a bridge for defendant. After plaintiff had done a minimal amount of construction, defendant notified plaintiff on February 21, 1924 not to proceed any further with the bridge construction. Nevertheless, plaintiff proceeded with construction. Plaintiff brought suit to recover the amount it claimed was due on the contract for work performed before November 3, 1924 and the trial court entered a verdict for plaintiff. **HOLDING:** On appeal, the court reversed stating that once plaintiff received notice of defendant's breach "it was its duty to do nothing to increase the damages flowing therefrom" and therefore plaintiff had no right to complete the bridge, thereby increasing its damages. [Thus, defendant should be liable only for the damages plaintiff would have suffered if plaintiff had stopped construction when defendant instructed plaintiff to do so.] The court quoted with approval from Professor Williston who said "There is a line of cases . . . which holds that, after an absolute repudiation or refusal to perform by one party to a contract, the other party cannot continue to perform and recover damages based on full performance. This rule is only a particular application of the general rule of damages that a plaintiff cannot hold a defendant liable for damages which need not have been incurred; or, as it is often stated, the plaintiff must, so far as he can without loss to himself, mitigate the damages caused by the defendant's wrongful act."
Tongish v. Thomas (1992) → (CB pg. 678) *Thomas entitled to full differential (market price – contract price) as recovery bc/ it encourages good seller practice*	**FACTS:** Tongish, a farmer, agreed to grow sunflower seeds to be purchased by Coop who in turn had a contract to deliver the seeds to Bambino Bean for the same price it paid Tongish, plus a handling fee which would be Coop's profit. When the market price of sunflower seeds rose, Tongish breached its contract with Coop. Coop sued and recovered $455 in damages for its loss of handling fees. On appeal, the Kansas Court of Appeals reversed and remanded to have damages determined based on the measure provided for in UCC §2-713 which is the difference between the market price at the time when the buyer learned of the breach and the contract price together with incidental and consequential damages but less expenses saved as a result of the seller's breach. Tongish appealed, claiming that the trial court was correct under UCC §1-106 [UCC remedies "shall be liberally administered to the end that the aggrieved party may be put in as good a position as if the other party had fully performed. . . ."] **HOLDING:** On appeal, the Kansas Supreme Court affirmed the Court of Appeals and approved its rationale in holding that Coop's damages for Tongish's failure to deliver should be computed under UCC §2-713 and not UCC §1-106. Where the seller knows that the buyer has a resale contract and the seller does not breach in bad faith, the measure of damages in UCC §2-713 is not applicable and the buyer is limited under UCC §1-106 to recovering its actual loss. The court discussed the history and theories behind §2-713 and rejected the approach followed in *Allied Canners & Packers*, which the court described as a minority rule. Although the market damages remedy in UCC §2-713 "may not reflect the actual loss to a buyer,

CASES	SUMMARIES
Tongish, continued	it encourages a more efficient market and discourages the breach of contracts." The court further noted that damages measured under UCC §2-713 "encourage the honoring of contracts and market stability."
Parker v. Twentieth Century-Fox Film Corp. (1970) → (CB pg. 683) *Employer carries the burden of proving the employee failed to mitigate their damages...* *Employee does not have to take work of a different or inferior kind*	**FACTS:** Defendant, Twentieth Century, entered into a contract dated August 6, 1965 with plaintiff for her to play the female lead in a motion picture musical production entitled "Bloomer Girl." In early April, Twentieth Century notified plaintiff that it would not perform under the contract and offered to employ her as the leading actress in a western movie entitled "Big Country" for the same compensation but with certain of the other terms being different. Plaintiff refused the offer and sued to recover her compensation. In its defense, Twentieth Century asserted that plaintiff failed to mitigate damages in that she unreasonably refused to accept the leading role in "Big Country." The trial court granted plaintiff summary judgment. **HOLDING:** On appeal, the court said that the measure of damages for a wrongfully discharged employee "is the amount of salary agreed upon for the period of service, less the amount which the employer affirmatively proves the employee has earned or with reasonable effort might have earned from other employment. . . ." An employee, however, need not look for nor take employment of a different or inferior kind. The employer has the burden of showing that "the other employment was comparable, or substantially similar, to that of which the employee has been deprived." The court held that the substitute employment defendant offered plaintiff was different—"Bloomer Girl" involved plaintiff's talents as a dancer and actress to be produced in L.A. while "Big Country" was a dramatic western-type role taking place in a mine in Australia. A female lead as a dramatic actress in a western style motion picture is not substantially similar to the lead role in a song and dance production. [Note: The court did not discuss whether an employee can refuse an employer's offer to rehire simply because it came from the employer who had breached the contract.] **DISSENT:** An employee need not accept employment of a different kind but it is not the law that the "mere existence of differences between two jobs in the same field is sufficient, as a matter of law" to excuse a discharged employee from mitigating damages by accepting the other job. The majority, the dissent believed, made no attempt to assess the significance of the differences between the two jobs. While there may be differences between two jobs, the relevant question is whether the differences "are substantial enough to constitute differences in the kind of employment or, alternatively, whether they render the substitute work employment of an *inferior kind . . . .*" (emphasis added)

(B) Foreseeability

Concepts:

- The losses caused by the breach must have been reasonably foreseeable to the defendant as a probable result of the breach at the time of contracting to be recoverable. (*Hadley v. Baxendale*)

- The injured party may recover damages for loss that "may fairly and reasonably be considered [as] arising naturally, i.e., according to the usual course of things, from such breach of contract itself." (*Hadley v. Baxendale*)

- Damages for loss other than those "arising naturally" from the breach are not recoverable unless the loss was "such as may reasonably be supposed to have been in the contemplation of both parties, at the time they made the contract, as the probable result of the breach of it." (*Hadley v. Baxendale*)

- The modern trend phrases the test in terms of foreseeability: "damages are not recoverable for loss that the party in breach did not have reason to foresee as a probable result of the breach when the contract was made." R2d §351(1)

- Loss may be foreseeable if it follows "in the ordinary course of events" or if it follows "as a result of special circumstances, beyond the ordinary course of events, that the party in breach had reason to know." R2d §351(2)

CASES	SUMMARIES
Hadley v. Baxendale (1854) → (CB pg. 688) The mill needing the drive shaft to operate is a "special circumstance" (most mills had back ups) & they did not make the Δ aware of it... thus the damages were unforeseeable & the lost profits should not be considered as damages	**FACTS:** Plaintiff, a mill operator, entered into a contract with defendant, a common carrier, whereby defendant was to deliver for plaintiff the mill's broken shaft to the manufacturer to make a new shaft. Plaintiff alleged that defendant failed to deliver the broken shaft to the manufacturer within a reasonable time and that plaintiff's mill remained closed an extra five days because of the delay causing plaintiff a loss of profits. A jury gave a verdict for plaintiff. **HOLDING:** The court stated that the non-breaching party should be entitled to damages which "may fairly and reasonably be considered either arising naturally, i.e., according to the usual course of things, from such breach of contract itself, or such as may reasonably supposed to have been in the contemplation of both parties, at the time they made the contract, as the probable result of the breach of it." If plaintiff at the time of contracting communicated to defendant any special circumstances under which the contract was being made, then the damages the parties would reasonably contemplate from a breach would be the injury which would ordinarily flow from a breach under these known circumstances. If the breaching party is unaware of any special circumstances, he "could only be supposed to have had in his contemplation the amount of injury which would arise generally, and in the great multitude of cases not affected by any special circumstances, from such a breach of contract." This is so because if the breaching party had known of special circumstances, it might have been able to address the breach and put in special terms as to the damages. In this case, plaintiff told defendant at the time of the contract that the article being delivered for transportation by defendant to the manufacturer was a broken shaft of a mill and that plaintiffs were the millers of the mill. Nothing was said as to whether the mill had stopped working or whether plaintiff had another shaft in its possession. Nothing was communicated to defendant to indicate that the mill's profits would be affected by any unreasonable delay in defendant's delivery of the broken shaft to the manufacturer. Thus, the parties could not reasonably have contemplated at the time of contract the possibility of lost profits: "For such loss would neither

CASES	SUMMARIES
Hadley, continued	have flowed naturally from the breach of this contract in the great multitude of such cases occurring under ordinary circumstances, nor were the special circumstances, which, perhaps, would have made it a reasonable and natural consequence of such breach of contract, communicated to or known by the defendants." The trial judge therefore should have instructed the jury that, based on the facts, the jury should not consider lost profits in determining the damages to which plaintiff was entitled.
Delchi Carrier Spa v. Rotorex Corp. (1995) → (CB pg. 692) *It was objectively forseeable that Delchi would rely on conforming goods to satisfy sales ther had already made, thus the damages are appropriate.*	**FACTS:** Rotorex entered into a contract to supply compressors to Delchi, an Italian air conditioner manufacturer. When Delchi discovered that the first shipment was non-conforming, it notified Rotorex but Rotorex refused to supply conforming compressors. Delchi sued Rotorex and obtained a judgment for over $1 million. On appeal, the Second Circuit stated that the case was governed by the United Nations Convention on Contracts for the International Sale of Goods (CISG) and that the court would consider, among other things, case law interpreting analogous UCC provisions where the CISG language is similar to the UCC. Under the CISG Article 74 of the CISG, breach of contract damages "may not exceed the loss which the party in breach foresaw or ought to have foreseen at the time of the conclusion of the contract, in the light of the facts and matters of which he then knew or ought to have known, as a possible consequence of the breach of contract." Thus, under the CISG, damages are limited by the *Hadley v. Baxendale* foreseeability principle. **HOLDING:** The court held that Delchi was properly awarded profits for unfilled orders because it was objectively foreseeable that Delchi would make sales based on the number of compressors it ordered from Rotorex. The court further noted that Delchi was entitled to recover expenses for shipping, customs, and storage with respect to the compressors returned to Rotorex, as well as some unreimbursed tooling expenses and the cost of useless insulation and tubing materials. These were allowable as incidental and consequential damages and did not duplicate the lost profits award. Finally, the court said that Delchi's labor expense incurred from an air conditioner production line shutdown was a reasonably foreseeable consequence of the non-conforming delivery of compressors. Whether the labor expense was a variable or fixed cost was a question that the district court had to decide on remand.
Kenford Co. v. County of Erie (1989) → (CB pg. 695)	**FACTS:** In August 1969, Erie County, Kenford, and Dome Stadium Inc (DSI) entered into a contract whereby Kenford would donate 178 acres of land to Erie County to use for construction of a domed stadium and in return the County agreed to build the stadium within twelve months and negotiate a 40 year lease with DSI to operate the facility. The lease was to provide for the County to receive not less than $63.75 million over 40 years which would include revenues from increased real property taxes resulting from increased assessment to the peripheral lands—lands owned by Kenford or its sole stockholder. If a lease was not agreed upon within three months, the County and DSI were obligated to execute the 20-year management agreement attached to the contract. When the County terminated the contract, Kenford and DSI sued and the trial court awarded Kenford $18 million for loss of appreciation of its peripheral property and awarded DSI lost profits under the the domed stadium, provided a guarantee that if any reason the stadium

CASES	SUMMARIES

Kenford Co., continued

Kenford & DSI hoped the land/dome would appreciate in value & they would profit...

but nothing guaranteed that appreciation profit

therefore it is unforseeable & the County of Erie is not liable for lost profits

The anticipated profits were speculative & could not be proven to a substantial degree of certainty

twenty year management contract. The appellate division reversed DSI's award for lost profits and directed a new trial on the Kenford's damage award for lost antici- pated appreciation in the value of its peripheral lands.

HOLDING: On appeal, the NY Court of Appeals said that "the nonbreaching party may recover general damages which are the natural and probable consequence of the breach." To recover damages beyond those naturally and directly flowing from the breach, they must have been in the parties' contemplation at the time of contracting as a probable result of a breach. Here the parties assumed that the new stadium would increase peripheral land values and property taxes. However, this does not necessarily mean that the County assumed liability for Kenford's loss of anticipated peripheral lands appreciation if the stadium was not built. The court pointed to its prior decision where DSI sought recovery for lost profits under the 20-year management contract. There the court noted that the contract did not pro- vide for the County's liability for DSI's loss of profits over a 20-year period and that in the absence of a contract provision "for such an eventuality, the commonsense rule to apply is to consider what the parties would have concluded had they consid- ered the subject." There the evidence did not demonstrate that the County's liability for 20 years of lost profits "would have been in the contemplation of the parties" at the time of contracting.

[Note: Apart from holding that the County's liability for DSI's profits was not within the parties' contemplation, it also held that they were speculative and failed to meet the legal requirement that to be recoverable damages must be proved "with reason- able certainty."]

Here, too, the contract had no provision—nor was there evidence —to demonstrate that the parties contemplated when contracting that the County was undertaking to be contractually liable for failure of Kenford's peripheral land to appreciate in value if the stadium was not built. The County knew that Kenford owned and intended to acquire peripheral lands; but this information alone, the court said was insuffi- cient "as a matter of law, to impose liability on the County for the loss of anticipated appreciation in the value of those lands since the County never contemplated at the time of the contract's execution that it assumed legal responsibility for these damag- es upon a breach of the contract." The court explained that "to hold otherwise would lead to the irrational conclusion that the County, in addition to promising to build were not built, Kenford would still receive all the hoped for financial benefits from the peripheral lands it anticipated to receive upon completion of the stadium." Since the leading case of *Hadley v. Baxendale*, cases have constantly stated that contract damages are limited to those reasonably foreseen or contemplated by the parties at the time of contract, thus limiting a party's liability for unassumed risk and dimin- ishing the business risk. Although Kenford anticipated benefits from the peripheral lands when the stadium was completed, the court concluded that "these expecta- tions did not ripen or translate into cognizable breach of contract damages since there is no indication whatsoever that the County reasonably contemplated in any relevant time that it was to assume liability for Kenford's unfulfilled land apprecia- tion expectations in the event that the stadium was not built."

(C) Certainty

Concepts:

- To be recoverable, plaintiff must establish the amount of the loss with "reasonable certainty." R2d §352

- Lost profits for a new enterprise may be recoverable where proven to a reasonable degree of certainty. (*Fera v. Village Plaza, Inc.*)

- If losses are speculative, then they are not recoverable.

CASE	SUMMARIES
Fera v. Village Plaza, Inc. (1976) → (CB pg. 705) The jury found the 𝜏's appraisal of anticipated lost profits to be reasonable & not speculative, which is the jury's job. Thus, the anticipated lost profits can be recovered	**FACTS:** In August 1965, plaintiff entered into a ten year lease in defendants' proposed shopping center for a "book and bottle" shop, a proposed new business for plaintiff. Defendants, however, refused to give plaintiff occupancy when the space was ready. Plaintiff sued, seeking among other things, anticipated lost profits, and obtained a jury verdict for $200,000. The Court of Appeals reversed and remanded for a new trial on the issue of damages only holding that the trial court erred by permitting lost profits for two reasons: first, "a new business cannot recover damages for lost profits for breach of a lease" and second, "because the proof of lost profits was entirely speculative." **HOLDING:** On appeal, the Supreme Court of Michigan disagreed and reversed. The court indicated that there is no rule which prevents "every new business from recovering anticipated lost profits for breach of contract." Even with respect to a new business, a party is entitled to recover damages provided it can prove those damages with reasonable certainty. The court stated that "the issue becomes one of sufficiency of proof." The court noted the trial court's observation that many days of testimony were devoted to the issue of whether plaintiff's profits were speculative. Testimony was conflicting as to whether plaintiff would have made profits if the contracts had been performed and as to whether a liquor license was available. The court noted that the jury had all of the conflicting evidence before it which it weighed and decided in plaintiff's favor. The jury apparently believed the plaintiff which was the jury's prerogative. Although the Supreme Court said that it might have found plaintiff's proof lacking if the judges were members of the jury, nevertheless it would not reverse the jury's verdict "'unless the factual record is so clear that reasonable minds may not disagree'" which was not the case. Justice concurring in part, dissenting in part: although anticipated profits from a new business may be determined with a reasonable degree of certainty, here, the lost profits from the liquor sales were speculative both regarding the availability of a liquor license as well as the possibility of profits from the liquor sales had a license been obtained.

Section 4. "Liquidated Damages" and "Penalties"

Concepts:

Liquidated Damages : *(Set amount of damages set in contract)* — *1. Can't know what the damages will be* *2. Have a reasonable guess* *3. Can't be punitive (too much)*

- A liquidated damages provision is a term in a contract where the parties agree what the damages will be in the event of a breach by one of them. The parties may set an amount or identify a formula to calculate the damages.

- There are several reasons contracting parties may agree to "liquidate" (make certain) damages as part of their contract: to eliminate the need for proof in the event of breach, to provide compensation for loss which would otherwise be unavailable because incapable of proof with reasonable certainty, to limit damages to the sum stated, and to save the time and expense of litigation. (*Dave Gustafson & Co. v. State*)

- A court will consider a damages provision to be punitive in nature and unenforceable where the agreed-to amount is significantly larger than necessary to compensate the injured party for its loss. The amount fixed by the parties must be "reasonable in the light of the anticipated or actual loss caused by the breach and the difficulties of proof of loss." R2d §356(1)

CASES	SUMMARIES
Dave Gustafson & Co. v. State (1968) → (CB pg. 710) *Appropriate use of liquidated damages*	**FACTS:** Gustafson contracted with the State to surface a new highway. The contract provided a graduated scale of "liquidated damages per day" of $210 for a contract over $500,000 but not more than $1 million. The trial court upheld the State's claim to liquidated damages for a 67 day delay. On appeal, the court affirmed and quoted an earlier case that "[a] provision for payment of a stipulated sum as a liquidation of damages will ordinarily be sustained if it appears that at the time the contract was made the damages in the event of a breach will be incapable or very difficult of accurate estimation, that there was a reasonable endeavor by the parties as stated to fix fair compensation, and that the amount stipulated bears a reasonable relation to probable damages and not disproportionate to any damages reasonably to be anticipated." **HOLDING:** Here the court believed that the contract provision was not a penalty but one for liquidated damages because delay damages for new highway construction "are impossible of measurement," the contract amount "indicates an endeavor to fix fair compensation for the loss, inconvenience, added costs, and deprivation of use caused by delay." The court noted that daily damages were graduated according to the size of the project and that it can be assumed that the larger the project, the more each day of delay adds to the loss and inconvenience and deprivation of use. For the same reasons, the court said that the stipulated amount was not "as a matter of law, disproportionate to any and all damage reasonably to be anticipated from the unexcused delay in performance."

Read Volkswagen on mental anguish & UCC Breach of Warranty

CASES	SUMMARIES

Lake River Corp. v. Carborundum Co. (1985)

→ (CB pg. 712)

Damages determined to be too high and punitive ; defendant could not control the crashing steel market

π must seek different compensatory damages ; like for the $89,000 spend on the bagging system

FACTS: Carborundum, a manufacturer of Fero Carbo (a powder used in making steel), entered into a contract whereby Lake River agreed to provide distribution services for Carborundum. Carborundum would ship Fero Carbo in bulk to Lake River which it would bag and ship to Carborundum's customers. At Carborundum's insistence, Lake River installed a new bagging system at a cost of $89,000. To ensure that Lake River could recover the cost and make a 20% profit over the contract price, the contract provided that Carborundum would deliver a minimum of 22,500 tons of Fero Carbo during the first three years. If this minimum was not shipped, the contract provided that "LAKE-RIVER shall invoice CARBORUNDUM at the then prevailing rates for the difference between the quantity bagged and the minimum guaranteed." At the expiration of the contract, Carborundum had only shipped 12,000 of the 22,500 tons it had guaranteed. Because of the minimum guarantee clause, Carborundum owed Lake River $241,000: this amount was determined by taking the $533,000 contract price if the minimum amount guaranteed had been delivered, less what Carborundum paid for the bagging of the quantity it had shipped. Lake River sued to recover the $241,000 as liquidated damages. The district court awarded Lake River the liquidated damages.

HOLDING: On appeal, the Seventh Circuit reversed and remanded. Judge Posner noted that the difficult issue was whether the minimum guarantee imposed a penalty for breach or was merely an effort by the parties to liquidate damages. Judge Posner noted that if the court were free to do so, it might question whether a modern court should refuse to enforce a penalty where the party is a substantial corporation. He discussed the various arguments that would question the advisability of refusing to enforce penalty clauses against sophisticated promisors. Noting that any innovation in common law must rest with the Illinois courts, he pointed out that Illinois continues to distinguish between penalties and liquidated damages. Under Illinois law, a valid liquidated damages clause "must be a reasonable estimate at the time of contracting of the likely damages from breach, and the need for estimation at that time must be shown by reference to the likely difficulty of measuring the actual damages from a breach of contract after the breach occurs. If damages would be easy to determine then, or if the estimate greatly exceeds a reasonable upper estimate of what the damages are likely to be, it is a penalty. . . . " Here the court concluded that the guarantee minimum clause was designed to ensure that Lake River would be entitled to more than its actual damages and that the formula provided was "invariant to the gravity of the breach." The court said that "[w]hen a contract specifies a single sum in damages for any and all breaches even though it is apparent that all are not of the same gravity, the specification is not a reasonable effort to estimate damages; and when in addition the fixed sum greatly exceeds the actual damages likely to be inflicted by a minor breach, its character as a penalty becomes unmistakable. . . . This case is within the gravitational field of these principles even though the minimum-guarantee clause does not fix a single sum as damages." Judge Posner went on the show that no matter when a breach by Carborundum occurred the contract formula always gave Lake River a reasonably significant amount more than if no breach had occurred. Thus the damage formula "over the interval between the beginning of Lake River's performance and nearly the end, the clause could be expected to generate profits ranging from 400 percent of the expected contract profits to 130 percent of those profits" excluding any value that the bagging system had.

CASES	SUMMARIES
Lake River Corp., continued	The court rejected Lake River's argument that under the contractual damage formula it would not receive this much because it would be required to mitigate its damages. The court seemed to reject this argument saying that "mitigation of damages is a doctrine of the law of court-assessed damages, while the point of a liquidated-damages clause is to substitute party assessment" which assessment would be impaired if defendant could reduce them because of the mitigation doctrine. Thus the court stated that the minimum guarantee clause should be construed as eliminating any duty of mitigation and in any event, "mitigation would not mitigate the penal character of this clause." The court remanded for the district court to determine Lake River's common law damages which would be based on the formula of contract price minus the costs Lake River saved by not having to complete the contract.
Wasserman's Inc. v. Township of Middletown (1994) → **(CB pg. 718)** *Are stipulated damages based on gross receipts reasonable?* *Probably not*	**FACTS:** The Town of Middletown and Wasserman entered into a store lease which Wasserman sublet to Jo-Ro. The lease provided that in the event the Township cancelled the lease, it would reimburse the lessee, pro-rata, for any improvements and pay damages of 25% of the lessee's average gross receipts for one year. The Township cancelled the lease but refused to pay the agreed upon damages. The Law Division granted summary judgment for Wasserman which was affirmed on a first appeal. The New Jersey Supreme Court granted certification and affirmed the renovation costs award but remanded to the Law Division the question of whether the stipulated damages based on the lessee's gross receipts was a valid liquidated damages clause. **HOLDING:** In its discussion, the court noted that a stipulated damages clause must be a reasonable forecast of the provable injury resulting from the contract breach to be enforceable: "New Jersey courts have viewed enforceability of stipulated damages clauses as depending on whether the set amount 'is a reasonable forecast of just compensation for the harm that is formed by the breach' and whether that harm 'is incapable or very difficult of accurate estimate.'" Further, the "[u]ncertainty or difficulty in assessing damages is best viewed … as an element of assessing the reasonableness of a liquidated damages clause." The more difficult it is to estimate or prove damages, the greater the likelihood the clause is reasonable. In determining reasonableness, the court stated that the modern trend is to assess it either at the time of contract formation or at the time of breach. In this case, whether measured at either point in time, damages based on gross receipts may be unreasonable because generally gross receipts are not reflective of actual losses caused by the breach because, among other things, gross receipts do not take into account plaintiff's operating or other expenses. The court remanded for the trial court to determine the reasonableness of the clause. Among other things, the trial court should consider "the reasonableness of the use of gross receipts as the measure of damages no matter when the cancellation occurs; the significance of the award of damages based on twenty-five percent of one year's average gross receipts, rather than on some other basis such as total gross receipts computed for each year remaining under the lease; the reasoning of the parties that supported the calculation of the stipulated damages; the lessee's duty to mitigate damages; and the fair market rent and availability of replacement space." The Township has the burden of proving that the stipulated damages clause was unreasonable.

■ CHAPTER 8. PERFORMANCE AND BREACH

Introduction:

This Chapter covers the performance phase of the contract. Here the parties are performing, their respective duties and obligations (promises) when one party claims that the other party has breached by failing to perform either when or what the other party is required to do so by the terms of the contract. Whether a breach has occurred and the consequences which flow from the breach are generally addressed under the topics of "conditions" and "promises."

Contract terms can be promises, conditions, or both. A promise is a commitment and gives rise to a duty, i.e., upon making a promise, the promisor assumes an obligation to act or not to act in a particular way. On the other hand, a condition is not a promise but is an event that must occur before a duty of performance will arise. Some contract terms are both: a "promissory condition" is a condition and also a promise that the condition will occur. In this case, there is an event that must occur before a party's performance becomes due and there is also a promise by the other party that the event will occur.

The distinction between a condition and a promise is critical: while failure to perform a promise, unless excused, is a breach, the non-occurrence of a condition is not a breach. If the condition fails to occur, then the promisor whose performance was conditioned is generally discharged from its duty to perform its promise without any obligation under the contract to compensate the promisee for any work the promisee has done. This can result in a forfeiture for the promisee while the promisor might not have been prejudiced at all by the failure of the condition. Accordingly, where there is doubt about whether a term is a condition or a promise, R2d §227(2) prefers an interpretation that finds the term to be a promise to avoid the harsh result of a forfeiture. The difficulty is determining whether the language is one of promise or condition or both. It becomes a matter of the intent of the parties and the rules of interpretation.

Section 1. Conditions

Concepts:

- A condition is "an event, not certain to occur, which must occur, unless its non-occurrence is excused, before performance under a contract becomes due." R2d §224

- When conditions are used to order the sequence of the parties' performance, they are classified as either conditions precedent, concurrent, or subsequent.

  — **Condition Precedent:** A "condition precedent" refers to a condition which must occur before the promisor's duty to perform arises.

  — **Concurrent Conditions:** Where the parties are to render their performances simultaneously—each for the other—their performance are known as "concurrent conditions." Each party's performance is a condition of the other's and must be performed or tendered at the same time.

  — **Condition Subsequent:** A "condition subsequent" is an event which discharges or extinguishes a duty of performance that has arisen.

■ When conditions are defined by the *manner* in which they arise, whether agreed to by the parties or implied by law, they are divided into express conditions—conditions the parties agreed to—and constructive conditions—conditions implied by law.

— **Express Conditions:** These conditions are created by agreement of the parties and can be recognized by the use of such contract language as "if," "on condition that," "provided that," "in the event that," and "subject to." Even if the contract language is not explicit, conditions may be implied from the language of the contract as a matter of interpretation. These conditions are referred to as "implied-in-fact" because the court implies the condition by implication from the other terms in the parties' agreement. They are treated as express conditions.

— **Constructive Conditions:** These are conditions created by the court and are referred to as conditions "implied-in-law" because they are not to be found either explicitly or implicitly in the parties' agreement. As opposed to express conditions, "constructive" conditions may permit a party to render something less than full performance and still be entitled to performance from the other party. Substantial performance of a promise, as distinguished from full performance, is sufficient to fulfill constructive conditions whereas nothing less than full performance is acceptable to satisfy an express condition. Substantial performance of a promise is acceptable to satisfy a constructive condition because the court created the condition — and only requires substantial performance to satisfy it — as opposed to an express condition which is agreed upon by the parties. However, although substantial performance satisfies the constructive condition, it is not sufficient to satisfy the party's promise to perform and thus, to the extent the promise was not performed, the party is in breach.

FRAMEWORK FOR ANALYSIS: Is the party's duty to perform subject to a condition?

ASK: Is the party's performance of a promise under the contract subject to the occurrence of an uncertain event such that unless and until the event occurs, that party's promised performance is not due?

If yes, then ask:

1. **Timing of the Condition?** Is there an order to the parties' performances?

   a. **Precedent?** Is the condition one which must be satisfied before the performance subject to that condition becomes due? If so, then it is a condition precedent and it must occur before a contractual duty becomes due. If not, then proceed to the next question.

   b. **Concurrent?** Are the promises dependent on each other such that one performance is a condition of the other? If so, then they are concurrent conditions of exchange and the parties' performances are due at the same time. Because the performances of the parties' promises are concurrent conditions of each other, both parties must show up ready, willing, and able to perform their promises. Where there is doubt as to the order of performances, an interpretation is preferred where the performances are to be performed simultaneously.

2. **Manner in which the Condition Arises?** Was the condition agreed to by the parties or created by law?

a. **Express Condition?** Is the event one that the parties have agreed to make a condition of performance by using such language as "if," "on condition that," "provided that," "in the event that," or "subject to"? If so, then strict compliance with the condition is required before the other party's duty to perform under the contract will arise. If not, proceed to the next question.

b. **Implied-in-fact Condition?** Is there contextual evidence in the contract that the parties intended a performance to be conditional even if they did not use express language creating a condition? If so, then the condition is implied-in-fact and is treated the same as an express condition where strict compliance is required. If not, proceed to the next question.

c. **Constructive Condition?** Are the circumstances and nature of the contract such that a condition should exist because if the parties had considered the issue, they reasonably would have intended it to be part of their agreement? If so, then the court will construct a condition and strict compliance is not required: substantial performance rather than full performance is permissible. If not, then the court will not supply a condition.

3. **Condition of Satisfaction?** Has the party made its promised performance conditional on its satisfaction of the other party's performance?

ASK: Is performance conditional on the party's subjective or objective satisfaction?

a. **Subjective Standard?** Is the contract one for personal services where the taste or judgment of the individual party is involved? If so, then the standard is one of subjective satisfaction. A party claiming to be dissatisfied must be acting in good faith which means honesty in fact. Thus the party must be honestly dissatisfied with the other party's performance to avoid its own performance.

b. **Objective Standard?** Is it a commercial contract such as one involving manufacturing or construction where objective criteria is available? If so, then the standard is one of objective satisfaction which requires the satisfaction of a reasonable person in the position of the obligor.

In case of doubt as to whether a party's subjective or objective satisfaction is required, the Restatement expresses a preference for use of the objective standard of reasonableness to avoid forfeiture. R2d §228

Note: If the promised performance is conditioned on the satisfaction of a third-party, i.e., where "A contracts with B to repair B's building for $20,000, payment to be made '*on the satisfaction of C, B's architect, and the issuance of his certificate*'" (R2d §227 ill.5), then the standard is generally read to be that of "honest satisfaction."[1]

---

[1] Allan Farnsworth, Contracts, §8.5 (4th ed. 2004). New York applies an objective test if forfeiture would result. *Nolan v. Whitney*, 88 N.Y. 648 (1882).

FRAMEWORK FOR ANALYSIS: Assuming that the party's duty to perform is subject to a condition, has the condition occurred?

ASK:

1. Is it the occurrence of an **express** or **implied-in-fact** condition? If so, then ask: Has there been **strict compliance**? If there has been strict compliance, then the condition has been fulfilled and the other party's duty to perform arises.

    If the condition has not been satisfied, then the other party's duty to perform does not arise unless the non-occurrence of the condition has been excused.

    • **Excused?** — Was the non-occurrence of the condition excused? If so, then the promisor will be obligated to perform despite the non-occurrence of the condition to its promised performance. The non-occurrence may be excused on a number of grounds. A condition may be excused if the promisor had a duty to facilitate the occurrence of the condition and hindered its fulfillment or failed to act in good faith by obstructing its fulfillment. Or a court may excuse a condition to avoid a disproportionate forfeiture unless the occurrence of the condition was a material part of the agreed exchange.

        —**Waived?** Was the non-occurrence of the condition excused by waiver? Has the promisor whose performance is conditional indicated by either words (express) or conduct (implied) that she will perform even if the condition does not occur? A party may waive a condition that solely benefits the party waiving it. If so, then the promisor is still obligated to perform despite the non-occurrence of the condition.

        —**Waiver Retracted?** Was the waiver retracted before the time for occurrence of the condition has expired? If so, the condition may be reinstated unless the other party has relied on the waiver such that retraction would be unjust. If not, then the condition remains waived.

2. Is it the occurrence of a constructive condition? If so, then ask:

    Has there been **substantial performance**? If the condition is not expressly stated but is constructed by the court, then there is room for flexibility and substantial performance may be sufficient to satisfy the condition. Where Party A and Party B are to render performances under an exchange of promises, each party's performance is conditioned on there being no uncured material failure of the other party to perform its promise due at an earlier time. If for example, Party A is to perform its promise first, then Party B's performance is conditioned on Party A substantially performing its promise.

(A) Effects of Conditions

Concepts:

The key to understanding promises and conditions lies in appreciating the consequences which flow from each with respect to the parties' future performances and entitlement to damages:

If a contract term is *only* a condition and the condition does not occur, then the party (obligor) whose performance was contingent on the condition is discharged but has no claim for breach against the other party (obligee) based on the non-occurrence of the condition. In other words, where a party's duty to perform is made conditional on the occurrence of an event and that event does not occur, then the party's duty to perform does not become due. There is no basis for claiming breach of contract because the non-occurrence of a condition is not a breach unless the other party (obligee) had promised—was under a duty—that the condition—event—occur.

If a contract term is *only* a promise and the promise is not performed in any respect, then the failure to perform is a breach of contract and the injured party has a claim for damages. As far as future performance by the injured party, it depends: where the parties are required to render performances under an exchange of promises and the breaching party was required to perform its promise first, then the injured party's own duty of further performance under the contract is not discharged unless the breach is "material" and the breaching party has no time to cure the breach. If the breaching party has time to cure and effects a timely cure, then the other party's duty to perform under the contract is due although it may still have a claim for damages caused by any delay in the breaching party's performance.

If the breaching party's failure to perform was not material, then the injured party must render its performance subject to the injured party's claim against the breaching party for damages for the breaching party's failure to perform its promise completely.

If a contract term is *both* a promise and a condition, that is, a "promissory condition," then the non-occurrence of the condition discharges the injured party from any future performance obligation under the contract and entitles that party to damages for any loss suffered as a consequence of the breach of the other party's (obligor's) promise—duty—that the condition would occur.

Applying the Concepts:

Consider the following example based on the case *Constable v. Cloberie* in the casebook on pages 733-734.

A shipowner promises to carry cargo from England to Cadiz in return for the cargo owner's promise to pay freight. Suppose that the cargo owner wants the shipowner to sail with the next wind. The cargo owner can seek to induce the shipowner to do so in several ways:

- **Condition:** *"Freight is payable only on condition that shipowner sails with the next wind."*

By making sailing with the next wind a condition of the cargo owner's duty to pay the freight, the cargo owner will not have to pay freight if the shipowner carries the cargo to Cadiz but delays sailing beyond the next wind. However, the cargo owner will have no right to any damages caused by the delay.

- **Duty:** *"Shipowner promises to sail with the next wind."*

By having the shipowner promise, that is, to undertake a duty to sail with the next wind, the cargo owner will have to pay freight if the shipowner carries the cargo to Cadiz but delays sailing beyond the next wind. However, the cargo owner will have a right to any damages caused by the delay.

A condition may cancel performance, and B-K cannot be claimed "if, unless"

A promise does not cancel performance, but there may be B-K claim for damage "I promise, stipulated"

■ **Condition and Duty:** *"Shipowner promises to sail with the next wind and freight is to be paid only on condition that the shipowner does so."*

By making sailing with the next wind both a promise and a condition of payment, if the shipowner fails to sail with the next wind, the cargo owner will have a right to any damages caused by the delay and will not have to pay the freight.

CASES	SUMMARIES
Luttinger v. Rosen (1972) → (CB pg. 726) 8 ½ % interest was a clear condition that was not met. Buyer made a good faith effort to attain it & did not, so the duty to perform is gone.	**FACTS:** Plaintiffs (buyers) contracted to purchase a piece of property from defendants (sellers) subject to the buyers obtaining a $45,000 first mortgage from a bank or other lending institution at an interest rate not to exceed 8½ percent. Buyers agreed to use due diligence in obtaining the mortgage. Buyers relied on their attorney who knew that only one institution would give a $45,000 mortgage on a single family house. If buyers did not obtain the specified financing, and if they timely notified sellers, the contract would be terminated. A mortgage commitment for $45,000 with interest at not less than 8¾ percent per annum was obtained. Buyers gave notice to sellers that they had been unsuccessful in obtaining a mortgage meeting the contract specification and demanded return of the down payment. Sellers offered through an undefined funding arrangement to make up the difference between the 8¾ percent the bank offered, and the 8½ percent contract rate, but buyers refused sellers' offer. Buyers brought suit and obtained judgment in its favor. **HOLDING:** On appeal, the court rejected the sellers' contention that buyers did not use reasonable diligence because buyers only applied to one bank. The evidence showed that the buyers' attorney was fully familiar with the types of mortgages lending institutions in and out of the area would give and thus concluded that due diligence was used. The court stated that applications to other lending institutions were not required since the law does not require the performance of a futile act. Finally, the court rejected the sellers' argument that the condition of the mortgage contingency clause was not met. The purchase was unambiguously conditioned on the buyers obtaining a mortgage as specified in the contract. Since buyers could not obtain a $45,000 mortgage at no more than 8½ percent, buyers were entitled to a refund. The buyers were not obligated to accept sellers' additional offer to fund the difference in interest payment.
Internatio-Rotterdam, Inc. v. River Grand Rice Mills, Inc. (1958) → (CB pg.729)	**FACTS:** In July, 1952, plaintiff (buyer) entered into a contract to purchase from defendant (seller) 95,600 pockets of rice for delivery at Lake Charles and/or Houston, Texas with shipment to be "'December 1952 with two weeks call from buyer'"; payment was to be made by a letter of credit that was to be opened immediately. After receiving buyer's instructions on December 10, the seller completed delivery of 50,000 pockets at Lake Charles with the last car unloaded on December 23. In the meantime, seller received no shipping instructions by December 17 for the 45,600 pockets to be delivered at Houston. On December 18, seller rescinded the contract for the Houston shipments but continued to make the Lake Charles deliveries. Buyer sued because seller refused to make the Houston shipments and the trial court dismissed the action.

CASES	SUMMARIES
Internatio-Rotterdam, continued Sellers notice + delivery Instructions were a condition precedent to the Houston deliveries .	**HOLDING:** On appeal, the court noted that buyer promised to give seller notice and that seller's duty to ship was conditioned on receipt of such notice. The court said that the notice requirement was what Professor Corbin would consider a "promissory condition"—buyer promised to give notice and and seller's duty to ship was conditioned on receipt of such notice. The issue was whether that condition was performed. Whether the condition was performed depended on whether seller's duty to ship was conditioned on notice no later than December 17 so that seller's performance would be completed within December or whether buyer could, under the contract, give notice later in December with seller having a duty to ship within two weeks of the notice. The court interpreted the contract and concluded that the "provision for December delivery went to the essence of the contract." The court explained, among other things, that when the contract was made in July the parties wanted protection of a specified delivery period—seller so that it could arrange its production schedules and avoid storage facility congestion, and buyer so that it could meet its commitments to its own customers. Since the court held that delivery within December was of the essence, "notice of shipping instructions on or before December 17 was not merely a 'duty'" of buyer, "it was a condition precedent to the performance which might be required" of the seller. Since buyer did not give notice by December 17, the condition to seller's duty of performance did not occur. The non-occurrence of the condition entitled seller to rescind, which seller did on December 18. The court rejected buyer's argument that because of its substantial part performance before December 17, it could not be held in default for not giving shipping instructions sooner. The court said that buyer's activities prior to December 17 were not performance but rather were preparations for performance of the contract. Thus, buyer's opening of a letter of credit was an arrangement for future performance and not an act of performance. The court noted that the seller gained no benefit from these preparatory activities. Finally, the court rejected the buyer's argument that seller's continuing shipments to Lake Charles after December 17 was an election by seller to continue the contract. Instead, the court found that seller had the option to split the deliveries between Lake Charles and Houston. The only reasonable inference from the facts was that the parties' duties with respect to the Lake Charles shipments were not dependent on the Houston shipments. The court concluded that the parties' "duties as to shipments at each port were paired and were reciprocal and that performance by the parties as to Lake Charles did not preclude the [seller's] right of cancellation as to Houston."

(B) Problems of Interpretation

Concepts:

- It is often difficult to determine whether a term is a promise or condition. Here, the intent of the parties is critical. Intent may be indicated by the parties' choice of language: words such as "if" or "unless" usually indicate the existence of a condition, while phrases such as "stipulate to" or "I promise that" indicate the intent to make an event a promise rather than a condition.

- Where there is doubt about whether a term is a condition or a promise, R2d §227(2) prefers an interpretation that finds a promise to avoid the harsh result of a forfeiture.

- Parties may include "satisfaction clauses" in their agreement requiring performance only upon the obligor's satisfaction. One issue which arises in such cases is whether the standard of satisfaction is subjective or objective.

- Determining whether the standard of satisfaction is objective or subjective generally depends on the subject matter of the contract. If it is a commercial contract such as one involving manufacturing or construction, then objective satisfaction, which requires the satisfaction of a reasonable person in the obligor's position, is required. Alternatively, if the contract involves personal services where the taste, fancy or judgment of the individual is involved, then subjective satisfaction is required. Still, even subjective satisfaction must be exercised in good faith which means honesty in fact, i.e., the party, if not satisfied with the other party's performance, must be honestly dissatisfied with the performance and not the bargain itself. Where the contract language is not clear whether the test is one of honest satisfaction or reasonable satisfaction, then the preference is for an objective standard of reasonableness to avoid the increased risk of forfeiture. R2d §228 cmt. b

CASES	SUMMARIES
Peacock Construction Co. v. Modern Air Conditioning, Inc. (1977) → (CB pg. 735) *Questions of fact - jury* *Questions of interpreting a contract - law* *Here, Gen. K had a duty to pay sub K's in a reasonable time, the gen K's payment from owner ≠ condition precedent*	**FACTS:** Peacock Construction, a builder, entered into two subcontracts with plaintiffs, each of which provided that final payment would be made to the subcontractors "within 30 days after the completion of the work included in this subcontract, written acceptance by the Architect and full payment therefor by the Owner." When the subcontractors completed their work, Peacock refused to make final payment, claiming that the owner had not made full payment to Peacock for the subcontractors' work. Peacock claimed that its duty to make final payment to each of the plaintiffs was expressly conditioned on Peacock's receipt of full payment from the owner. [Since the owner did not make full payment, the condition to Peacock's duty to perform—to pay plaintiff—never occurred.] The trial court entered summary judgment for plaintiffs and the Court of Appeals affirmed. The Court of Appeals held that the payment provisions did not establish a condition but rather "constitute absolute promises to pay, fixing payment by the owner as a reasonable time for when payment to the subcontractors is to be made." **HOLDING:** On appeal to the Florida Supreme Court, Peacock argued that the Court of Appeals was incorrect because the issue of whether the parties intended there to be conditions precedent was an issue of fact which should be determined by a jury. The court noted that the contract provision was susceptible of two meanings: it could be "interpreted as setting a condition precedent or as fixing a reasonable time for payment." The court recognized that the meaning of language is a factual question but nevertheless the general rule is that interpretation of a writing is a question of law not of fact. Thus an issue of interpretation relating to the parties' intention can be determined from the written contract "as a matter of law, when the nature of the transaction lends itself to judicial interpretation" and "that contracts between small subcontractors and general contractors on large construction projects are such transactions." In most cases, the parties' intent is that the owner's payment to the general contractor is not a condition precedent to the general contractor's duty to pay the subcontractor. The reason for this is that subcontractors cannot stay in business without payment for their work and thus ordinarily will not assume the risk of the owner's failure to pay the general contractor. The court noted, however, that its opinion did not prevent parties from agreeing otherwise: if they wished to shift the risk

CASES	SUMMARIES
Peacock Construction Co., continued	of payment failure by to the owner to the subcontractor, then they must "unambiguously express that intention."
Gibson v. Cranage (1878) → **(CB pg. 738)** Bad satisfaction clause, but enforceable. Very Subjective	**FACTS:** Plaintiff agreed to take a small portrait of defendant's deceased daughter and make it into a large one. The parties agreed that defendant would not have to pay unless the picture was satisfactory to the defendant. When the picture was finished, defendant was dissatisfied with it. Plaintiff was unable to clearly determine defendant's objections to the picture but nevertheless sent the picture to the artist to have it changed. When plaintiff received the picture from the artist, he showed it to defendant who initially refused to look at it but during the trial he examined it and still objected to it. The court said that even if the picture was an excellent one, under the contract, the only one who had the right to decide that was the defendant. If he did not find it to his satisfaction, he was not obligated to pay for it.

(C) Mitigating Doctrines

CASES	SUMMARIES
McKenna v. Vernon (1917) → **(CB pg. 745)** Condition must be upheld consistently to be enforceable	**FACTS:** McKenna agreed to build a moving picture theater for Vernon. The work was to be done under the direction of an architect and payment of each installment of the contract price was subject to the architect's certificate. When McKenna sued Vernon for the final payment, the trial court gave judgment to McKenna for $2500. Vernon appealed, claiming that McKenna was not entitled to payment because there was no architect certificate that the building had been completed. **HOLDING:** On appeal, the court stated that although payments were to be made only on the architect certificate, six of the seven progress payments had made without a certificate. The court said that since the owner had repeatedly waived the requirement during the progress of the work that payment was to be made only on an architect certificate, he could not insist on it now with respect to the final payment.
Hicks v. Bush (1962) → **(CB pg. 747)**	**FACTS:** Hicks entered into a completely integrated agreement with shareholders of Clinton G. Bush Co. to merge their corporate interests into a new company called Bush-Hicks Enterprises. Hicks transferred his stock to the new company but the other parties did not. Hicks sued for specific performance. At trial, defendants claimed that the agreement was subject to an oral condition that the agreement would not become effective until $672,500 of "equity expansion funds" were first raised. This sum was never raised. Although Hicks denied that anything was said about such a condition prior to signing the agreement, the trial court, based on the evidence, found that the parties had orally agreed upon the condition and therefore the contract never came into existence.

CASES	SUMMARIES
Hicks, continued Oral condition accepted under parol evidence bc/ it did not contradict terms of the written contract	**HOLDING:** Upon appeal, the NY Ct of Appeals stated that the law was clear that "[p]arol testimony is admissible to prove a condition precedent to the legal effectiveness of a written agreement. . . if the condition does not contradict the express terms of such written agreement. . . ." The court noted that the oral condition in this case dealt with a matter on which the agreement was silent and thus there was no contradiction between the terms of the written agreement and the oral condition. Still, Hicks argued that the written agreement provided that if the new company did not accept the stock subscriptions within 25 days, the agreement would be terminated and that this condition was irreconcilable with the oral condition that the written agreement would not be effective until the expansion funds were raised. The court rejected this argument and said that the two conditions were not contradictory—namely that the contract would not be effective until the expansion funds were raised and the added condition which required stock subscriptions acceptance within 25 days. Thus parol evidence as to the existence of the oral agreement was admissible.

Section 2. Constructive Conditions of Exchange

Concepts:

- Constructive conditions are conditions created by the court and not explicitly or implicitly by the parties' agreement. They are also referred to as conditions "implied-in-law."

- As opposed to express conditions, a "constructive" condition is satisfied even when a party renders something less than full performance and entitles her to performance from the other party. Substantial performance is sufficient for satisfaction of constructive conditions whereas nothing less than full performance is acceptable to satisfy an express condition. Substantial and not complete performance is sufficient to satisfy a constructive condition because the court created the condition as opposed to an express condition which is agreed upon by the parties.

- A promisor commits a breach when, without justification or excuse, she fails to tender **any** part of a promised performance when performance is due or tenders a defective performance. However, not all breaches are "equal"; some are trivial and others are serious. This difference is important because it affects the promisee's duties and rights under the contract. Consider the following:

  — If a promisor materially fails to perform, then the promisee may withhold her own performance, but if it is too late for the performance to occur, the promisee may terminate the contract, and sue for damages for total breach.

  — If a promisor commits a material breach, but it is not too late for the performance to occur, then the promisee may suspend her own performance, await the promisor's cure of the defect in performance, and seek damages for partial breach for any loss suffered as a result of the delay by the promisor to perform.

— If a promisor commits a non-material breach (substantially performs), then the promisee must tender her own performance but can seek damages for any loss suffered as a consequence of the promisor's failure to completely perform.

FRAMEWORK FOR ANALYSIS: Was there a breach of contract?

ASK: Has a party failed to perform her promise when performance was due? If the party has failed to perform, without excuse or justification, when the promised performance was due, then she is in breach of contract and the aggrieved party is entitled to seek a remedy.

If a party has materially failed to perform, then the aggrieved party may withhold her own performance, and if there is no further time for the breaching party to cure, the aggrieved party may terminate the contract and seek damages for total breach.

To determine whether a breach was material, a court considers a number of factors: (R2d §241)

- **Deprivation of Expected Benefit?** What is the extent to which the injured party will be deprived of the expected benefit from the contract?

- **Adequate Compensation?** What is the extent to which the injured party can be adequately compensated for the loss of that benefit?

- **Unfair Forfeiture?** What is the extent to which the breaching party will suffer forfeiture if not allowed to recover the agreed exchange under the contract? Where a breaching party's performance falls short of substantial performance, a court may still be able to avoid forfeiture and allow some recovery on the contract if the contract is "divisible."

  Is the contract divisible? Can the parties' performances be apportioned into corresponding pairs of part performances that may properly be regarded as agreed equivalents? If so, the doctrine of substantial performance can be applied to the corresponding pairs to avoid forfeiture. If not, the separation of tasks and payments were merely "progress payments" and the rule of substantial performance is not applicable. See Section (B) Divisibility.

- **Likelihood of Cure?** What is the likelihood that the breaching party will cure its failure?

- **Willfulness of the Breach?** What is the extent to which the breaching party meets standards of good faith and fair dealing? Was the breach intentional or willful?

1. Was the breach material? If, in considering the above factors, the breach was material, then the non-breaching party may suspend her own performance. However, even if it is a material breach, the breaching party may have time to cure, e.g., if time is not of the essence. Proceed to Question 3.

2. Was the breach immaterial? If, in considering the above factors, the breach is immaterial, then there has been substantial performance. In this case, the promisee must tender her own performance but can seek damages for any loss suffered because of the promisor's less than complete performance.

3. If there is still time to cure a material failure of performance, then the aggrieved party may suspend its performance but not yet terminate the contract. Ask: Can the defective or incomplete performance be cured?

- **Yes**—If the time for performance under the contract is not yet due, the breaching party may offer to cure her performance. If so, then the other party may be required to allow her to do so but is still entitled to recover any damages suffered as a consequence of the delay in complete performance.

- **No**—If the time for performance has passed or the need for timely performance is so essential—that is, time is of the essence—that any delay would result in a discharge of the contract, then there is no possibility for cure. In this case, the non-breaching party's remaining duties under the contract are discharged.

CASES	SUMMARIES
Kingston v. Preston (KB 1773) → (CB pg. 750) *Defendant's performance was subject to the constructive condition that the P provide the security payment*	**FACTS:** Plaintiff and defendant entered into an agreement whereby defendant was to deliver to plaintiff "his stock and business" and plaintiff was to give to defendant security for the payment that plaintiff was obligated to make. Plaintiff did not deliver the security and defendant did not turn over its business to plaintiff. Plaintiff sued defendant for breach, claiming that the defendant's promise to deliver his stock and business and plaintiff's promise to give security were mutual and independent such that plaintiff's failure to perform its promise was no bar to a breach of contract action against defendant who would have a remedy for plaintiff's breach in a separate action. **HOLDING:** The court granted judgment for defendant because it concluded that plaintiff's performance was a condition precedent to defendant's duty to perform. Lord Mansfield explained that there were three types of promises (covenants)—(1) mutual and independent promises, where either party could recover damages from the other for injury he may have received by a breach of covenants to him and where it is no excuse for the defendant to allege a breach of the covenants on the part of the plaintiff. (2) dependent promises where performance of one promise depends on the prior performance of another and (3) mutually dependent promises, covenants which are to performed at the same time meaning that if one party was ready and offered to perform and the other refused, the one who was ready may sue the other party for breach. Whether promises are dependent or independent, the court noted, must be gleamed from "the evident sense and meaning of the parties." The court explained that in this case defendant was not expected to turn over his business to plaintiff without receiving security for payment. Plaintiff's giving such security, therefore, was a condition precedent to defendant's duty to deliver the business to plaintiff.
Stewart v. Newbury (1917) → (CB pg. 752) *W/ no payment agreement made, substantial performance must be completed before payment*	**FACTS:** Stewart, a builder, entered into a contract to do excavation work for Newbury. The contract was silent as to the time or manner of payment. There was conflicting testimony as to whether the payments were to be made monthly. The trial court rejected Newbury's request that the jury be instructed that if there was no such agreement, Stewart was not entitled to any payment until the contract was completed. Instead, the court instructed the jury that if there was no agreement as to the time of payment, plaintiff would be entitled to part payment at reasonable times as the work progressed and if such payments were refused, he could abandon the work and recover the amount for the work performed.

CASES	SUMMARIES
Stewart, continued "Tender Condition?" idk	**HOLDING:** On appeal, the NY Court of Appeals said "this is not the law" and explained that the contract was "an entire contract" and that where there is a contract "to perform work and no agreement is made as to payment, the work must be substantially performed before payment can be demanded. . . ." Because of this and another error, the court reversed and ordered a new trial.

Section 3. Mitigating Doctrines

(A) Substantial Performance

CASES	SUMMARIES
Jacob & Youngs v. Kent (1921) → (CB pg. 757) Room for error w/ trivial, innocent deviations in a big contract	**FACTS:** Builder (plaintiff) sued to recover a balance of approximately $3,500 remaining on a $70,000 contract pursuant to which builder constructed a country residence for homeowner (defendant). The contract specifications called for all plumbing to be wrought iron pipe of Reading manufacture. As a result of builder's subcontractors' oversight, some of the pipe was the product of other manufacturers. The trial court excluded evidence that the brands installed were of the same quality, appearance, and value as the Reading brand and directed a verdict for the homeowner. The Appellate Division reversed. **HOLDING:** On appeal, the NY Court of Appeals noted that a party never fulfills his duty [promise] by less than full performance. However, a trivial and innocent omission may not always be a failure of a condition to be followed by forfeiture. [Note: if a party's duty to perform is subject to a condition, and that condition does not occur, then that party's duty to perform will not arise.] The court explained that "the margin of departure within the range of normal expectation upon a sale of common chattels will vary from the margin to be expected upon a contract for the construction of a mansion or a 'skyscraper.' There will be harshness sometimes and oppression in the implication of a condition when the thing upon which labor has been expended is incapable of surrender because united to the land [as is the case here], and equity and reason in the implication of a like condition when the subject-matter, if defective, is in shape to be returned. From the conclusions that promises may not be treated as dependent to the extent of their uttermost minutiae without a sacrifice of justice, the progress is a short one to the conclusion that they may not be so treated without a perversion of intention." There is no formula where to decide to draw the line between the important and the trivial; it all depends on the setting. However, where a contract's purpose would be frustrated, the law will not tolerate change. Whether literal fulfillment will be implied by law as a condition depends on various factors including "the purpose to be served, the desire to be

CASES	SUMMARIES

Jacob, continued

gratified, the excuse for deviation from the letter, the cruelty of enforced adherence." Only after weighing these factors can a court determine whether literal fulfillment of a party's performance should be implied by law as a condition to the other party's duty to perform. Of course, parties are free to provide by appropriate language that literal performance is a condition to the duty. The court noted that the law will mitigate the rigor of implied-in-law conditions for a party whose default is unintentional and trivial but that a willful transgressor will not be permitted relief from any deviation. [In other words, substantial performance by one party of its duty—and not full performance— will be implied as the condition precedent to the other party's duty to perform.]

DISSENT: Builder's omission was either intentional or the result of gross negligence. Builder installed between 2,000-2,500 feet of pipe with only 1,000 feet being contract compliant. The fact that the installed pipe may be just as good as Reading is irrelevant since the homeowner was entitled to the pipe he wanted. In this case, the rule "of substantial performance, with damages for unsubstantial omissions, has no application."

Bartus v. Riccardi (1967)

→ (CB pg. 763)

Substitute goods can be offered, with notice, in good faith.

Imperfect Tender

FACTS: Plaintiff, a representative of Acousticon, a manufacturer of hearing aids, agreed to sell a Model A-660 Acousticon hearing aid to defendant. Defendant had been tested and was told that this was the best hearing aid for his condition. On February 2, 1966, defendant was fitted at plaintiff's office with Model A-665 which he was told was an improved model. Defendant denied that he understood that the hearing aid given to him was a different model number. After using the new model, defendant complained to plaintiff that the hearing aid was giving him a headache and he returned it to plaintiff. Plaintiff offered to get Model A-660 for him; defendant did not respond. By letter dated 2/14/66, Acousticon, after having been told of defendant's complaint, wrote to defendant and told him that they would replace the model he had been given or would obtain a Model A-660 for him. Defendant decided he did not want any hearing aid from plaintiff and refused to accept any replacement, regardless of the model. Plaintiff brought suit to recover the balance due on the contract.

HOLDING: The issue on appeal was whether plaintiff, having delivered a different hearing aid from what was ordered, could recover when he subsequently tendered the model that met the contract terms. The court explained that although defendant had the right under UCC §2-601 to reject the hearing aid, plaintiff had the right under UCC §2-508(2) to substitute a conforming tender although the contract period had expired if he had reasonable grounds to believe that the non-conforming tender would be accepted and if he seasonably notified defendant of his intention to substitute a conforming product. The court stated that the plaintiff had reasonable grounds to believe that the defendant would accept the newer model and acted seasonably to notify defendant of plaintiff's tender of a conforming model. Thus plaintiff complied with UCC §2-508(2) and was entitled to judgment.

(B) Divisibility

Concepts:

- Even if a party's performance falls short of that required by the doctrine of substantial performance, a court can avoid forfeiture and allow some recovery on the contract if the contract is "divisible."

- A contract is divisible if the performances to be exchanged can be divided into "corresponding pairs of part performances so that the parts of each pair are properly regarded as agreed equivalents." R2d §240

- Often in construction contracts requiring a long period of time between the beginning of work and completion, parties may agree to structure payments during the course of the project. These are referred to as "progress payments" and do NOT correspond to the value of the work performed but rather are tied to progress points in the overall work project. Such progress payments do not make the contract "divisible."

CASES	SUMMARIES
Gill v. Johnstown Lumber Co. (1892) → (CB pg. 767) *Performance / payments parked the contract Severed* *Gill can be paid for what he delivered + cannot recover for anything else*	**FACTS:** Pursuant to a written contract, Gill agreed to drive approximately 4 million feet of logs to defendant's boom at Johnstown. The trial court, finding that the contract was entire, held that Gill was in default when a flood carried a considerable proportion of the logs past the Johnstown Lumber Co.'s boom so that a complete delivery was not made. Gill appealed. **HOLDING:** The issue on appeal was whether the contract was entire or severable. The court stated that if the contract was entire, the trial court was correct, but if it was severable, then plaintiff was entitled to have its claim submitted. The court held that the contract was severable and reversed the trial court. Quoting from Parsons on Contracts, the court said that to determine whether a contract is entire or severable (also referred to as "divisible"), the following criterion should be applied: "'If the part to be performed by one party consists of several and distinct items, and the price to be paid by the other is ① apportioned to each item to be performed, or ② is left to be implied by law, such a contract will generally be held to be severable. . . . But if the consideration to be paid is single and entire the contract must be held to be entire, although the subject of the contract my consist of several distinct and wholly independent items.'" Here, the court said that Gill's work under the contract consisted of several items, including driving different types of logs, carrying other kinds of timber from points above Johnstown to defendant's boom at Johnstown, as well as driving cross-ties from one designated point to Bethel and points below Bethel. Payment for this work was not an entire sum but was apportioned among several items, thus making the contract severable: (1) for oak logs-$1.00 per thousand feet; (2) for all other logs $0.75 for a thousand feet; (3) for cross-ties driven to Bethel $0.3 each; and (4) for points below Bethel at $0.5 for each cross-tie. Since the contract was severable, Gill would be entitled to the stipulated rate for all delivered logs and ties but would not be entitled to any compensation for the logs that he had driven part of the way but

CASES	SUMMARIES
Gill, continued	which were carried by the flood past the defendant's boom. In other words, compensation "for driving each log is an entire sum per thousand feet for the whole distance and is not apportioned or apportionable to parts of the drive."

(C) Restitution

CASES	SUMMARIES
Britton v. Turner ***(1834)*** → **(CB pg. 769)**	**FACTS:** Plaintiff agreed to work for defendant for one year at a salary of $120. After nine and a half months, plaintiff quit without justification. Plaintiff sought recovery in quantum meruit for the reasonable value of the work he performed until he terminated his employment. The jury found for plaintiff in the amount of $95. Defendant did not offer any evidence as to any damages it suffered because plaintiff quit before he performed the entire contract. Defendant objected to the trial court's jury instructions which permitted plaintiff to recover *in quantum meruit*. **HOLDING:** On appeal, the court noted that assuming plaintiff voluntarily failed to perform the entire contract, he clearly was not entitled to recover upon the contract itself because he never completed his one year performance which was a condition to defendant's duty to pay plaintiff the agreed upon $120 (note that the contract was entire and not divisible). The issue was whether under these circumstances, plaintiff could recover a reasonable sum for the services he actually performed under a theory of quantum meruit. In determining the question, the court considered the existing law which held for such labor contracts as at issue here that "the party who voluntarily fails to fulfill the contract by performing the whole labor contracted for, is not entitled to recover anything for the labor actually performed, however much he may have done towards the performance. . . ." The court found that such a rule was unequal and unjust, reasoning that if plaintiff had not even started performing, his liability to defendant would probably have been no more "than some small expense and trouble incurred in procuring another to do the labor which he contracted to perform." But here plaintiff worked 9½ months for defendant who received $95 worth of services according to the jury. Thus if defendant succeeded on this technical rule requiring the contract's full performance, he would be able to retain without payment nearly five-sixths of plaintiff's performance, a sum which would not only be "utterly disproportionate to any probable, not to say possible damage which could have resulted from the neglect of the plaintiff to continue the remaining two and a half months, but altogether beyond any damage which could have been recovered by the defendant, had the plaintiff done nothing toward the fulfillment of his contract." Consequently, the court held that "where a party undertakes to pay upon a special contract for the performance of labor, or the furnishing of materials, he is not to be charged upon such special agreement until the money is earned according to the terms of it. . . ." However, if a party under such a contract receives labor or materials from which it "derives a benefit and advantage, over and above the damage which has resulted from the breach of the contract by the other party, the labor actually

CASES	SUMMARIES

Britton, continued

Normally, if a party willfully breaches w/o completing performance on an "entire contract," then they cannot recover.

Here though, the D received benefit & it would be unfairly prejudicial not to award P for services rendered.

done, and the value received, furnish a new consideration, and the law thereupon raises a promise to pay to the extent of the reasonable worth of such excess." [In sum, plaintiff would be entitled to the value of the benefit that defendant received from plaintiff's performance less any damage that plaintiff caused defendant by plaintiff's breaching the contract in failing to perform for the entire year.]

The court explained "the technical reasoning — that the performance of the whole labor is a condition precedent, and the right to recover anything dependent upon it; that, contract being entire, there can be no apportionment; and that, there being an express contract, no other can be implied, even upon the subsequent performance of service — is not properly applicable to this species of contract, where a beneficial service has been actually performed; for we have abundant reason to believe, that the general understanding of the community is that the hired laborer shall be entitled to compensation for the service actually performed, though he do not continue the entire term contracted for, and such contracts must be presumed to be made with reference to that understanding, unless an express stipulation shows the contrary. . . ." Accordingly, while plaintiff was entitled to recover the reasonable value of his services even though he materially breached the contract, defendant was entitled to set off against that amount any damages it incurred for having to procure another party to complete the work that plaintiff did not do. However, since defendant did not introduce evidence as to any damage he suffered because of plaintiff's breach, defendant was not entitled to any deduction from the $95 awarded to plaintiff for the reasonable value of his services.

Kirkland v. Archbold (1953)

→ (CB pg. 776)

Entire, not severed
↓
bc there is a single consideration: "6K for a finished house"

Bc this is a construction contract, there's no need to show substantial performance - just that benefit was conferred

FACTS: Plaintiff agreed to repair defendant's house for which the owner agreed to pay $6,000, payable as follows: $1,000 after ten (10) days of work, another $10,000 after 20 days of work, another $10,000 after 30 days of work, and the remainder on completion. After owner had paid plaintiff $800, she prevented plaintiff from finishing the job and plaintiff sued. The trial court held that defendant had properly prevented plaintiff from continuing to work because plaintiff had materially failed to perform. Nevertheless, the court gave plaintiff judgment for $200, holding that plaintiff had earned the first $1,000 installment.

HOLDING: On appeal, the court reversed and remanded the case for further proceedings. It held that the lower court erred in holding that the contract provisions were severable simply because the parties had a schedule of payments based on the progress of the work. This did not change the character of the contract which was an entire contract—the total consideration of $6,000 was to be paid for the entire work under the contract. Conceding that plaintiff failed to substantially perform the contract (i.e., he materially failed to perform it), the issue was whether plaintiff, as a defaulting party, was entitled to recover for his partial performance. While earlier case law refused to allow a defaulting plaintiff to bring a contract action except where there has been substantial performance on his part, the court acknowledged the increasing number of other courts of last resort which have allowed a material

CASES	SUMMARIES
Kirkland, continued	ly defaulting plaintiff— who therefore cannot recover on a breach of contract theory—to recover on a *quantum meruit* theory. Quoting from *Williston on Contracts*, the court said that "[t]he drastic rule of forfeiture against a defaulting contractor who has by his labor and materials materially enriched the estate of the other party should in natural justice, be afforded relief to the reasonable value of the work done, less what damage the other party had suffered. . . ." The court concluded that the trial court's judgment was therefore contrary to law and remanded the case for further proceedings.
	Note: Based on the cited authorities, recovery on a *quantum meruit* theory may be limited to a non- willful defaulting contractor.

Section 4. Suspending Performance and Terminating the Contract

CASES	SUMMARIES
Walker & Co. v. Harrison (1957) → (CB pg. 782) Walkers failure to Maintain the Sign, In this case, did not amount to a material breach.	**FACTS:** Plaintiff, Walker, agreed to construct, install, and lease to defendants, Harrison, who were in the dry cleaning business, an approximately 19 foot "neon sign with electric clock." The lease provided for monthly rental payments of $148.50 and Walker agreed to maintain the sign in "first class advertising condition." Soon after the sign was installed, it was hit with a tomato, rust was visible on the chrome, and there were spider cobwebs in its corners. Harrison repeatedly requested Walker to service the sign and, failing to respond to the repeated calls, Harrison refused to make any monthly payment after the first one. Walker elected to accelerate the rental payments pursuant to paragraph G of the parties' rental contract and sued to recover the entire balance. The trial court entered judgment for Walker.
	HOLDING: The court affirmed on appeal, noting that a material failure of performance by one party justifies the other party's refusal to perform. Determining whether a breach was material is based on a number of factors as set forth in Section 275 of the First Restatement of Contracts [see R2d §241]. The court said that although Walker's delay in rendering the maintenance service was irritating, it agreed with the trial court that it did not amount to a material breach so as to justify Harrison in refusing to pay the rent. Harrison's refusal was itself a material breach. As to damages, the court noted that the trial court had reduced the acceleration of rentals due "by the amount that service would have cost Walker during the unexpired portion of the agreement" and Walker did not complain about such diminution.

Acceleration - upon a missed payment, creditor may request the payment of remaining dues immediatley

CASES	SUMMARIES

K&G Construction Co. v. Harris (1960)

→ (CB pg. 786)

Gen. Contractors promise to pay was dependent on sub Contractors fulfillment of obligations

FACTS: K&G, the owner and general contractor of a housing project, contracted with Harris and Brooks to do excavating and earth moving work. The contract provided among other things that ① "all work shall be performed in a workmanlike manner" and (2) that "Subcontractor will submit to Contractor, by the 25th of each month, a requisition for work performed during the preceding month" and that Contractor would pay 90% of the requisitioned amount by the 10th of the month in which the requisition was received. On August 9, during the course of grading, the Subcontractor caused the collapse of a wall and other damage to the Contractor's house. Because of the bulldozer damage, which Subcontractor refused to repair or pay for, the Contractor did not pay on August 10 the Subcontractor's requisition which was due for work it did prior to July 25. Nevertheless, the Subcontractor continued to work until September 12 when it stopped working because the progress payment due on August 10 was not made. The trial court denied the Contractor recovery of the $450 it paid to have the excavation work completed by another excavating company and granted Subcontractor's counterclaim for damages for not being permitted to finish the job.

HOLDING: The issue on appeal was whether the contractor had the right under the circumstances to refuse to make the August 10 progress payment. The court stated the parties' promises and counter-promises in a contract may be independent of each other or mutually dependent upon each other: "They are independent of each other if the parties intend that performance by each of them is in no way conditioned upon performance by the other. . . . A failure to perform an independent promise does not excuse non-performance on the part of the adversary party. . . . Promises are mutually dependent if the parties intend performance by one to be conditioned upon performance by the other. . . ." The court noted that Lord Mansfield in Kingston v. Preston "decided that performance of one covenant might be dependent on prior performance of another, although the contract contained no express condition to that effect" and that "[t]he modern rule, which seems to be of almost universal application, is that there is a presumption that mutual promises in a contract are dependent and are to be so regarded, whenever possible." The court held that the bulldozer damage constituted a breach of the contract requirement that the work be done in a "workmanlike manner" and that such breach was material. It cited to and quoted from Corbin on Contracts that a failure of performance is always a breach and that if it is "'of such great importance'" it may constitute what Corbin calls "a 'total' breach" but nevertheless the injured party may opt to treat the non-performance as only a "'partial' breach." In this case, the court said that "[i]n permitting the subcontractor to proceed with work on the project after August 9, the contractor, obviously, treated the breach by the subcontractor as a partial one. As the promises were mutually dependent and the subcontractor had made a material breach in his performance, this justified the contractor in refusing to make the August 10 payment; hence, as the contractor was not in default, the subcontractor again breached the contract when he, on September 12, discontinued work on the project, which rendered him liable (by the express terms of the contract) to the contractor for his increased cost in having the excavating done. . . . ."

CASES	SUMMARIES
K&G Construction Co., continued	**QUESTIONS TO THINK ABOUT:** *Did the contractor treat the subcontractor's breach as a partial one by allowing the subcontractor to continue working after August 9 until September 12?* *If so, why was the contractor justified in still refusing to make the progress payment? In other words, why wasn't the contractor in default, thus excusing the subcontractor from continuing to work?*
***Iron Trade Products Co. v. Wilkoff Co.** (1922)* → (CB pg. 793) *No proof π knowingly acted in bad faith, + no proof that the supply of rails was exhausted*	**FACTS:** Plaintiff entered into a written contract to buy 2,600 tons of rails at $41.00 a ton from defendant. Defendant did not deliver any of the rails. Plaintiff sued and recovered a judgment because it was compelled to purchase the rails at a higher price. The trial court rejected defendant's defense and entered judgment for plaintiff. Defendant appealed. **HOLDING:** On appeal, defendant claimed that it was excused from delivering the rails because the supply of rails was very limited and it could only obtain the contract quantities in two places in the United States. Pending the time of delivery when defendant was negotiating for purchasing the rails, plaintiff purchased 887 tons and agreed to buy a larger quantity from the very same people that defendant was negotiating with, thereby reducing the available supply and increasing the cost of the rails. The court noted that the defendant's affidavit failed to allege that plaintiff knew "that the supply of rails was limited or any intent on its part to prevent, interfere with, or embarrass defendant in the performance of the contract; and there [was] no suggestion of any understanding, express or implied, that defendant was to secure the rails from any particular source, or that plaintiff was to refrain from purchasing other rails," which the court said plaintiff was not required to do. The court then quoted "the true rule" from Williston: "'[i]f a party seeking to secure all the merchandise of a certain character which he could entered into a contract for a quantity of the required goods, and subsequently made performance of the contract by the seller more difficult by making other purchases which increased the scarcity of the available supply, his conduct would furnish no excuse for refusal to perform the prior contract.'" The court concluded that here defendant was not prevented from performing because of plaintiff's purchases, although it may have added to its difficulty and expense; plaintiff's purchases did not exhaust the supply of rails and any increased costs were no excuse for defendant's failure to perform.
New England Structures, Inc. v. Loranger → (CB pg. 796)	**FACTS:** Loranger, a general contractor on a school project, entered into a contract with New England Structures ("New England"), whereby New England agreed to install a roof deck. The contract provided among other things that if New England failed "to supply enough properly skilled workmen" Loranger was entitled, on five days' written notice, to terminate New England's right to proceed with its performance under the contract. About a month after New England began working, Loranger sent a telegram stating that it was terminating New England's right to proceed and giving as

CASES	SUMMARIES
New England Structures, continued P only stated one reason for the breach, but can rely on other unstated reasons as long a D does not rely on stated breach	its justification New England's failure to provide sufficient skilled workman to maintain satisfactory progress. The trial court instructed the jury that Loranger could not justify the termination on any grounds other than the one stated in the termination notice such as New England's "failure to stagger the joints of the bulb tees or failure to weld properly" unless these reasons were inherent in the failure to provide enough skilled workmen. Loranger excepted to the judge's instruction. **HOLDING:** On appeal, the court noted that there is some case authority for the trial court's instructions that Loranger, having identified one basis for termination of the subcontract, could not then rely on other grounds, except to the extent that the other grounds may directly affect the first ground asserted. The basis for this principle is estoppel or waiver. However, the court stated that Massachusetts law "somewhat more definitely require[s] reliance or change of position based upon the assertion of the particular reason or defense before treating a person, giving one reason for his action, as estopped later to give a different reason." The court therefore held that Loranger was entitled to assert grounds in support of its termination of New England which were not mentioned in Loranger's notice of termination unless New England establishes that it relied to its detriment on the one asserted ground. The trial court should have instructed the jury that they could consider other grounds for termination of the subcontractor and defenses to New England's claim other than the basis claimed in the notice of termination "unless they found as a fact that New England had relied to its detriment upon the fact that only one particular ground for termination was mentioned in the telegram." Finally, the court noted that once the five-day notice of termination was given, New England did not have a right to attempt to cure its default during that five-day period.

Section 5. Prospective Nonperformance

Concepts:

- An anticipatory repudiation occurs when the promisor expresses to the promisee the intent, either through words or conduct, that a promised performance will not be forthcoming. Since this occurs before the actual time set for performance, it is referred to as an "anticipatory breach" or "prospective non-performance."

- A repudiation by the promisor can be either through words or conduct. R2d §250 ("a repudiation is (a) a statement by the obligor to the obligee indicating that the obligor will commit a breach that would of itself give the obligee a claim for damages for total breach under §243, or (b) a voluntary affirmative act which renders the obligor unable or apparently unable to perform without such a breach.")

- The promisor's statement must be sufficiently clear, absolute, and certain so as to be reasonably understood that the promisor will not or cannot perform it promised performance. Mere expressions of doubt as to willingness or ability to perform are insufficient.

FRAMEWORK FOR ANALYSIS: Determining whether there has been an anticipatory repudiation

ASK: Has one party expressed an intent not to perform the contract before the time performance is due? Has one party taken affirmative action that renders her unable to perform without a breach?

1. Was there an express or implied repudiation?

- **Express repudiation?** Did the party express a clear, positive, unequivocal refusal to perform? The party's language must be sufficiently clear and positive to indicate that it cannot or will not render the promised performance to constitute a repudiation. If so, then the other party has several options. Proceed to "*4. Responding to a Repudiation.*"

- Language of one party that is equivocal or merely expresses doubt concerning a prospective ability to perform is insufficient to constitute a repudiation. However, it may give the other party reasonable grounds for insecurity and such party may seek assurances. Proceed to "*2. Assurances of Performance.*"

- **Implied Repudiation?** Has the party voluntarily done something which makes it actually or apparently impossible for her to perform without giving rise to a claim for total breach? If so, then the party has repudiated. Proceed to "*4. Responding to a Repudiation.*"

If the act falls short of these requirements, it may still give reasonable grounds for insecurity and the aggrieved party may seek assurances of performance. Proceed to "2. Assurances of Performance."

2. **Assurances of Performance:** Has a party's expectation of receiving due performance under the contract been impaired? If there are reasonable grounds to believe that the other party's promised performance will not be forthcoming, the party in doubt is entitled to demand assurances.

- **Sale of Goods?** Under UCC §2-609 a party may in writing demand adequate assurances of due performance. While awaiting assurances, it may suspend its own performance for which it has not already received the agreed return performance if commercially reasonable.

- **Common Law?** Under R2d §251, the demand for assurances need not be in writing. The party who demands assurances must do so in accordance with its duty of good faith and fair dealing. Comment d. This may make a written demand the preferred method.

Have adequate assurances of performance been provided?

- **Sale of Goods?** Under UCC §2-609, a party has a reasonable time, not exceeding thirty days, in which to provide adequate assurances after receiving a justified demand. Failure to provide such assurances is a repudiation of the contract.

- **Common Law?** The R2d follows the UCC in requiring assurances to be given within a "reasonable time" but it does not impose the thirty day limitation. Failure to provide such assurances allows the aggrieved party to treat it as a repudiation.

3. **Retracting a Repudiation:** Has the repudiating party attempted to retract the repudiation? The retraction may be oral or written but the other party must have knowledge of it to be effective. A valid retraction restores the contract and the non-repudiating party has no damage claims except for any harm (such as delay) incurred by the repudiation. While it is possible to retract a repudiation, there are limits to when a retraction is possible. Ask:

- **Reliance?** Has the aggrieved party acted upon the repudiation? If the aggrieved party has acted in reliance on the repudiation by materially changing its position, commencing an action, or indicating to the repudiating party that it considers the repudiation final, then it is too late for the repudiating party to retract. If the aggrieved party has not changed its position, then the repudiating party can nullify the repudiation by giving notice of retraction.

4. **Responding to a Repudiation:** If a party has repudiated before the time for performance has arrived, what are the non-repudiating party's options?

- **Treat as Terminated?** Can the non-repudiating party treat the contract as terminated and bring an action for damages? R2d §253(1)

— The injured party may treat its remaining duties under the contract as discharged and bring suit immediately for damages for total breach. When bringing suit, the injured party must show that it would have been ready, willing, and able to perform but for the repudiation. R2d §253(2)

— The injured party may not bring suit immediately if the party has repudiated either a unilateral contract or a bilateral contract that has been fully performed by the injured party and the breaching party's only remaining duty is the payment of installments not related to each other. The injured party must await the time for performance to sue for damages. This is the exception to the general rule that a party may bring suit immediately for an anticipatory repudiation. R2d §243(3) cmt d

- **Urge Retraction?** Can the non-repudiating party try to save the deal by insisting that the repudiating party perform and urge it to retract its repudiation? The non-repudiating party can insist on performance and urge retraction. If the repudiating party retracts, the contract remains in force. If the repudiating party fails to retract, the injured party can still treat the repudiation as a breach and seek damages.

- **Ignore and Await Performance?** Can the non-repudiating party ignore the repudiation and await the time for performance? The non-repudiating party can ignore the repudiation but may run into the problem of failing to mitigate damages.

QUESTIONS TO THINK ABOUT:

How soon must the non-repudiating act to mitigate damages?

Under UCC §2-610(a), the aggrieved party may "for a commercially reasonable time await performance[.]" Comment 1 adds: "[b]ut if he awaits performance beyond a commercially reasonable time he cannot recover resulting damages which he should have avoided."

What is the appropriate time to measure Buyer's damages when Seller anticipatorily repudiates and Buyer does not cover?

Buyer's damages under UCC 2-713(1) states that "the measure of damages for . . . repudiation by the seller is the difference between the market price at the time when the buyer learned of the breach and the contract price together with any incidental and consequential damages . . . but less expenses saved in consequence of the seller's breach."

When has the buyer "learned of the breach"? (See Cosden Oil & Chemical Co. below)

(A) Anticipatory Repudiation

CASES	SUMMARIES
Hochster v. De La Tour (QB 1853) → (CB pg. 800) *Options* *1. Sue immediatley* *2. Sue when the breach occurs* *3. Excuse performance*	**FACTS** On April 12, defendant agreed to employ plaintiff commencing June 1 as a courier and in that capacity plaintiff was to travel with defendant for three months. On May 11, defendant wrote plaintiff that he would not use his services. On May 22, plaintiff sued defendant for breach. The jury found for plaintiff. **HOLDING:** On appeal, the court gave judgment for plaintiff, thereby rejecting defendant's argument that there could be no breach of contract prior to June 1, the date performance was due. The court explained that "[i]f the plaintiff has no remedy for breach of the contract unless he treats the contract as in force, and acts upon it down to the 1st June, 1852, it follows that, till then, he must enter into no employment which will interfere with his promise" to commence traveling with defendant on June 1. Instead, it would be more rational and beneficial to the parties, once defendant repudiates the contract, that plaintiff should be free of any duty to perform while retaining the right to sue defendant for breach. Instead of plaintiff's remaining idle and spending money on useless preparation, he should be "at liberty to seek service under another employer, which would go in mitigation of the damages to which he would otherwise be entitled for a breach of the contract." The court noted that a person who repudiates a contract has no basis for complaining that the other party put faith in the repudiating party's renunciation and sued immediately for breach of contract; thus, the court said "it seems reasonable to allow an option to the injured party, either to sue immediately, or to wait till the time when the act was to be done, still holding it as prospectively binding for the exercise of this option, which may be advantageous to the innocent party, and cannot be prejudicial to the wrongdoer." Finally, the court rejected the argument that an action before June 1 should not be allowed because of the difficulty of calculating damages. The court pointed out that the calculation would be no more difficult if an action were brought before September 1. "In either case, the jury in assessing the damages would be justified in looking to all that happened, or was likely to happen, to increase or mitigate the loss of the plaintiff down to the day of trial."
Kanovos v. Hancock Bank & Trust Co. (1985) → (CB pg. 805) *He was not ready, willing, & able to perform (purchase)*	**FACTS:** Defendant, Hancock Bank, was the holder of all the stock of 1025 Hancock Inc. ("Stock") which owned an apartment building known as Executive House. Hancock Bank gave plaintiff, Kanovos, a right of first refusal to purchase the Stock within 60 days. In November 1976, Hancock Bank entered into a contract to sell the Stock to a third person and sold it without giving Kanovos the opportunity to purchase it. In order to match the offer the bank had received for the Stock, Kanovos would have had to pay the bank $760,000. The trial court ruled that Kanovos' ability to pay the $760,000 was not material and that Kanovos was not required to have been ready, willing, and able to pay that amount to the bank within 60 days to match the offer the bank had accepted. **HOLDING:** The issue on appeal was whether Kanovos' financial ability to perform was material. The court concluded that it was material because Kanovos was not

CASES	SUMMARIES
Kanavos, continued	entitled to recover from the repudiating bank "unless he could have complied with his concurrent obligation to pay for the stock (or, as is not the case here, unless the bank's conduct substantially prevented Kanovos from being able to meet his obligation)." The court explained that when the bank received an acceptable offer for the stock it was obligated to give Kanovos the right to match the offer. If Kanovos wanted the stock, he would have had to tender the purchase price and the bank would have been required to deliver the stock. Of course Kanovos would not have been required in this particular case to actually tender the purchase price because the bank had already sold the stock to a third party. Thus, while "Kanovos did not have to show that he was ready, willing, and able to purchase the stock on the day the bank repudiated its agreement with him by selling the stock . . . . [t]hat principle does not mean, however, that his ability to purchase the stock during the option period is irrelevant." Kanovos' financial ability to match the offer which the bank accepted was material to his right to recover. Noting that the circumstances concerning his ability to raise $760,000 were far better known to him than to the bank, the court held that Kanovos had the burden to prove his financial ability to purchase the stock and that such proof was "an essential part of establishing the defendant's liability." Noting that there was evidence from which the jury could have found that Kanovos had the ability to finance the stock purchase, the court remanded the case to determine "whether, if he had had proper notice of his right to purchase the stock, Kanovos would have been ready, willing, and able to do so during the option period."
Cosden Oil & Chemical Co. v. Karl O. Helm Aktiengesellschaft (1984) → **(CB pg. 810)**	*Note: For the purposes of this case summary, the conventions for referring to UCC provisions will follow that of the court opinion.* **FACTS:** In early 1979, Helm Houston, Buyer, entered into a contract with Cosden Oil, Seller, for the purchase of 1250 metric tons of high impact polystyrene under four orders numbered 04 through 07. Cosden shipped product under the 04 order but refused to make final delivery by March 16 as requested and instead canceled the 04 order by the end of March. As to orders 05 through 07, Cosden had informed Helm in February that it did not have sufficient product to fill those orders. Cosden sued Helm for payment of the delivered polystyrene and Helm counterclaimed. The jury found that Cosden had anticipatorily breached orders 05 through 07 and that Cosden's cancellation of order 04 for Helm's failure to pay for the second 04 delivery was a repudiation. The district court granted Helm damages measured by "the difference between the contract price and the market price at a commercially reasonable time after Cosden repudiated. . . ." Since the jury found that Helm's purchases in February and March of high impact polystyrene from other sources constituted "other" purchases and not "cover," Helm's recovery for Cosden's repudiation was governed by UCC Section 2.713 and not Section 2.712. Section 2.713 provides that subject to 2.723, a buyer's damages for seller's repudiation is measured by "the difference between market price at the time when the buyer learned of the breach and the contract price together with any incidental and consequential damages . . . but less expenses saved in consequence of the seller's breach." [emphasis added]

CASES	SUMMARIES

Cosden, continued

Contract price – Commercially reasonable price

HOLDING: On appeal, the court noted that there were three possible interpretations of the statutory language "learned of the breach." The court rejected interpreting those words to mean "learned of the repudiation" because to do so "would undercut the time that 2.610 gives the aggrieved buyer to await performance." It noted that under 2.610 when a seller repudiates and a buyer does not cover, the buyer is entitled to await performance for a commercially reasonable time but "cannot recover resulting damages which he should have avoided"—thus implying that the buyer could recover damages where the market rises during the commercially reasonable time period. The court said that Section 2.610 must be read together with Section 2.713, the result being that a buyer "learns of the breach" at "a commercially reasonable time after he learns of the seller's anticipatory repudiation." The court pointed out that the issue would normally be presented in a rising market and, to the extent that damage rules influence market decisions, measuring market price at a commercially reasonable time after repudiation gives the buyer the opportunity to consider his alternatives without worrying that if he does not cover his damages will be measured at the time of repudiation.

Although the court recognized that there were good arguments to interpret the words "learned of the breach" to mean "time of performance" as was the pre-UCC rule, to do so would mean that "phrases in Section 2.610 and 2.712 lose their meaning." Thus under 2.610 there would be no reason to limit a buyer to a commercially reasonable time or under Section 2.712(a) to require the buyer to act "without unreasonable delay" in making cover after a repudiation. The court recognized that its interpretation does not "explain the language of Section 2.723(a) insofar as it relates to aggrieved buyers." However, that Section only deals with the rare cases where the case is tried before performance is due. The court concluded that "[i]n light of the Code's persistent theme of commercial reasonableness, the prominence of cover as a remedy, and the time given an aggrieved buyer to await performance and to investigate cover before selecting his remedy, we agree with the district court that 'learned of the breach' incorporates Section 2.610's commercially reasonable time."

McCloskey & Co. v. Minweld Steel Co. (1955)

→ (CB pg. 818)

FACTS: Plaintiff, a general contractor, entered into three contracts with defendant, Minweld, a steel fabricator and erector, whereby plaintiff agreed to provide and erect all of the structural steel needed for two buildings to be built on the grounds of a Pennsylvania state hospital. Each of the contracts provided under Article VI that "'[a]ll labor, materials and equipment required under this contract are to be furnished at such times as may be directed by the Contractor, and in such a manner so as to at no time delay the final completion of the building.'" In May, Minweld, the subcontractor, received the contract drawings and specifications. On June 8, McCloskey wrote Minweld asking when the structural steel would be delivered and an estimated time for when erection would be complete. Minweld replied on June 13, submitting a schedule of estimated steel deliveries which were to start by September 1 and of an estimated completion date of November 15. Plaintiff wrote Minweld on July 20 "threatening to terminate the contracts unless the latter [Minweld] gave unqualified assurances that it had effected definite arrangements for the procurement, fabrication and delivery within thirty days of the required materials." On July 24,

CASES	SUMMARIES

McCloskey, continued

P rightly sought assurance for performance -

but D's response was not a repudiation, it was a good faith effort to perform in a tough market

(Must be absolute, unequivocle refusal to perform)

Minweld wrote plaintiff that it was having difficulty securing the necessary steel and asked for plaintiff's help in procuring the steel. Minweld also wrote that "'[w]e are as anxious as you are that there be no delay in the final completion of the buildings or in the performance of our contract. . . .'" Minweld had unsuccessfully tried to purchase steel from Bethlehem Steel, U.S. Steel, and Carnegie-Illinois. Rightly concerned about the tightening steel market because the Korean War had broken out on June 24, 1950, Minweld knew that without plaintiff's help in getting assistance from the Pennsylvania State agency that owned the hospital, "Minweld was in a bad way for the needed steel." Plaintiff claimed that Minweld's July 24 letter, "read against the relevant facts," was a positive statement not to perform and thus a repudiation. Plaintiff sued for anticipatory beach and the trial court granted judgment for Minweld.

HOLDING: The Third Circuit affirmed on appeal. The court said that Minweld's July 24 letter did not convey the idea of contract repudiation. The court noted that Minweld realistically faced the steel shortage problem and asked for the general contractor's help which the court indicated should have been given. The court noted that "[d]espite the circumstances there is no indication in the [July 24] letter that Minweld had definitely abandoned all hope of otherwise receiving the steel and so finishing its undertaking." For example, one of the steel producers may have relented and sold to Minweld or another supplier may have been found. The court believed that plaintiff's refusal to help eliminated any chance that Minweld had when it took the position that Minweld had repudiated rather than trying to get the State Authority to help. The court said that to constitute a repudiation under Pennsylvania law "'there must be an absolute and unequivocal refusal to perform or a distinct and positive statement of an inability to do so.'" In this case, the court found that Minweld's conduct was "plainly not that of a contract breaker under that that test." Plaintiff further argued that its July 20 letter asking Minweld for assurances that it had made arrangements for delivery within thirty days constituted the fixing of a date for performance under Article VI of the contracts. The court said that the thirty day date, if fixed, was not repudiated. At best, Minweld said it was not able to give assurances as to preparatory arrangements which does not constitute the repudiation of a promised performance. The court noted that there was nothing in the contract that required Minweld to give such assurances.

(B) Assurance of Due Performance

CASES	SUMMARIES
By-Lo Oil Co. v. Partech, Inc. (2001) → (CB pg. 825) By-lo had reasonable grounds to be ~~insur~~ insecure & request assurance, but 2 years away from Y2k is not grounds to demand an answer + force an action.	**FACTS:** ParTech contracted with By-Lo to furnish it with accounting software and continuing support for a set monthly fee. In September 1997, concerned about being Y2K compliant, By-Lo's controller, Thomas Masters wrote to ParTech requesting that Eng, ParTech's Host Accounting Systems director, contact Masters to discuss By-Lo's concern about the year 2000. When Eng did not respond, Masters wrote to her on January 7, 1998 demanding a response "'by January 31, 1998 of Par[Tech]'s commitment that the software [By-Lo] own[s] will function after December 31, 1999 with no problems (emphasis added).'" By letter dated January 30, 1998, Eng told Masters that she could not answer Masters' question of whether ParTech would change the software to handle the year 2000 because ParTech's upper management would make that decision when they had the data necessary to make an informed decision. Eng assured Masters that once a decision was made, he would be notified. Masters traveled to ParTech's Texas headquarters and tried to get a more definite assurance but was told again that he would be notified when a decision was made. In June 1998, concerned about Y2k, By-Lo purchased a new computer system. On November 20, 1998, unaware of what By-Lo had done, ParTech wrote By-Lo stating it would supply the needed software and that the software would have to be installed before January 1, 1999 because "the programs run on a 'date check plus one' system. . . ." On December 18, ParTech sent the needed software with instructions. By-Lo sued ParTech in May 1999—after realizing that it had brought suit in May 1998 against the wrong ParTech—claiming that ParTech's actions were an anticipatory breach. By-Lo claimed it had reasonable grounds for insecurity because of the Y2K deadline and Portech's failure to answer By-Lo's 9/7/97 letter and phone calls. ParTech moved for summary judgment which the district court granted. In reaching its decision, the district court assumed for the sake of argument that By-Lo had reasonable grounds for insecurity but held that "ParTech's assurance—given almost two years before what By-Lo had indicated was the date it was concerned about—that it was looking into the matter was adequate assurance under the UCC." **HOLDING:** On appeal, the court noted that under Michigan's UCC §2-609, each party has a duty not to impair "the other's expectation of receiving due performance" and that if a party has reasonable grounds for insecurity he can demand in writing that the other party give it "adequate assurance of due performance," which must be given within a reasonable time. The court explained that here, whether a party such as By-Lo had reasonable grounds for insecurity and whether a party such as ParTech gave adequate assurance may be decided as a matter of law even though generally these are factual questions for the trier of the fact to determine. In determining whether By-Lo had reasonable grounds for insecurity, the court said that "[t]he question to be answered is whether a reasonable merchant in By-Lo's position would 'feel that his expectation of receiving full performance was threatened'" by a post contract event. Essentially, By-Lo argued that it had grounds for insecurity because if ParTech did not perform in two years as promised, it would be costly for By-Lo. The court rejected this argument saying that future performance is usually the case in any contract so that "it is clear that the mere fact that performance was to come due is not sufficient under 2-609." The court tried to determine what grounds might have been sufficient for By-Lo to have reasonable insecurity. Such grounds

CASES	SUMMARIES

By-Lo Oil Co., continued

considered in combination with the contract's own provision calling for continuing support which suggested that such support would be necessary for the proper functioning of the software. However, the question for the court was still "whether January 7, 1998 was that time." In analyzing the question, the court said it would look to (1) whether sufficient time remained to make alternative arrangements (2) whether By-Lo would need all that time to install any ParTech modifications or updates (3) whether ParTech had ever been unreliable and (4) whether By-Lo had reason to believe that ParTech would not be able to perform. Based on these factors, the court concluded that By-Lo had no reasonable grounds for insecurity as of January 7, 1998. By-Lo did not complain about ParTech's service nor was there any indication that it could not timely obtain another system if ParTech did not respond promptly or make any corrections ParTech required. Only ParTech's initial delay in answering By-Lo may be viewed as an indication of an inability to perform but there was "little reason for By-Lo to be concerned at such an early date—so little that no reasonable jury could have found for By-Lo." As to the issue of adequate assurance, the court said that it must answer the question "'what are the minimum kinds of promises or acts on the part of the promisor that would satisfy a reasonable merchant in the position of the promisee that his expectation of receiving due performance will be fulfilled?'" In determining whether an assurance is adequate, the court should consider the promisor's reputation, the grounds for insecurity and the types of assurance available. Based on these factors, the court upheld the district court's decision as matter of law that "ParTech's assurance that it was evaluating the matter was adequate despite the fact that it was less than requested [by By-Lo]."

Rocheux Int'l of N.J. v. U.S. Merchants Fin. Group (2010)

→ (CB pg. 831)

FACTS: Merchants ordered large amounts of raw plastic in 2005 and 2006 from Rocheux, a plastics distributor. Rocheux delivered some of the plastics that Merchants ordered but Merchants failed to pay for most of the 2006 deliveries. In 2005 and 2006, Rocheux delivered more than $1.5 million worth of plastics to a warehouse that Merchants had designated. Merchants did not pay for these deliveries either. On September 24, 2006 Rocheux demanded payment by September 29, 200[6] for the 2006 deliveries and the warehouse goods and gave Merchants notice that if they did not pay, Rocheux would sell the warehouse goods pursuant to UCC §2-706, which it did, leaving a deficiency of almost $390,000. By the time Rocheux brought the instant suit, Merchants owed more than $2 million for the plastics that Rocheux delivered in 2006 as well as the shortage from the warehouse sale. In its defense, Merchants claimed that Rocheux improperly repudiated the parties' contract. Merchants argued that Rocheux did not demand adequate assurances of performance under UCC §2-609, challenging both the language Rocheux used in its correspondence and its grounds for insecurity. Specifically, Merchants pointed to the 9/21/06 letter that Rocheux's president sent to Merchants in which he said that unless past due invoices were paid by September 29, Rocheux would sell the goods in the warehouse and recover any deficiency from Merchants.

CASES	SUMMARIES

Rocheux Int'l,
continued

Whether D's
correspondence provided
assurance or constituted
repudiation is a matter
for the jury to decide.

HOLDING: The court rejected Merchants' proposition that "a party's breach of a collateral contract does not authorize the aggrieved party to refuse performance under a separate and distinct contract." The court relied on UCC §2-609 comment 3 to explain that consistent with commercial standards and practices, a ground for insecurity need not arise from the contract in question and therefore a buyer who is delinquent in payment under a separate contract nevertheless "impairs the seller's expectation of due performance." The court further noted that Rocheux's September 21 letter showed that Rocheux's insecurity arose from Merchants' non-payment of both the 2006 deliveries and the warehouse goods so that Rocheux's insecurity arose under the contracts in question and not a separate contract. The court concluded that "[c]onsidering the parties' course of dealings, which included Defendants' undisputed failure to pay more than $2 million of the purchase price for the 2006 deliveries and the warehouse goods, this Court cannot say that Rocheux's insecurity was unreasonable as a matter of law." The court further explained that in Rocheux's September 21 letter, as well as its prior e-mail of August 2, Rocheux identified its reasons for insecurity, namely Merchants' failure to pay for the 2006 deliveries and the warehouse goods. While the term "adequate assurance" was not used in the August 2 email or the September 21 letter, the court noted that courts generally do not apply "formalistic requirements for the demand of adequate assurances, instead opting for a case-specific approach that considers a party's demand in the context of its course of dealings with the adverse party." The court concluded that "[c]onsidering the parties' course of dealings, which included multiple in-person meetings . . . concerning Defendants' failure to pay accounts on time, the Court cannot say as a matter of law that Rocheux's correspondence of August 2 and September 21, 2006 did not constitute a demand for adequate assurance."

The court also rejected Merchants' contention that it provided adequate assurances to Rocheux of Merchants' continued performance in its October 4 letter where it offered "to pay on a C.O.D. basis or extend a letter of credit." Notably, Merchants did not offer to provide a letter of credit for the warehouse goods. Further, although an insecure party may request C.O.D. payments, the court said that there is no authority for the proposition "that an insecure party must accept an assurance of C.O.D. where the delinquent party has fallen in arrears for more than $2 million on goods delivered at the time that the insecure party sought assurances of performance." The court concluded that in view of Merchants' failure to pay the outstanding invoices it could not say as a matter of law that Rocheux's demand for a letter of credit covering both 2006 deliveries and the warehouse goods was unreasonable. The court added, however, that it could not determine as a matter of law that Merchants' October 4 letter did not provide adequate assurance. The court held "that a reasonable jury could conclude that Defendants' October 4 letter provided adequate assurance and did not repudiate the parties' contracts." It therefore denied both parties' cross-motions for summary judgment concerning the warehouse goods.

■ CHAPTER 9. BASIC ASSUMPTIONS: MISTAKE, IMPRACTICABILITY, AND FRUSTRATION

Concepts: Mistake

- In cases of mistake, which is defined as "a belief that is not in accord with the facts," the parties have reached an agreement but one or both of the parties entered that agreement on an erroneous assumption about one or more facts that existed at the time of contracting. R2d §151

- The mistake must relate to a fact in existence at the time of contract. It cannot be an error in business judgment or an incorrect prediction about the future. Parties make inaccurate predictions all the time and the mistake doctrine will not provide a basis for setting aside the contract in this case. Second, the mistake must be with respect to a basic assumption on which the contract is made and have a material effect on the agreed exchange of performances. Third, it must be a case where the aggrieved party neither assumed the risk of the mistake nor would it be fair or appropriate to allocate it to her.

- A mistaken belief may be held by one party, a unilateral mistake (R2d §153), or shared by both parties, a mutual mistake (R2d §152)

- A claim of mutual mistake allows avoidance of the contract by the adversely affected party if the mistaken belief relates to facts in existence at the time of contract, concerns a basic assumption on which the contract was made, has a material effect on the agreed exchange, and the aggrieved party did not bear the risk of the mistake.

FRAMEWORK FOR ANALYSIS:

A. Mistake of Fact

ASK: Did one or both of the parties have an erroneous belief as to the facts that existed at the time of contracting? If so, then ask, was it a:

1. **Mutual Mistake?** If the mistake was shared by both parties as to a basic assumption on which the contract was made, does it have a material effect on the agreed exchange of performances?

   - If so, then the contract is voidable by the adversely affected party unless she bears the risk of the mistake.

   Ask the following to determine whether the party bears the risk:

   — **Allocated by Agreement?** Was the risk of a mistake allocated to her by agreement of the parties?

   — **"Conscious Ignorance"?** Was she aware at the time of contract that she had only limited knowledge with respect to the facts to which the mistake relates, but treated her limited knowledge as sufficient?

   — **Risk Allocated by the Court?** Would it be reasonable under the circumstances for the court to allocate the risk of mistake to the party seeking to avoid the agreement?

2. **Unilateral Mistake?** If the mistake was held by one party as to a basic assumption on which she made the contract, does it have a material effect on the agreed exchange of performances that is adverse to her?

- If so, the contract is voidable by her if she does not bear the risk of mistake under one of the tests identified above for mutual mistake and either:

  — the effect of the mistake is such that enforcement of the contract would be unconscionable or

  — the other party had reason to know of the mistake or it was her fault that caused the mistake.

If the answer is "no" to both, then the defense of unilateral mistake is not applicable.

B. Mistake of Written Expression

ASK: Has there been a mistake as to the recorded expression of the parties' agreement?

1. **Scrivener's Error?** Is there a clerical or scrivener's error that results in a written agreement that fails to express the parties' agreement correctly? If so, then the appropriate remedy is reformation of the writing to reflect the agreement actually reached.

2. **Mutual Mistake?** Are both parties mistaken with respect to the reduction to writing of their agreement? Where a writing that evidences an agreement in whole or in part fails to express the agreement because of a mistake of both parties as to the contents or effect of the writing, the court may, at the request of a party, reform the writing to express the agreement.

Section 1. Unilateral Mistake

CASES	SUMMARIES
Sumerel v. Goodyear Tire & Rubber Co. (2009) → (CB pg. 842)	**FACTS:** In a products liability action relating to the plaintiffs' heating systems, plaintiffs obtained a jury verdict holding Goodyear liable, among other things, for 36% of certain "other costs and losses" suffered by plaintiffs, Berzins and Dickes, and 48% suffered by plaintiffs, Sumerels and Mr. Kaufman. The trial court entered a judgment upon the jury's verdict but did not award pre-judgment interest on the "other costs and losses." **HOLDING:** On appeal, a division of the Court of Appeals remanded the case to the trial court to determine the accrual dates for pre-judgment interest and to calculate that interest. After remand, Thomasch, Goodyear's lead attorney, discussed with Mayhort, plaintiffs' lead attorney, a possible compromise on the accrual dates. Thomasch proposed accrual dates and informed Mayhort of the amount of pre-judgment interest resulting from those dates and from the jury's 36% and 48% allocations of fault. During the follow up discussions between Brooks, an attorney with Goodyear's co-counsel, and Gray, an associate of Mayhort, Brooks told Gray that based on his calculation, Goodyear owed approximately $2.7 million. Within a

CASES	SUMMARIES

Sumerel, continued

E-mail ≠ offer, just two parties trying to resolve a mathmatical dispute ...

Cannot "snap up" a contract just b/c it would be good for you

Goodyear did not bear the risk of Mistake, & it would be unfairly oppressive to enforce it.

Normally, Unilateral Mistakes are not grounds for recission

few days Gray advised Brooks that the $2.7 million was larger than Gray's calculation by "about six figures." There appeared to be no dispute, however, as to the accrual dates. On October 23, Brooks called Gray and speculated that the discrepancy might be attributable to plaintiffs' failure to include the amount awarded to Mr. Kaufman. Gray made a comment to the effect that that could or might be right but without Gray's calculation, Brooks could not be sure whether the discrepancy was accounted for. Nevertheless, on November 2, 2006, Brooks sent an e-mail to Gray stating "'[h]ere are our charts providing the numers [sic] that Goodyear believes are appropriate. . . . Please review these, then let's discuss.'" Mayhort noticed that Goodyear's numbers did not agree with plaintiffs' numbers and recognized that Goodyear's calculations were incorrectly based on a 100% allocation of the "other costs and losses" instead of the actual 36% and 48% allocation. The error resulted in overstating Goodyear's liability by more than $550,000. Neither Gray nor any of plaintiffs' co-counsel called Brooks as he had requested in his letter. Instead, Mayhort called Thomasch and left a voice mail message that plaintiffs accepted Goodyear's November 2 offer and followed up with a fax to Thomasch confirming plaintiffs' acceptance. Subsequently, Brooks and Gray had a discussion regarding what was needed to conclude the case. They agreed that a satisfaction of judgment was needed which Brooks prepared and sent to Gray on November 16 "with a notation that the document was a draft for discussion purposes only." That same day, Brooks realized his calculation error and sent Gray a corrected version of the charts and a revised satisfaction of judgment. On November 21, Mayhort wrote Brooks demanding that Goodyear adhere to the alleged settlement agreement. Goodyear refused and plaintiffs' moved to enforce the alleged settlement agreement. The court granted plaintiffs' motion.

On appeal, the court rejected plaintiffs' contention that Goodyear's November 2 e-mail with the attached erroneous charts was an offer. At the time Brooks's e-mail was sent to Gray, the parties were only beginning to exchange calculations based on the agreed accrual date while trying to determine the source of the six-figure discrepancy. "Thus," the court said "Brooks's e-mail, using qualifying and indefinite language, noted that the calculations were what Goodyear believes are appropriate'" which shows that there was no definitive offer. Furthermore, Brooks's e-mail requested a return call ("let's discuss") and did not solicit an acceptance. All this shows that the parties were still in preliminary discussions, especially trying to identify the discrepancy source. The court's conclusion that Brooks's e-mail and charts did not constitute an offer was also supported by the rule that "'an offeree may not snap up an offer that is on its face manifestly too good to be true.'" Here, even assuming that there was an offer, it was too good to be true. The parties had already agreed on the accrual dates and plaintiffs' counsel recognized that Brooks' calculations were erroneous, resulting in a more than $550,000 error. On the undisputed facts, the court said that Brooks's e-mail and charts raised a presumption of error because they were inconsistent with the jury's award and the prior discussions Thomasch had with Mayhort and with other calculations in the charts where the corect jury's allocations of fault were used. Because of these obvious inconsistencies, plaintiffs at minimum were required to inquire before trying to accept the alleged offer. Absent "such an inquiry, there was no offer capable of acceptance here."

CASES	SUMMARIES
Sumerel, continued	Goodyear argued that even if the email and charts were an offer, the agreement would be unenforceable on the grounds of unilateral mistake. The court cited and quoted from Professor Corbin, pronouncements by the Colorado Supreme Court, and R2d §153 and §154. For example, under the Second Restatement, a party can avoid a contract based on a material unilateral mistake if he does not bear the risk of the mistake and enforcement of the contract would be unconscionable, or the other party had reason to know of the mistake. Here, the court found not only did plaintiffs know of the mistake but the agreement would be unconscionable because it would give plaintiffs a windfall of over $550,000. Finally, the court rejected plaintiffs' contentions that "Brooks chose to charge ahead in conscious ignorance, believing that his limited knowledge was sufficient." The court noted that someone had to do the first calculation and Brooks did so while asking Gray to review them and call him to discuss the numbers. The November 2 e-mail showed that Brooks was still trying to identify the source of the discrepancy. Rather than "an agreement through conscious ignorance" Brooks "sought further dialogue because he knew of the discrepancy in the parties' calculations." The court reversed and remanded for the purpose of having the parties file a satisfaction of judgment reflecting the amounts which Goodyear already paid.

Section 2. Mutual Mistake

CASES	SUMMARIES
Stees v. Leonard (1874) → (CB pg. 850) Contractor held liable, drawing the land to erect the building was a hardship, but not impossible.	**FACTS:** Pursuant to a contract, defendants agreed to build a building on plaintiff's lot in accordance with the plans and specifications annexed to the contract. The building collapsed after defendants had built three stories. The next year defendants began again and the building once again fell to the ground when they had built three stories. Defendants had complied with the contract specifications which provided that the foundation walls should have footing six inches thick. Defendants claimed that the building fell because "the soil upon which it was to be constructed was composed of quicksand, and when water flowed into it, was incapable of sustaining the building. . . ." Plaintiffs sued, claiming among other things that defendants were negligent and the jury found for plaintiffs. **HOLDING:** On appeal, the court said that this case was governed by the established rule that "[i]f a man bind himself, by a positive, express contract, to do an act in itself possible, he must perform his engagement, unless prevented by the act of God, the law, or the other party to the contract. No hardship, no unforeseen hindrance, no difficulty short of absolute impossibility will excuse him from doing what he has expressly agreed to do." The court observed that any hardship to a contractor in this type of case falls to the contractor and not the law because the contractor has

CASES	SUMMARIES

Stees, continued

taken on an absolute duty when he could have qualified it. In rejecting the defense that the footing that defendants constructed conformed to the contract specifications, the court said that the defendants agreed to "'erect and complete the building'" which required them to do everything necessary to complete it, even though they had constructed the footings in accordance with the contract. This meant that even if the building could be built only by draining the land, plaintiffs were obligated to do so "'because they have agreed to do everything necessary to erect and complete the building.'"

QUESTION TO THINK ABOUT: *The contractor did not claim mistake as the basis to be relieved of its obligation. Why not? Was it because both parties knew that draining the land was necessary for construction of the building?*

Renner v. Kehl
(1986)

→ (CB pg. 853)

Mutual Mistake is grounds for recission,

P will not have to buy the land, but cannot recover consequential damages (drilling wells)

FACTS: Defendants agreed to sell their interest in unimproved land in Arizona to plaintiffs. Sellers understood that plaintiffs were interested in purchasing the land only to cultivate jojoba which required an adequate water supply. Both parties believed "that sufficient water was available beneath the land to sustain jojoba production." Plaintiffs drilled five test wells but none produced enough water to sustain jojoba production. Plaintiffs sued and the trial court granted them rescission which was affirmed by the Court of Appeals.

HOLDING: On appeal to the Arizona Supreme Court, the court said that "[i]n Arizona a contract may be rescinded when there is a mutual mistake of material fact which constitutes 'an essential part and condition of the contract.'" It noted that the trial court found that both parties believed that jojoba could be grown commercially on the land and that there was sufficient water to sustain such production. The court applied R2d §152 and said that the parties' belief "that adequate water supplies existed beneath the property was 'a basic assumption on which both parties made the contract'. . . and their mutual mistake 'ha[d] such a material effect on the agreed exchange of performances as to upset the very bases of the contract.'" Accordingly, plaintiffs were entitled to rescission based on mutual mistake. The court went on to discuss the question of the sellers' reimbursement to the purchasers. It stated that "[w]hen a party rescinds a contract on the ground of mutual mistake he is entitled to restitution for any benefit that he has conferred on the other party by way of part performance or reliance. . . . Restitutionary recoveries are not designed to be compensatory; their justification lies in the avoidance of unjust enrichment on the part of the defendant. . . . Thus the defendant is generally liable for restitution of a benefit that would be unjust for him to keep, even though he gained it honestly." The question is how to measure this restitutionary interest. First, the rescinding party must return, or offer to return to the other party "any interest in property that he has received in the bargain." Here, plaintiffs have to return the land and in addition pay the fair rental value of it during the time they had possession. On the other hand, plaintiffs must be compensated for the reasonable value of any land improvement they made relying on the contract measured by "'the extent to which the other party's property [here the defendants'] has been increased in value or his other interest advanced.'" [citing R2d §371(b)] Thus plaintiffs were "entitled to their down payment, plus the amount by which their efforts increased the value of [defendants']

CASES	SUMMARIES
Renner, continued	property, minus an amount which represents the fair rental value of the land during their occupancy." The court also held that "absent proof of breach for fraud or misrepresentation a party who rescinds a contract may not recover consequential damages. . . ." Note: In a footnote the court stated, without explanation, that the parties' failure to investigate the water supply before entering the contract "does not preclude rescission where the risk of mistake was not allocated among the parties and the mistake is material and relates to a basic assumption on which the contract was made." (citing R2d §152 cmt. a and ill.1).

Section 3. Impracticability of Performance

Impractacability is a Sellers claim

Concepts:

■ Contract liability is strict liability. Contract duties are absolute and one is liable in damages for any breach even if she is without fault and even if circumstances have changed to make the contract more burdensome or less desirable than expected.

■ One exception to this strict view which would allow an obligor's duty to perform to be discharged is where some changed circumstance has occurred — the non- occurrence of which was a basic assumption of the agreement — and has made the obligor's performance "impracticable." The party seeking discharge must show that actual performance of the contract would be so significantly different from what was originally expected as to defeat the party's legitimate expectations in entering the agreement.

Why not Stees v. Leonard ?
by 1874

FRAMEWORK FOR ANALYSIS:

Was there an event that occurred that made "performance as agreed" impracticable? If so, proceed to "**A . Supervening Impracticability.**"

Was there a fact that existed at the time of contracting that made performance as agreed impracticable? If so, proceed to "**B. Existing Impracticability.**"

A. Supervening Impracticability

ASK: Did the event occur after the the contract was formed?

If the event occurred subsequent to the contract's formation, then a party's duty to perform may be discharged based on supervening impracticability if the following four requirements are met:

• An event has made the promisor's "performance as agreed" impracticable. After identifying the promisor's agreed performance, ask:

— Are there alternative ways for the promisor to perform? If a party had alternatives, then the fact that one alternative became impracticable will not excuse the party if another remains available. In this case, the promisor's agreed performance has not become impracticable. If, however, there are no alternatives, there may be a basis for excuse. Proceed to the next question.

— Has performance become more expensive? Additional expense in the cost of performance does not rise to the level of impracticability. (R2d §261 cmt.d) Under the Code, "[i]ncreased cost alone does not excuse performance unless the increase is due to some unforeseen contingency which alters the essential nature of the performance." (UCC §2-615 cmt 1) Market fluctuations will not excuse performance since they are the types of risk for which parties make contracts.

- The nonoccurrence of the event was a "basic assumption" on which the contract was made. Ask: what was the basic assumption on which the contract was made? Consider:

— **Government Act?** Did the parties assume that the government would not directly intervene such as by a governmental order or regulation and prevent performance?

— **Necessary Person?** Did the parties assume that a person necessary for performance would neither die nor become incapacitated before the time of performance?

— **Necessary Thing?** Did the parties assume that a thing necessary for performance would remain in existence and in such condition that performance could occur?

- The impracticability resulted without the fault of the party seeking to be excused. Ask: did the impracticability result without the fault of the party seeking to be excused? The party seeking to be discharged must not be the source or basis of the impracticability.

- The party has not assumed a greater obligation than the law imposes. If a party has expressly undertaken to perform even if performance becomes impracticable, impracticability will not be an excuse. To determine whether a party who is claiming to be discharged assumed the risk of impracticability, ask the following:

— **Foreseeability?** Was the event foreseeable? Foreseeability is a factor in assessing whether the promisor assumed the risk of its occurrence, but it is not determinative. Even if the parties could have imagined the event occurring, it may not be one that they expected to happen. Ask: did the parties consider the event to have a real likelihood of occurring?

— **Risk Bearer?** Was the risk within a party's control? If so, then that party should bear the risk of its occurrence because it could have shifted the risk to a third party by contract (i.e., protecting oneself by getting insurance). For example, if a wholesaler contracts to sell goods that it obtains from a particular supplier, then the wholesaler can contract with the supplier to secure its source of supply. UCC §2-615 cmt. 5: stating when "a particular source of supply is exclusive . . . and fails through casualty," there is no excuse "unless the seller has employed all due measures to assure himself that his source will not fail."

— **Risk Allocated?** Was there a clause in the contract allocating risk for some events and not others? If a clause excuses a party from specified events, it is possible to imply that the party assumed the risks of other events.

— **Assumed the Risk?** Do the surrounding circumstances justify an inference that the party assumed the risk?

B. Existing Impracticability

ASK: Did a fact exist at the time of contract the non-existence of which was a basic assumption on which the contract was made? Did the existence of the fact render a party's performance impracticable?

If the fact existed at the time of the agreement, then a party's duty to perform may not arise based on existing impracticability. If so, a party must meet the same four requirements as in the case of supervening impracticability (the fact made the "performance as agreed" impracticable; the non-existence of the fact was a basic assumption on which the contract was made; the impracticability resulted without the fault of the party seeking to be excused; and the party has not assumed a greater obligation than the law imposes) with one additional requirement: the party must not know or have reason to know at the time of contracting of the fact(s) making performance impracticable. If the party did not know or have reason to know, then the excuse of existing impracticability is available. (*Mineral Park Land Co. v. Howard*) R2d §266 cmt. a

CASES	SUMMARIES
Mineral Park Land Co. v. Howard (1916) → (CB pg. 863)	**FACTS:** Defendants had a contract to construct a concrete bridge across a ravine. Defendants entered into a contract with plaintiff in which they agreed to take from plaintiff's land all the gravel and earth necessary to do the fill and cement work for the concrete bridge. After removing over 50,000 cubic yards, defendants did not remove any more and plaintiff brought suit because defendants did not take all that they needed for the bridge. The trial court found that although plaintiff's land had in excess of 100,000 cubic yards of earth and gravel, only 51,131 cubic yards were above water level and that removing more than the 51,131 would have involved "an expense of 10 or 12 times as much as the usual cost per yard." The trial court said that it was not practical for defendants to take all the sand and gravel from plaintiff though not impossible. The trial court also found "that the parties were not under any mutual misunderstanding regarding the amount of available gravel, but that the contract was entered into without any calculation on the part of either of the parties with reference to the amount of available earth and gravel on the premises." It held that defendants were not justified in failing to take all of their requirements. **HOLDING:** The issue on appeal was whether the facts justified excusing defendant's failure to take all the earth and gravel required by the contract. The California Supreme Court said that the trial court apparently thought that the case was governed by the principle "that where a party has agreed, without qualification, to perform an act which is not in its nature impossible of performance, he is not excused by difficulty of performance, or by the fact that he becomes unable to perform." The court pointed out, however, that this case fell within the rule that "where performance depends upon the existence of a given thing, and such existence was assumed as the basis of the agreement, performance is excused to the extent that the thing ceases to exist or turns out to be non-existent. . . ." Here the parties to the contract assumed that the needed quantity of earth and gravel was available for use and that availability must be viewed "in a practical and reasonable way." Defendants could not extract

[handwritten left margin: Stees v. Leonard ?]

[handwritten under case name: The existence of readily-obtainable gravel was the basis for the agreement, & once it stopped existing further performance became impracticable]

CASES	SUMMARIES
Mineral Park Land Co., continued	the gravel "except at a prohibitive cost. To all fair intents then, it was impossible for defendants to take it." The court added that defendants could not excuse themselves by simply showing that their duty became more expensive than anticipated or would entail a loss. It is only where the added cost is so great—as it was here—that in effect performance is impracticable and the case is no different from one where earth and gravel are not there.
Taylor v. Caldwell **(KB 1863)** → **(CB pg. 866)** Music Hall burning down case. Performance Excused	**FACTS:** The court said that if it appears from the nature of the contract that it could not be performed without the continuing existence of a "specified thing" then the contract is to be interpreted not as being unqualified "but as subject to an implied condition that the parties shall be excused in case, before breach, performance becomes impossible from the perishing of the thing without default of the contractor." The court also noted that the implied condition may be the life of a human being. The court found "that the parties contracted on the basis of the continued existence of the Music Hall at the time when the concerts were to be given; that being essential to their performance" and "that the Music Hall having ceased to exist, without fault of either party, both parties are excused, the plaintiffs from taking the gardens and paying the money, the defendants from performing their promise to give the use of the Hall and Gardens and other things. Consequently the rule must be absolute to enter the verdict for the defendant."
Transatlantic Financing Corporation v. United States **(1956)** → **(CB pg. 871)**	**FACTS:** On July 26, 1956, Egypt nationalized the Suez Canal. On October 2, in the midst of the international crisis resulting from Egypt's seizure of the canal, Transatlantic, operator of the SS CHRISTOS, and the U.S. entered into a voyage charter providing for the shipment of a cargo of wheat from a gulf port in the U.S. to an Iranian port. The contract gave only the destination but not the route to be followed. On October 27, the CHRISTOS sailed using a route which would pass through the Suez Canal. In late October, Israel invaded Egypt, and Great Britain and France invaded the Suez Canal zone. On November 2, Egypt closed the Suez Canel to travel. On November 7, Transatlantic contacted Postosky, a Department of Agriculture employee, seeking additional compensation for changing course to the Cape of Good Hope. Postosky told Transatlantic that he did not believe they were entitled to any additional compensation. The CHRISTOS changed course and arrived in Iran on December 30. Transatlantic sued the U.S. for the additional expenses it incurred when it had to divert its ship from the Suez Canal to a different route. The trial court dismissed the suit.

HOLDING: On appeal, the court found that Transatlantic's performance of the contract was not legally impossible and therefore it was not entitled to any relief. The court stated that in applying admiralty principles, particularly the "doctrine of deviation," it was required to imply into the contract "the term that the voyage was to be performed by the 'usual and customary' route" which at the time was the Suez Canal. Transatlantic argued that when it proceeded by going around the Cape "in compliance with the Government's demand under claim of right, it conferred a benefit upon the United States for which it should be paid *in quantum meruit.*" The court explained that the doctrine of impossibility of performance has been relaxed |

CASES	SUMMARIES
Transatlantic Financing, continued	and now a performance is legally impracticable "'when it can only be done at an excessive and unreasonable cost.'" Further, when the issue of commercial impracticability is raised, "the court is asked to construct a condition of performance based on the changed circumstances" a process which requires satisfying three factors: first, something unexpected must have occurred—"a contingency"; second, the risk of that contingency must not have allocated by agreement or custom; and, third, the occurrence of that contingency must have made performance commercially impracticable. All three requirements must be met before the party's duty to perform will be excused based on a claim of impracticability.

In applying the requirements to the facts, the court found that the first requirement was met even though the contract did not specify a route. It was assumed that the CHRISTOS would follow the usual and customary route from Texas to Iran which was through the Suez Canal. When the canal closed, the expected method of performance was impossible. The court then addressed the question of whether the risk of this unforeseen event had been allocated and if not, whether performance by alternative routes would be impracticable. The court said that the allocation of risk may be expressed in the contract or implied from it. It may also be found in the surrounding circumstances, including custom and usage of trade. Here the contract did not refer to the Suez route and there is nothing in the contract from which it could be implied that the availability of the Suez was a condition of Transatlantic's performance. Furthermore, there was nothing in the custom or trade usage or in the surrounding circumstances from which a court could imply that the Suez was a condition of performance.

The court noted that the case law indicated the Cape route was generally regarded as the alternative route when the Suez was closed. Still, the fact that the Suez route was the expected route was "hardly adequate proof of an allocation to the promisee of the risk of closure. In some cases, even an express expectation may not amount to a condition of performance. The doctrine of deviation [an admiralty insurance practice] supports our assumption that parties normally expect performance by the usual and customary route, but it adds nothing beyond this that is probative of an allocation of the risk" of the routes unavailability. Instead, the court indicated that the surrounding circumstances might have indicated that the "Canal's closure may be deemed to have been allocated to Transatlantic." It could be assumed that the parties were well aware that the Suez "might become a dangerous area." But the court said the fact that the parties saw or recognized the risk "does not necessarily prove its allocation." Parties do not always cover all possibilities, "often simply because they are too busy." Egypt's nationalizing of the Suez did not necessarily indicate that the Canal would be closed. However, the surrounding circumstances indicated that Transatlantic was willing "to assume abnormal risks, and this fact should legitimately cause us to judge the impracticability of performance by an alternative route in stricter terms than we would were the contingency unforeseen."

Finally, the court found that the Suez closure did not make the contract's performance commercially impracticable under the circumstances: the goods could withstand the longer, less temperate voyage, the vessel and crew were fit to travel around the Cape, and Transatlantic could purchase insurance to cover the contingency of

CASES	SUMMARIES
Transatlantic Financing, continued	the Suez closing. As far as the added expense of traveling an extra 3,000 miles by using the Cape route, the court said: "[w]hile it may be an overstatement to say that increased cost and difficulty of performance never constitute impracticability, to justify relief there must be more of a variation between expected cost [$305,842.92] and the cost of performing by an available alternative [here an additional $43,972.00] than is present in this case, where the promisor can legitimately be presumed to have accepted some degree of abnormal risk, and where impracticability is urged on the basis of added expense alone." The court concluded, as did most courts considering disputes arising from the Suez closing, that performance had not been made impracticable. In denying Transatlantic's claim for quantum meruit, the court observed that recovery in quantum meruit would have been proper for the entire performance but not here where Transatlantic had already been paid the contract price and was seeking reimbursement or the extra expense of going around the Cape. The court characterized this as Transatlantic's attempt "to take its profit on the contract, and then force the Government to absorb the cost of the additional voyage." Since the court was not about to cast "the entire burden of commercial disaster on one party in order to preserve the other's profit," the court found no basis for relief for Transatlantic.
Selland Pontiac-GMC, Inc. v. King (1986) → (CB pg. 880)	**FACTS:** Selland, buyer, agreed to buy four school bus bodies from King which the contract provided would be manufactured by Superior Manufacturing. There was no clause excusing King from performing if King's suppliers failed to supply the bus bodies. Relying on the contract, Selland ordered from General Motors four bus chassis on which the bus bodies were to be mounted. They arrived in June and early July 1983. On July 7, Superior Manufacturing went into receivership and although there was a dispute as to what transpired afterwards, the trial court found that Selland acquiesced to a production delay. The bus bodies were never manufactured and in December, Selland's customer canceled their order for the buses. Selland sold the chassis at a loss. Selland sued King for breach and the trial court granted judgment for King. **HOLDING:** On appeal, the court affirmed the lower court's findings that the parties' contract "identified Superior as King's supplier, and that the contract contemplated that the bodies would be manufactured by Superior" and that this finding was "supported by the contract which states that Superior bus bodies were being sold." It also sustained the trial court's findings that Selland acquiesced in delay of delivery. The court noted that "[s]upply of Superior bus bodies was a basic assumption on which the contract was made" so that when Superior stopped manufacturing, the supply of these bodies became impracticable. The court further noted that the parties had no knowledge of Superior's financial position at the time of contract. The court concluded that the trial court properly applied UCC §2-615.

CASES	SUMMARIES
Canadian Industrial Alcohol Co. v. Dunbar Molasses Co. (1932) → (CB pg. 885)	**FACTS:** Plaintiff Canadian Industrial Alcohol Co. contracted to purchase from Dunbar approximately 1,500,000 gallons of molasses "'of the usual run from the National Sugar Refinery, Yonkers, NY.'" After shipping approximately 344,000 gallons to Canadian, which was Dunbar's entire allotment from the refinery, Dunbar did not deliver any more molasses because National had reduced its production. Canadian brought suit and Dunbar argued that its duty to perform "was conditioned, by an implied term, on the refinery's producing enough molasses to fill the plaintiff's order." The trial court granted judgment for Canadian. **HOLDING:** On appeal, the New York Ct of Appeals court said that Dunbar "wholly failed to relieve itself of the imputation of contributory fault. . . ." Dunbar did not show that it made any effort to procure a contract from the refinery from the time of plaintiff's order for molasses to the time shipments began. It appeared that Dunbar gambled that the refinery's output would remain the same from year to year. The court said that "[t]he defendant is in no better position than a factor who undertakes in his own name to sell for future delivery a special grade of merchandise to be manufactured by a special mill. The duty will be discharged if the mill is destroyed before delivery is due. The duty will subsist if the output is reduced because times turned out to be hard and labor charges high. . . ." The court affirmed judgment for Canadian.
Eastern Air Lines, Inc. v. Gulf Oil Corp. (1975) → (CB pg. 889)	**FACTS:** On June 27, 1972, Eastern Airlines and Gulf Oil entered into a contract whereby Gulf was to furnish Eastern with jet fuel. The parties agreed that the contract would contain "a reference to reflect changes in the price of the raw material from which jet fuel is processed, i.e., crude oil in direct proportion to the cost per gallon of jet fuel." Both Eastern and Gulf knew that crude price increases were "'a way of life'" and intended Eastern to bear the increases "in a direct proportional relationship of crude oil cost per barrel to jet fuel cost per gallon." The parties chose as an indicator "'the average of the posted prices for West Texas sour crude'" of Gulf, Shell Oil, and Pan American Petroleum and provided that "'[t]he posting of crude prices under the contract 'shall be as listed for these companies in Platts Oilgram Service—Crude Oil Supplement. . . .'" Platt's Oilgram published a periodical for the oil industry which contained each oil company's published price bulletin which reflected the current price per barrel at which such oil company would pay for a particular type of crude oil. In August 1973, the US Government—which for years had imposed various price controls on domestic crude oil—implemented a "two-tier" price control system which differentiated between "old oil" and "new oil." "Old oil"— which was the number of barrels that a well-produced in May 1972—had its price frozen at a fixed level and "new oil"— which was any increased oil production above the May 1972 benchmark production—was not price-controlled. Further, with respect to each barrel of new oil produced, the government authorized an equivalent number of "old oil" to be released from price control. For example, if a well produced 100 barrels in May 1972, all production from that well since August 1973 up to 100 barrels of oil would be considered "old oil" but if there was any increase in production from that well, i.e., to 150 barrels, it would result in there being 50 barrels of "new oil"—not controlled—and of the remaining 100 barrels, 50 would

CASES	SUMMARIES

Eastern Airlines, continued

now be designated "released oil"—and not controlled—and only the remaining 50 barrels would still be designated "old oil" and still subject to control.

In October 1973, the Arab countries imposed an embargo on exporting crude oil to the U.S. causing an immediate energy crisis in this country. "New and released oil (uncontrolled) soon reached parity with the price of foreign crude, moving from approximately $5 to $11 a barrel from September, 1974 to January 15, 1974." Since the government instituted "two-tier," the price of "old oil" remained fixed by government action, with oil companies resorting to postings reflecting the prices they will pay for the new and released oil, not subject to government controls. Those prices, referred to as "premiums" were the subject of supplemental bulletins which were similarly posted by the oil companies and provided to interested parties, including Platts. However, Platts had not published in its bulletin the pricing of any of the premiums by the U.S. oil companies, including those companies designated in the parties' agreement. Instead, the information which had appeared regarding the price of West Texas Sour crude oil "has been the price of 'old' oil subject to government control."

In early March, 1974, Gulf demanded that Eastern agree to a price increase or it would not supply jet fuel to Eastern. Eastern sued Gulf for breach and Gulf contended, among other things, that the contract was "commercially impracticable" within the meaning of UCC §2-615. Gulf first argued "that the price escalator indicator (posting in Platt's Oilgram Crude Oil Supplement) no longer reflects the intent of the parties by reason of the so-called 'two-tier' pricing structure . . ."

HOLDING: The court rejected this argument stating that it was clear from the contract itself "that they [Gulf and Eastern] intended to be bound by the specified entries in Platt's, which has been published at all times material here, which is published today, and which prints the contract reference prices. Prices under the contract can be and still are calculated by reference to Platt's publication."

As to Gulf's argument that the contract was commercially impracticable because crude oil prices had increased, the court said that from the record it could not determine Gulf's cost to produce a gallon of jet fuel for Eastern or whether Gulf's sale of jet fuel to Eastern was profitable. In claiming commercial impracticability because of increased costs, Gulf had the burden of showing what losses it would suffer if it had to perform the contract. The evidence that Gulf presented on the issue of its "costs" included intra-company profits which were allocated among 400 plus Gulf corporate subsidiaries, the amount of which was never revealed. The court said that "under no theory of law can it be held that Gulf is guaranteed preservation of its intra-company profits, moving from the left-hand to the right-hand, as one Gulf witness so aptly put it. The burden is upon Gulf to show what its real costs are, not its 'costs' inflated by its internal profits at various levels of the manufacturing process and located in various foreign countries." Thus, Gulf did not establish the necessary hardship to prove commercial impracticability under UCC §2-615. The court further pointed out that even if there was commercial impracticability, Gulf would not succeed "because the events associated with the so-called energy crises were reasonably foreseeable at the time the contract was executed." The court said

CASES	SUMMARIES
Eastern Airlines, continued	that any consequences of a foreseeable contingency takes the case out of UCC §2-615 because the so-called injured party could have protected itself in the contract. Here there was an abundance of evidence as to what was occurring in the Middle East and the disruption in the commercial trade of fuel oil. The court stated that it could take judicial notice "that oil has been used as a political weapon with increasing success by the oil-producing nations for many years, and Gulf was well aware of and assumed the risk that OPEC nations would do exactly what they have done." The court also rejected Gulf's argument that " two tier" was not foreseeable since Gulf had been urging the U.S. Government to decontrol domestic oil prices and was in constant contact with government agencies regarding oil policies and could have protected itself from any contingency. Knowing all the facts, Gulf nevertheless "tied the escalation to certain specified domestic posting in Platt's." The court further noted that UCC §2-614(2) was irrelevant because that "Section dealing with 'means or manner of payment' speaks, by way of illustration, to the blocking by governmental interference with the contemplated mode of monetary exchange," for example, where payment is to be in gold specie and the government forbids payment in gold.

Section 4. Frustration of Purpose

FRAMEWORK FOR ANALYSIS: Can a party's duty to perform be discharged based on frustration of purpose?

Note: In contrast to the defense of impracticability discussed above, performance by a party claiming frustration of purpose is practicable and such party can perform as contemplated.

Frustration of purpose may be based on facts existing at the time of contract (R2d §266(2)) or on events rising after the time of the contract (R2d §265).

ASK: Can the party claiming discharge due to frustration of purpose satisfy all four requirements?

1. **Supervening Event?** Was there a supervening event that substantially frustrated the party's principal purpose in forming the contract? The supervening event must totally or nearly totally destroy the purpose of the contract. In determining whether a party's principal purpose has been substantially frustrated, ask the following:

   —**Remaining Benefit?** Can the party still benefit from the contract even if the supervening event has prevented the party from benefiting in the same way that was anticipated? If so, then the party still has a purpose for the contract and excuse is not available. If not, then excuse may be available if the other criteria are met. Proceed to the next question.

   —**Total or Nearly Total Frustration?** Is the frustration nearly total? It is not enough that a profitable contract has turned out to be a losing one. One cannot claim frustration of purpose simply because a deal has turned out not to be profitable. If the frustration is not total or nearly so, then excuse is not available. If it is, then excuse may be available if the other criteria are met. Proceed to the next question.

— **Shared Purpose?** Was the purpose or object of the contract known and recognized by both parties at the time of contract? The purpose cannot be a secret purpose, known by only one party. If the purpose is not known, then excuse is not available. If it is known, then excuse may be available if the other criteria are met. Proceed to the next question.

- **Basic Assumption?** Ask: did an event occur that substantially frustrated a party's principal purpose? If so, was it a basic assumption on which the contract was made that the event would not occur? The nonoccurrence of the event must have been a basic assumption on which the contract was made. If not, then excuse is not available. If so, then excuse may be available if the other criteria are met. Proceed to the next question.

- **Fault?** Did the frustration result without the fault of the party seeking to be excused? If not, then excuse is not available. If so, then excuse may be available if the other criteria are met. Proceed to the next question.

- **Assumed the Risk?** Did the party seeking to be discharged assume a greater obligation than the law imposes? Even if a party's principal purpose has been frustrated, a court might not excuse that party's performance if the party assumed the risk of the occurrence of the frustrating event. Consider the following:

  — **Foreseeability?** Was the supervening act or event reasonably foreseeable at the time of contract? Did the parties consider the event to have a real likelihood of occurring? Even if the parties could have imagined the event occurring, it may not be one that they expected to happen.

  — **Allocation of Risk?** Is it possible to determine how the risk was allocated based on the parties' objective in forming the contract?

  — **Usage of Trade?** Is there an applicable usage of trade which allocates risk? If so, then it may be considered in allocating risk.

CASES	SUMMARIES
Krell v. Henry *(1903)* → (CB pg. 899) *[handwritten: Dismissed - the purpose of the D renting the flat was to watch the coronation & the P knew this]*	**FACTS:** On June 20, plaintiff rented a flat in Pall Mall to defendant for June 26-27, the days on which the coronation of Edward VII was to take place and pass by the flat that plaintiff was renting. The contract made no reference to the coronation or to the purpose for which plaintiff was renting out the flat. Because the King fell ill, the coronation did not take place on the dates contemplated and defendant refused to pay the balance of the rent due. The court said that it was necessary to first determine "the substance of the contract"—from the contract or inferences from the surrounding circumstances—and then to ask the question whether "that substantial contract needs for its foundation the assumption of the existence of a particular state of things. If it does, this will limit the operation of the general words [in the contract], and in such case, if the contract becomes impossible of performance by reason of the non-existence of the state of things assumed by both contracting parties as the foundation of the contract, there will be no breach of the contract thus limited." Here the plaintiff had posted an announcement on the third floor of his

CASES	SUMMARIES

Krell, continued

property "to the effect that windows to view the Royal coronation procession were to be let, and that the defendant was induced by that announcement to apply to the housekeeper on the premises, who said that the owner was willing to let the suite of rooms for the purpose of seeing the Royal procession for both days, but not nights, of June 26 and June 27." The court said that the parties' contract amounted to a "license to use rooms for a particular purpose and none other" and that the parties regarded the procession taking place on the days announced to be the foundation of the contract. Thus the unconditional contract language requiring defendant to pay for the rooms on those days was not "used with reference to the possibility of the particular contingency which afterwards occurred."

QUESTION TO THINK ABOUT: *Performance was not impossible since defendant was able to make use of the room even though the coronation was canceled yet the court spoke in terms of performance being impossible. Did the court mean that where purpose is frustrated, a party has the same defense as a party claiming impracticability?*

Swift Canadian Co. v. Banet (1955)

→ (CB pg. 902)

FACTS: Seller, a Canadian corporation, entered into a contract with defendant buyer, Keystone, whereby Keystone agreed to purchase a certain quantity of lamb pelts, "F.O.B. Toronto" to be shipped via the Pennsylvania railroad to Keystone in Philadelphia. The contract also provided (1) that neither party would be liable for governmental orders or acts and (2) that the risk of loss for pelts sold "F.O.B. seller's plant" passed to buyer when the pelts were loaded on cars at the plant. After Canadian had shipped part of the pelts ordered, the U.S. issued regulations that had the effect of preventing Keystone from importing the lamb pelts into the U.S., and for that reason Keystone refused to take any more pelts and seller did not ship any more pelts. Seller sued buyer for breach and the court granted buyer's motion for summary judgment. Seller appealed.

HOLDING: The court reversed on appeal and entered judgment for seller. The court noted that when seller did not load the pelts because buyer had indicated it would refuse to accept them, seller was entitled to the same rights as if it had loaded the pelts because "[a] party is not obligated to do the vain thing of performing, assuming that he is ready to perform, when the other party has given notice of refusal to accept performance." Buyer claimed, however, that the "shipping directions in the contract showed that what the parties had in mind was such kind of performance by the seller as would start the goods to the buyer in Philadelphia" and since the government prevented importation, buyer was excused from performing. The court said that the contract provision providing for shipment via Pennsylvania railroad to buyer with destination Philadelphia was simply a shipping direction and buyer could have directed shipment to any other destination it wanted. Such shipping directions are inserted for the buyer's convenience and the buyer could change it at any time. The court noted that the contract provision of "F.O.B. Toronto" was the equivalent of "F.O.B. Seller's plant." It referred to Williston on Sales who observed that "when goods are delivered 'free on board' pursuant to contract the presumption is that the property passes thereupon." The court explained that nothing was

CASES	SUMMARIES
Swift Canadian, *continued*	shown to rebut this presumption and accordingly, the seller would have fully performed when the pelts were delivered F.O.B. in Toronto and "both the risk of loss and the possibility of profit if the market advanced, were in the buyer from then on." If the buyer chose not to reroute the destination to any place other than the U.S., and the buyer's expectation of a profitable transaction was disappointed, the seller, having performed or being ready, willing, and able to perform, was still entitled to the "value of his bargain."
Chase Precast Corp. ***v. John J. Panonessa*** ***Co. (1991)*** → (CB pg. 905) Frustration of Purpose	**FACTS:** In 1982, defendant Panonessa had contracts with the Commonwealth's Department of Public Works ("Department") for resurfacing of two Sections of Route 128 which provided that Panonessa would replace a grass median strip with precast concrete median barriers. The contract with the Department also contained a standard provision which permitted the Department to eliminate any work it found unnecessary. Panonessa entered into two contracts with Chase pursuant to which Chase agreed to supply 25,800 linear feet of concrete median barriers. The contracts between Chase and Panonessa did not contain a provision similar to the standard provision found in the Panonessa-Department contract. After the highway work began, protests and litigation against the installation of the barriers commenced. Panonessa requested Chase to cease concrete barrier production for the project which Chase did. On June 23, the Department eliminated the concrete median barriers from the Panonessa contract. Before Chase stopped production on June 8, it had produced about one-half of the concrete barriers for which Panonessa had paid them. Chase sued for breach. The trial court held for Panonessa based on impossibility of performance. **HOLDING:** The Appeals Court affirmed but noted that the trial court's decision was more accurately based on the doctrine of frustration of purpose than the doctrine of impossibility of performance. On appeal to the Massachusetts Supreme Court, the court affirmed and noted that while it had recognized the doctrine of frustration of purpose it had never really clearly defined the doctrine. Relying on other jurisdictions, the court explained the doctrine as "when an event neither anticipated nor caused by either party, the risk of which was not allocated by the contract, destroys the object or purpose of the contract, thus destroying the value of performance, the parties are excused from further performance." The court provided another definition of frustration of purpose from R2d §265 and noted that this definition was virtually identical to the UCC's defense of commercial impracticability found in §2-615 which the Massachusetts Supreme Court held was consistent with the common law concept of impossibility of performance. Thus the court said that the "Restatement's formulation of the doctrine [of frustration] is consistent with this court's previous treatment of impossibility of performance and frustration of purpose." The court pointed out that both doctrines concerned the effect of supervening events and that "[t]he difference lies in the effect of the supervening event." The court said that when dealing with frustration, performance is still possible but the fortuitous event has destroyed the expected value of the performance to the party claiming to be excused. The court pointed that "since the two doctrines differ only in the effect of the fortuitous supervening event, it is appropriate to look to our cases dealing with impossibility for guidance in treating the issues that are the same in a frustration

CASES	SUMMARIES
Chase Precast Corp., continued	of purpose case." Noting that Panonessa was not responsible for the Department's elimination of the concrete barriers, the court explained that whether Panonessa could rely on the frustration defense hinged on whether the barrier elimination was a risk which the contract allocated to Panonessa. To make this determination, the relevant questions to be answered were whether the contingency was foreseen as a real possibility and, if it was, did the parties specifically assign the risk to the promisor by failing to provide for the contingency explicitly. Here, although the Department had the right to eliminate items found unnecessary, the Chase-Panonessa contracts did not have a similar provision. Nevertheless, Chase knew of the Department's power to eliminate contract items and was aware of the Department standard contract. The court added that even if the parties were aware of the Department's right "to eliminate contract items, the judge could reasonably have concluded that they did not contemplate the cancellation for a major portion of the project of such a widely used item as concrete median barriers, and did not allocate the risk of such cancellation."

CASES	SUMMARIES
Northern Indiana Public Service Co. v. Carbon County Coal Co. (1986) → (CB pg. 910) *P gambled by entering into a 20-year fixed contract... Frustration of purpose is not here to bail them out*	**FACTS:** The Northern Indiana Public Service Co. (NIPSCO), an Indiana electric utility, entered into a contract with Carbon County Coal in which NIPSCO agreed to buy approximately 1.5 million tons of coal each year for 20 years at a fixed price of $24/ton, subject to various escalation provisions which fixed the price in 1985 at $44/ton. In December 1983, the Public Service Commission (Commission) issued "economy purchase orders" that required NIPSCO to make good faith efforts to buy electricity from other utilities at prices lower than it cost NIPSCO to generate electricity. Apparently, NIPSCO was able to buy electricity below the cost of generating electricity from coal but, because of the "economy purchase orders," of which it had not sought judicial review, NIPSCO had no expectation that the Commission would allow it to recover its costs of buying coal from Carbon through the electrical rates it charged its customers. In April 1985, NIPSCO sued Carbon "seeking a declaration that it was excused from its obligations under the contract either permanently or at least until the economy purchase orders ceased preventing it from passing on the costs of the contract to its ratepayers." At trial, the jury's verdict was in favor of Carbon for $181 million. The court rejected Carbon's request for specific performance in lieu of damages.

HOLDING: On appeal, the court addressed the contractual *force majeure* clause which provided that NIPSCO could cease taking delivery for any cause beyond its control, including civil authority orders which prevented it, in whole or in part, from using the coal. NIPSCO argued that the "economy purchase orders" prevented it at least, in part, from using the coal that it had agreed to buy from Carbon. The court explained, however, that the "economy purchase orders" did not prevent NIPSCO from using the coal; it only prevented it from passing on its costs to the ratepayers. Thus, such orders did not trigger the force majeure clause. By entering into the fixed price contract with Carbon, NIPSCO gambled that fuel costs would rise but instead they fell. The court pointed out that the failure of such a gamble was not a force majeure event. It explained that had the Commission directed NIPSCO to close its plant because of a safety hazard that would be a force majeure event. But here the Commission only prevented NIPSCO from making consumers bear |

CASES	SUMMARIES
Northern Indiana Public Service Co., continued	the risk that NIPSCO assumed when it entered into a fixed price fuel contract. Thus, the court, said that NIPSCO could not complain because the risk that occurred was one that NIPSCO voluntarily took on at the time of contract.

The court then discussed the trial court's refusal to present NIPSCO's impracticability and frustration defenses to the jury, holding that Indiana does not allow a buyer to claim impracticability and does not recognize the defense of frustration. The Seventh Circuit referred to UCC §2-615—the UCC's commercial impracticability defense—noting that it refers only to sellers, not buyers—and that in the present case, NIPSCO's defense was "more properly frustration than impracticability." However, it pointed out that it did not have to decide whether the Indiana Supreme Court would adopt the doctrine of frustration since in any event NIPSCO did not establish that the facts fell within the scope of the doctrine. Nor did the court have to decide "whether a force majeure clause should be deemed a relinquishment of a party's right to argue impracticability or frustration, on the theory that such a clause represents the integrated expression of the parties' desires with respect to excuses based on supervening events; or whether such a clause either in general or as specifically worded in this case covers any different ground from these defenses; or whether a buyer can urge impracticability under Section 2-615 of the Uniform Commercial Code, which applies to this suit." The court concluded that the doctrine of impossibility and related doctrines being "devises for shifting risk in accordance with the parties' presumed intentions" had no place in this case because the parties had a fixed price contract. Such contracts explicitly assign "the risk of market price increases to the seller and the risk of market price decreases to the buyer. . . ." Having placed the risk of decreased costs on NIPSCO, NIPSCO cannot be excused from performing because "the cost of generating electricity turned out to be lower than NIPSCO thought when it signed the fixed-price contract with Carbon. . . ."

STOP

Section 5. Half Measures

CASES	SUMMARIES
Young v. City of Chicopee (1904) → (CB pg. 918)	**FACTS:** Plaintiff agreed with defendant to repair a wooden bridge that was part of a highway crossing the Connecticut River. Under the contract, work could not commence until the materials needed for at least one-half of the repairs had to be "'upon the job.'" Plaintiff complied with this condition and distributed the lumber along the bridge and the river banks. During the repairs, the bridge burned down without the fault of either party. **HOLDING:** The issue on appeal before the Massachusetts Supreme Court was whether plaintiff could recover for the lumber it had distributed but had not been used. While this lumber had been brought "upon the job," it was subject to

CASES	SUMMARIES
Young, continued	plaintiff's control and remained plaintiff's lumber until it was "brought into the bridge." The court noted that the condition requiring plaintiff to bring the lumber before work was commenced had "no material bearing upon the rights of the parties in relation to the lumber" but was inserted simply to ensure that the work progressed rapidly. The court noted that the contract was an entire one and both parties were excused from further performance when the bridge burned down. However, plaintiff was still entitled to recover for its part performance based upon a principle which "rest[s] upon the doctrine that there is an implied contract upon the owner of the structure upon which the work is to be done that it shall continue to exist, and therefore, if it is destroyed, even without his fault, still he must be regarded as in default, and so liable to pay for what has been done." The court then referred to another principle which holds that whatever a party performed properly is regarded in law as having been done at the other party's request thus creating a liability to pay for its value. The court stated that however the principle is stated, the owner's liability in a case like this "should be measured by the amount of the contract work done which at the time of the destruction of the structure had become so far identified with it as that, but for the destruction, it would have inured to him as contemplated by the contract." Therefore, defendant should be liable for the work and materials "actually wrought into the bridge." The court concluded, however, that the lumber that plaintiff owned did not inure to defendant's benefit at the time of the fire and thus its loss was not to be borne by defendant.

■ CHAPTER 10. THIRD PARTIES: RIGHTS AND RESPONSIBILITIES

Section 1. Third-Party-Beneficary Contracts

Concepts:

- The general rule is that privity of contract is required to provide a party with standing to sue and enforce contractual rights. This is because contract rights and duties exist only between the contracting parties and do not extend to those who are not parties to the contract.

- Third-party intended beneficiaries are an exception to this rule, and may be able to sue on their own behalf to enforce the contract.

- In determining whether a third party has acquired the right of enforcement, the critical factor is whether the contract was made for the benefit of the third party. The contracting parties must have intended at the time of the contract's formation for the contract to benefit the third party. While some third parties may incidentally benefit from a contract's performance, they are considered only incidental beneficiaries having no right of enforcement. Only intended beneficiaries have the right of enforcement.

Framework for Analysis: Was there a third-party beneficiary to the contract?

ASK: Was a third party to the contract identified at the time the contract was formed? Did the contracting parties intend to benefit a third party?

(a) If so, and if the promisee of a contractual promise intends to give a non-party the benefit of the promised performance, then that person is an intended third-party beneficiary; or

(b) If performance of the promise will satisfy the promisee's duty to pay money to the beneficiary, then that beneficiary is an intended third-party beneficiary. R2d §302

If new parties are introduced after the original contract is formed, through a post contract delegation of duties or assignment of rights, see Sections 2 and 3 below.

Note: The first Restatement classified beneficiaries that could recover as either donee or creditor beneficiaries (§133(1)(a); §133(1)(b)) whereas the Restatement Second does not differentiate between donee and creditor beneficiaries. Instead, the Restatement Second uses the term "incidental beneficiary" to describe one that does not acquire rights under a contract (R2d §315) and "intended beneficiary" to describe one that does acquire rights under a contract. R2d §302

- **Type of Beneficiary?** Was the beneficiary an intended or incidental beneficiary?

  — **Intended Beneficiary?** Was the beneficiary an "intended" beneficiary? Only an intended beneficiary has the right of enforcement and can sue the promisor directly.

  — **Incidental Beneficiary?** If the beneficiary is not an intended beneficiary, it is an incidental beneficiary. If so, then the contract was not intended for that party's benefit and she has no legally enforceable rights.

- **Vesting?** Has the intended beneficiary's rights vested or can they be varied by the contracting parties? The contracting parties may, by subsequent agreement, discharge or modify the contract without regard for the beneficiary. However, such power terminates if before notification of the discharge or modification, the intended beneficiary has done any of the following:

    — **Assent?** Has the beneficiary manifested assent to the promise at the request of the promisor or promisee?

    — **Suit?** Has the beneficiary brought suit to enforce the promise?

    — **Reliance?** Has the beneficiary materially changed position in justifiable reliance?

    Note: Under the first Restatement, a donee beneficiary's rights vested as soon as the contract was made and could not be varied without the beneficiary's consent unless a right to vary the contract was reserved. §142

CASES	SUMMARIES
Lawrence v. Fox (1859) → (CB pg. 928) *The promise to make a payment on behalf of a lender is consideration* *Lawrence is a 3rd party creditor beneficiary*	**FACTS:** Holly lent Fox $300 and told Fox at the time that he, Holly, owed that amount to the plaintiff, Lawrence, and that it was due the next day. At the time of the loan, Fox promised to pay the $300 to Lawrence the next day. When Fox did not do so, Lawrence sued him. At trial, defendant Fox moved to dismiss, claiming that there was no evidence showing that Holly was indebted to Lawrence, that defendant's promise to Holly to pay Lawrence lacked consideration, and that there was no privity between Lawrence and Fox. The jury found for plaintiff and judgment was affirmed on appeal to Superior Court. **HOLDING:** On appeal, the NY Ct of Appeals held, contrary to Fox's objection, that there was competent evidence to establish a debtor-creditor relationship between Holly and Lawrence. The court also rejected Fox's claim that its promise was not enforceable because there was no consideration to support it. The court, relying on Justice Savage's opinion in Farley v. Cleveland, explained that if Fox had made his promise to Lawrence rather than, or in addition to Holly, then there would have been precedent for Lawrence to recover against Fox. The loan by Holly to Fox would have been consideration for Fox's promise to Lawrence because consideration for a promise "need not move from the promisee to the promisor." The court also further rejected Fox's claim that his promise was not enforceable for lack of privity between Lawrence and Fox. Even though Fox's promise had not been made to Lawrence, the court allowed him to recover against Fox on a theory based on trust principles where, in the case "'that a promise made to one for the benefit of another, he for whose benefit it is made may bring an action for its breach.'" **DISSENT:** The promise that Lawrence was suing on was not made to him nor did Lawrence furnish the consideration for the promise. The dissent argued that Holly could have decided at any time to direct that Fox pay the $300 directly to Lawrence and that if Holly had done that "the defendant's promise to pay according to the direction would have ceased to exist." The dissent further noted that while "plaintiff would receive a benefit by a complete execution of the arrangement, . . .the arrangement itself was between other parties, and was under their exclusive control." In this case, there is no legal basis for a third person to sue upon the promise.

CASES	SUMMARIES

Seaver v. Ransom (1918)

→ (CB pg. 931)

Seaver is a 3rd party donee beneficiary

FACTS: Judge Beman drafted a will for his wife in which she left to her husband, Beman, the use of the house for life, with the remainder to the American Society for the Prevention of Cruelty to Animals. When the will was read to her, Mrs. Beman said that she wanted to leave the house to her niece, the plaintiff. Although Beman was prepared to draft another will, Mrs. Beman was concerned that she would not live long enough to sign it. Her husband told her that "if she would sign the will, he would leave plaintiff enough in his will to make up the difference." She signed the will but when Beman died his will had no provision for plaintiff. At trial, plaintiff was awarded a judgment based on the theory that equity had impressed a trust on the property in plaintiff's favor because Beman had obtained the property by inducing his wife to execute the will by promising to give plaintiff $6,000, the value of the house. On appeal, the court noted that imposition of a trust was improper because Beman had received no property through the will upon which equity could impose a trust: he had received only the use of the house for his lifetime. However, a breach of contract action was another matter. The Appellate Division upheld the trial court's judgment based on the general rule in Lawrence v. Fox and thus "the judgment could stand upon the promise [Beman] made to the wife, upon a valid consideration, for the sole benefit of plaintiff."

HOLDING: On appeal, the NY Ct of Appeals noted that the Lawrence v. Fox doctrine had been subsequently limited and the beneficiary's right to enforce a contract for its benefit was "not clearly or simply defined." The court said that when plaintiff brought suit, the doctrine was limited to cases, among others, involving contracts made for the benefit of a person's wife or child where "[t]he natural and moral duty of the husband or parent to provide for the future of wife or child sustains the action on the contract made for their benefit." The court pointed out that the childless Mrs. Berman's desire to provide for her favorite niece was no different in law or equity from a parent's moral duty to provide for a child in its will. Thus if plaintiff were Mrs. Beman's child, while the law would not have required Mrs. Berman to provide for her in her will, the child "could have enforced a covenant in her favor identical with the covenant of Judge Beman in this case." The court said that it could not reconcile enforcing a contract for the benefit of a wife "based on the moral obligations arising out of [a] near relationship, with a decision against the niece here on the ground that the relationship is too remote for equity's ken." The court explained that if Mrs. Beman had willed the house to her husband and he had accepted the devise, he would have been personally liable to pay that amount to plaintiff because in substance she had "bequeathed the promise to plaintiff, and not because close relationship or moral obligation sustained the contract. The distinction between an implied promise to a testator for the benefit of a third party to pay a legacy and an unqualified promise on a valuable consideration to make provision for the third party by will is discernible, but not obvious." In all these cases, the American authorities tend to sustain the gift and permit the donee beneficiary to recover on the contract. Accordingly, plaintiff was entitled to judgment whether it was an action for damages or an action "to convert the defendants into trustees for plaintiff's benefit under the agreement."

Skip 935 - 956

CASES	SUMMARIES
Detroit Institute of Arts Founders Society v. Rose (2001) → (CB pg. 935)	**FACTS:** NBC, owner of the original Howdy Doody puppet, and Rose entered into an agreement whereby Rose would arrange to dispose of the different Howdy Doody puppets which had been used on the show — all except for the original Howdy Doody. Rose was to notify NBC whether the puppet "Double Doody," used as a stand-in at times for Howdy Dowdy, was to be housed in the puppet museum of the Detroit Institute together with Howdy. After Rose's death, the Detroit Institute sued because it had not yet received the Double Doody puppet. **HOLDING:** In granting partial summary judgment for the Institute, the district court noted that a contract can be made for the benefit of a third party who is entitled to enforce the obligor's contractual obligations. Although the contract does not need to contain express language creating a direct obligation to the third-party beneficiary, such an obligation can be created only "if both parties to the contract intended to create a direct obligation from the promisor to the third party." The court noted that the parties' intent was to be determined from the contract terms in light of the circumstances surrounding the making of the contract.
Sisney v. State (2008) → (CB pg. 941)	**FACTS:** CBM and South Dakota entered into a contract whereby CBM agreed to provide food services to the State's Department of Correction (DOC) facilities including prisons. In April 2007, CBM began furnishing food for prisoners requesting a kosher diet. Sisney, an inmate, brought suit claiming that the kosher diet contained between 400 and 500 calories less than was required under the State/CBM contract and that the food did not comply with his religious beliefs. Defendants moved to dismiss, asserting among other things, that Sisney had no standing to sue under a public contract between the State and CBM. The court granted defendant's motion, concluding that Sisney was not a third-party beneficiary of the State/CBM contract. **HOLDING:** The South Dakota Supreme Court affirmed on appeal, finding that Sisney did not have third-party beneficiary status. The court cited to the South Dakota statute which provided that where a contract is made expressly for a third party's benefit, he can enforce the contract at any time prior to the parties' rescinding it. This rule, therefore, required that when entering into the contract, the parties intended to expressly benefit the third party. The court noted that the contract Sisney sought to enforce was a public contract and "the contract did not expressly indicate that it was intended for Sisney's direct benefit or enforcement. On the contrary, the contract reflects that it was made for the express benefit of the State, and the collective benefit that inmates may have received was only incidental to that of the State." The court noted that in a public contract an enforcement right "can only arise from the plain and clear language of the contract. . . . Consequently, when a public contract is involved, private citizens are presumed not to be third-party beneficiaries." Even though government contracts in some measure intend to benefit directly or indirectly every member of the public, a third party right to enforce it is "not properly inferred because of the potential burden that expanded liability would impose."

CASES	SUMMARIES

Sisney v. Reisch (2008)

→ (CB pg. 944)

FACTS: In 2000, the Department of Corrections (DOC) and Heftel, an inmate at the South Dakota State Penitentiary (SDSP), entered into a settlement agreement (the "Heftel Agreement") in which the DOC agreed to provide a kosher diet which would include prepackaged certified kosher meals to any Jewish inmate requesting it. In February 2007, CBM, SDSP's food service supplier, stopped serving prepackaged kosher meals and instead purportedly cooked a kosher meal in SDSP's kitchen. Sisney sued, claiming that CBM's change in the food service was a violation of the Heftel Agreement and Sisney's religious beliefs. The circuit court dismissed the suit without reaching the question of whether Sisney was a third-party beneficiary entitled to enforce the Heftel Agreement. Sisney appealed.

HOLDING: On appeal, the court noted that a third party may enforce an agreement if he can clearly show that it was entered into expressly for his benefit. After noting that third-party beneficiary status may be conferred upon a class of individuals, the court stated that the contract terms "'must clearly express intent to benefit that party or an identifiable class of which the party is a member.'" Here the court cited to various express provisions of the Heftel agreement which "raised the inference that the Heftel Agreement was intended to expressly benefit all Jewish inmates who requested a kosher diet." Thus, Sisney, who claimed to be member of the class, had standing to enforce the agreement.

Verni v. Cleveland Chiropractic College

→ (CB pg. 951)

FACTS: Dr. Makarov, a college employee, taught a dermatology class in which plaintiff, Verni, had enrolled. After being dismissed from the college, Verni sued Makarov claiming that Makarov had breached his employment agreement with the college by failing to observe certain standards of decency required of the faculty in dealing with students. Verni obtained a verdict against Makarov.

HOLDING: On appeal, the court held that Verni was not a third-party beneficiary of Makarov's employment contract with the college. The court noted that whether Verni was a third-party beneficiary depended on whether the contract clearly expressed an intent to benefit him or an identifiable class of which he was a member. Absent an express declaration of intent in the contract, a strong presumption exists that the parties intended to benefit only themselves and not a third party. The court examined Makarov's contract which provided that he would be a full-time faculty member and set forth the amount of time he had to be on campus, his teaching duties, and his salary. The contract did not "clearly express any intent that Dr. Makarov was undertaking a duty to benefit Verni or a class of students." Verni argued, however, that Makarov's contract required him to comply with Cleveland's faculty handbook policies and that Makarov failed to treat students fairly and courteously as the handbook required. The court stated that even assuming that the faculty handbook was part of Makarov's employment agreement, the handbook language did not "overcome the strong presumption that the contract was executed solely for the parties' own benefit." The court noted that all of the college's students were incidental beneficiaries of faculty members' contracts with the college but that alone did not entitle a student to enforce the contract, a right which only an intended beneficiary can exercise. The court concluded that Makarov's employment agreement did not confer

CASES	SUMMARIES
Verni, continued	third-party beneficiary status on Verni "because the terms of the contract do not directly and clearly express the intent to benefit Verni or any class of which Verni claims to be a member."
Grigerik v. Sharpe (1998) → (CB pg. 953)	**FACTS:** Grigerik entered into a contract to purchase an undeveloped tract of land from Lang and Lang agreed to obtain town approval to build on the land. Since the land was near a reservoir, the town sanitarian required submission of an engineer's site plan for drainage. Lang hired Sharpe to prepare the site plan which included the design of a septic sewer-disposal system. Lang told Sharpe that Lang needed the site plan to get approval for the land as a building lot and that if he got the necessary town approval, he had a buyer for the land. The town sanitarian approved Sharpe's site plan and Grigerik purchased the land. However, a new town sanitarian denied Grigerik a building permit because "the tract was not suited to a septic system." Grigerik sued Sharpe claiming, among other things, that he was a third-party beneficiary of the Lang/Sharpe contract. The jury found for Grigerik but the Appellate Court reversed, holding that the trial court erred by allowing Grigerik "to recover as a foreseeable, rather than an intended beneficiary of the contract" and also erred "in favor of the defendants, by requiring that both parties, rather than just the promisee of the contractual obligation in question, intended to benefit the plaintiff." **HOLDING:** On appeal, the Ct Supreme Court rejected the Appellate Court's view and held that the intent of both parties to the contract, not just one of the parties, determines whether a third party is afforded third-party beneficiary status under the contract. In so holding, the Ct Supreme Court noted that R2d §302(1)(b) "suggests that the right to performance in a third-party beneficiary is determined both by the intention of the contracting parties and by the intention of one of the parties to benefit the third party." The Ct Supreme Court, however, agreed with the Appellate Court that foreseeability is a tort concept and that the jury's finding that Grigerik was a foreseeable beneficiary was insufficient to confer rights as a third-party beneficiary. The court said that to import the concept of foreseeability into contracts "would significantly reduce contracting parties' ability to control, through the negotiated exchange of promises and consideration, the scope of their contractual duties and obligations." The court reversed and remanded with instructions to enter judgment for defendants on the breach of contract claim.

Section 2. Delegation of Duties

Concepts:

- An obligor is free to delegate performance of her contractual duties as long as it does not violate an express provision of the contract, the reasonable expectations of the obligee, or public policy.

FRAMEWORK FOR ANALYSIS: Has one of the contract parties purported to delegate performance of her duties under the contract to someone who was not an original party to the contract?

ASK: Has a party (obligor) delegated performance of its duty under the contract to another person? Is it the type of duty that can be delegated?

- **Personal?** Is the duty one that is "personal" in nature such that it involves the obligee's taste, skill, or discretion? If the obligor's performance involves unique skills or the personal services of professionals like lawyers, doctors, and portrait painters, then performance of the duty is non-delegable. In these cases, the obligee should not be required to accept performance from anyone other than the original obligor. If the performance is impersonal, then performance of the duty can be delegated unless the delegation materially alters the performance that the obligee will receive.

- **Public Policy?** Does the delegation violate public policy? If so, then it is non-delegable.

CASES	SUMMARIES
Sally Beauty Co. v. Nexxus Products Co. (1986) → (CB pg. 964)	**FACTS:** In July 1981 Sally Beauty acquired Best Barber Beauty and succeeded to Best's rights under an agreement that Best had with Nexxus to be the exclusive distributor of Nexxus hair care products in virtually all of Texas. When Best merged into Sally Beauty, Nexxus terminated the distributorship agreement because Sally Beauty was a wholly-owned subsidiary of Alberto-Culver, a major manufacturer of hair care products and thus a direct competitor of Nexxus in the hair care market. Sally Beauty sued Nexxus for breach; Nexxus moved for summary judgment, claiming that its distribution agreement with Best "was a contract for personal services" and thus was non-assignable without Nexxus's consent. The district court granted the motion, finding that the parties did not have a simple commercial contract, but was "based upon a relationship of personal trust and confidence." Sally Beauty appealed.
	HOLDING: On appeal, the Seventh Circuit stated that it could not affirm the motion on the grounds that the district court had relied on. Although the district court might have been reasonable to conclude that Best and Nexxus had based their contract on a personal relationship of trust and confidence and that Reichek's [Best's President] participation was essential to Best's performance, this was "a finding of fact" for the jury. Nevertheless, the court concluded that the contract was not assignable as a matter of law — but for a different reason. Applying the "'dominant factor'" test, the court found that the distribution contract was a transaction in goods because the sales aspect of the contract predominated and was therefore governed by the Uniform Commercial Code. The court observed that under the exclusive distribution agreement, Best had an obligation to use its "best efforts" in promoting the sale of Nexxus products and it was this duty which Nexxus did not want Sally Beauty to perform. The court held that the delegation of Best's duties was prohibited by UCC §2-210. In so doing, the court explained that the obligee's consent would be required before the duty of performance under an exclusive distributorship could be delegated to a market competitor. Therefore, Sally Beauty's status as an Alberto-Culver wholly owned subsidiary, which made Sally's "best efforts"

CASES	SUMMARIES
Sally Beauty Co., continued	subject to Alberto-Culver's control, was sufficient to bar Best's delegation of its duties under the distribution contract. The court rejected Sally's argument that it should be permitted to show at a trial that "it could perform and would perform the contract as impartially as Best." The court stated that "[w]hen performance of personal services is delegated, the trier merely determines that it is a personal services contract. If so, the duty is per se nondelegable. There is no inquiry into whether the delegate is as skilled or worthy of trust and confidence as the original obligor: the delegate was not bargained for and the obligee need not consent to the substitution." Thus, although Sally Beauty may have believed that it could operate impartially, there could be no guarantee of what would happen if Alberto-Culver made demands on Sally Beauty that competed with the needs of Nexxus. The law, the court said, may not force Nexxus to take the risk of an unfavorable outcome. **DISSENT:** Judge Posner stated that "notions of conflict of interest are not the same in law and in business." He observed that even though Sally Beauty was an Alberto-Culver subsidiary, it distributed hair care from other companies which appeared to compete with Alberto-Culver as much as Nexxus did. What the law may consider a fatal conflict of interest, may very well be a legitimate practice in business. Judge Posner believed that the risk of harm to Nexxus by the acquisition of Best by Sally Beauty was very slight. He noted that "there is no principle of law that if something happens that trivially reduces the probability that a dealer will use his best efforts, the supplier can cancel the contract. . . ." At best, Nexxus may have had grounds to demand adequate assurances under UCC §2-609.

Section 3. Assignment of Rights

Concepts:

- An assignment is a transfer of a contractual right or benefit.

- The party who transfers the right is the "obligee" under the original contract and, upon assignment, is called the "assignor." The party who acquires the right is called the "assignee." The party who owes the duty to the obligee under the original contract and now owes it to the assignee is called the "obligor."

(A) Assignability of Rights; Means of Assignment

FRAMEWORK FOR ANALYSIS: Has one of the contract parties, the obligee, transferred her rights under the contract to someone who was not an original party to the contract?

ASK: Has the obligee manifested an intent to make a present transfer of a contract right? An assignment extinguishes the right in the obligee (assignor) and vests it exclusively in the assignee. This gives the assignee a direct right against the obligor under the contract.

To determine whether the assignment was valid and enforceable, ask the following:

- **Effective?** Was it an effective assignment? An effective assignment requires the owner of the right to use words of present transfer and to describe the right to be transferred adequately. Consider whether the language manifests an intent by the assignor to divest herself completely and immediately of the right and establish it in the assignee. While the word "assign" need not be used, were such words as "sell," "transfer," "convey," or "give," used? If not, then it may only be an attempted or purported assignment and was ineffective. If so, then proceed to the next question.

- **Type of Right?** Is it the type of right that may be assigned? Generally, a contractual right may be assigned. There are some circumstances where a contract might not be assigned such as if it would materially alter the other party's (obligor's) duty or risk.

  ASK:

  — **Public Policy?** Would the assignment violate public policy or be forbidden by statute?

  — **Adverse Effect?** Would the purported assignment materially change or materially increase the risk or burden of the obligor's duty? In cases where the obligor's duty depends on the obligee's personal discretion, substituting an assignee for the obligee might result in a material change in the obligor's duty. If so, a court might find the assignment ineffective. The same is true in cases where the obligor's risk or burden under the contract is materially affected as in insurance contracts.

- **Precluding Assignment?** If there is no contractual prohibition, then contract rights can be assigned because the general rule is free assignability. Is there a term in the parties' contract that provides in words or substance that the contract is non-assignable? If so, then absent a statute, an assignment may be ineffective, depending on the precise contract language. *Bel-Ray Company v. Chemrite (Pty) Ltd.*

  ASK:

  — Does the contract language indicate that "assignment of rights under this contract is prohibited"? If so, then while an assignment would be a breach of contract and the obligor could seek damages, the transfer of rights, that is, the assignment itself, would be effective. However, this language should be construed to bar the delegation of duties and not the assignment of rights unless a contrary intent is indicated.

  — Does the contract language indicate that "assignment of rights under this contract is void"? If so, then the assignment is ineffective.

- **Notice?** If there is a valid assignment, has the obligor been given notice of the assignment? If so, then she is bound to render performance to the assignee instead of the assignor. If not, then she has no reason to know that her performance is due to the assignee. If she renders her performance to the assignor before receiving notice of the assignment, her obligations are discharged and she does not have to perform again for the assignee.

CASES	SUMMARIES
Herzog v. Irace (1991) → (CB pg. 971) Assignment language showed intent	**FACTS:** Attorneys Irace and Lowry represented Jones in a motorcycle personal injury action. The action was settled. Jones subsequently dislocated his shoulder which was unrelated to the motorcycle accident and went to see the plaintiff, Dr. Herzog, who concluded that Jones needed surgery. In a letter dated June 1988, Jones wrote "I, Gary Jones, request that payment be made directly from settlement of a claim currently pending for an unrelated incident, to John Herzog, D.O.. . . ." Herzog notified Irace and Lowry of the "assignment of benefits" and performed the surgery. Subsequently, Jones directed Irace and Lowry not to disperse any funds to Dr. Herzog whereupon Dr. Herzog sued to enforce the alleged assignment of benefit. On an agreed stipulation of facts the trial court entered judgment for Dr. Herzog, holding that "the June 14, 1988 letter constituted a valid assignment of the settlement proceeds"; this judgment was affirmed on appeal to the Superior Court. **HOLDING:** The Supreme Judicial Court of Maine affirmed on appeal. In so doing, the court stated that "[a]n assignment is an act or manifestation by the owner of a right (the assignor) indicating his intent to transfer that right to another person (the assignee)." Once the obligor receives notice of the assignment, he cannot pay the amount assigned to the assignor and if he does so, the assignee may seek recovery directly from the obligor. The court further stated that "[i]n Maine, the transfer of a future right to proceeds from pending litigation has been recognized as a valid and enforceable equitable assignment." However, Irace and Lowry argued that Jones did not manifest intent to relinquish control over the assigned funds and that the June 14th letter did no more than "request payment from a specific fund." In rejecting this argument, the court said that taken in context, the word "'request' did not give the court reason to question Jones's intent to complete the assignment. . . ." The court concluded that the evidence supported the trial court's finding on the validity of the assignment. The court rejected Irace and Lowry's contention that their ethical obligation to follow their client's instruction not to disperse the funds prevented them from honoring the assignment. Instead, the court stated that Irace and Lowry were duty bound to honor the valid assignment and thus the lower court was correct in concluding that the assignment was enforceable against them.
Bel-Ray Company v. Chemrite (Pty) Ltd. (1999) → (CB pg. 978)	**FACTS:** Bel-Ray produced specialty lubricants using highly confidential technology and formulas. Bel-Ray entered into agreements with Chemrite of South Africa to blend and distribute Bel-Ray's products in South Africa. In 1996, Lubritene acquired Chemrite's business, including rights under the Bel-Ray/Chemrite agreements and Bel-Ray was notified of the transfer. Bel-Ray sued Lubritene, charging it with various torts and obtained a court order directing Lubritene to arbitrate these claims based upon an arbitration provision in the latest of the Bel-Ray/Chemrite agreements. **HOLDING:** On appeal, the court noted that ChemRite had assigned the ChemRite/Bel-Ray agreements to Lubritene and that if the assignments were effective, the order directing arbitration should be affirmed. Lubritene argued that the Bel-Ray/Chemrite agreements had a provision requiring Bel-Ray's written consent to any assignment of Chemrite's interest under those agreements. The court looked for guidance to the New Jersey Superior Court's Appellate Division for the effect of contract provisions which limit or prohibit assignments. In deciding a case, the

CASES	SUMMARIES
Bel-Ray Company, continued	Appellate Division had looked to R2d §322 which provides that unless the parties manifest a different intent, breach of an anti-assignment clause only gives the obligor a right to sue for damages for breach but does not make the assignment ineffective. Thus, a party's "power" to assign — as distinguished from its "right" to assign — is limited only where the parties manifest a different intention. The court pointed out that "[i]n adopting §322, New Jersey joins numerous other jurisdictions [including New York] that follow the general rule that contractual provisions limiting or prohibiting assignments operate only to limit a parties' [sic] right to assign the contract, but not their power to do so, unless the parties' manifest an intent to the contrary with specificity" such as stating that any assignment would be "void" or "invalid." Absence of such specific language, contractual provisions prohibiting assignments will simply be interpreted as promises not to assign. Here the agreement only provided that Chemrite could not assign rights without Bel-Ray's written consent but did not state "that an assignment without Bel-Ray's written consent would be void or invalid." Thus Chemrite's assignment to Lubritene was enforceable and Lubritene was bound to arbitrate Bel-Ray's claims.

(B) Obligor's Duty to Assignee: Some Variations

CASES	SUMMARIES
Delacy Investments, Inc. v. Thurman & Re/Max Real Estate Guide, Inc. (2005) → (CB pg. 982)	**FACTS:** In November 2001, Thurman, a real estate agent, entered into an agreement with Delacy Investments d/b/a Commission Express (CE) pursuant to which Thurman gave CE a security interest in all his current and future accounts receivable. CE filed a UCC financing statement, thus perfecting its security interest. In February 2003, Thurman entered into an independent contractor agreement with Re/Max, a real estate brokerage company, which provided that Thurman would be entitled to payment of commissions to the extent they exceeded past due financial obligations that Thurman had to Re/Max. The portion that did not exceed past due financial obligations were deemed to belong to Re/Max. In April 2003, Re/Max acknowledged that CE had a security interest in Thurman's account receivable from a home sale on Javalin Avenue. In addition, in April 2003, CE and Thurman entered into an agreement pursuant to which CE agreed to purchase a $10,000 receivable related to Thurman's sale of the Keller Lake property. In June, Re/Max terminated Thurman and claimed that any commissions Re/Max earned from Thurman's services did not exceed Thurman's past due financial obligations to Re/Max; consequently, Thurman was not entitled to any compensation from the Keller Lake sale and nothing was to be paid to CE pursuant to the assignment. CE sued Re/Max. The district court found that Thurman was entitled to no commission at the Keller Lake property and that CE could obtain no greater right than Thurman in that commission. The court quoted from UCC §9-404 which provides that generally "an assignee's rights are subject to '(1) all terms of the agreement between the account debtor and the assignor. . . [.]'"

CASES	SUMMARIES
Delacy Investments, Inc., continued	**HOLDING:** On appeal, the court affirmed the district court's grant of summary judgment for Re/Max. In so holding, the court stated that "'it is black-letter law that an assignee of a claim takes no other or greater rights than the original assignor and cannot be in a better position than the assignor.'" Thus, since under UCC §9-404 (a)(1), CE's rights were subject to the Re/Max-Thurman agreement, CE was not entitled to recover from Re/Max because any commissions Re/Max earned as a result of Thurman's efforts did not exceed Thurman's past due obligations to Re/Max. The court rejected CE's argument that UCC §9-404(a)(2) did "not permit an account debtor [ReMax] to contract away the rights of an assignee after having received notice of a previously-executed assignment." Here Re/Max had notice of the Thurman/CE agreement before Re/Max entered into the independent contractor agreement with Thurman. The court rejected this argument, finding that UCC 9-404 (a)(2) did not govern the parties' dispute. Instead, under UCC §9-404 (a)(1), it was clear that CE's right as an assignee was subject to the terms of the agreement between Re/Max and Thurman, which limited Thurman's commissions that exceeded his past due financial obligations. CE could not take greater rights nor be in a better position than Thurman by recovering a commission which Thurman was not entitled to himself.
Chemical Bank v. Rinden Professional Association (1995) → **(CB pg. 993)**	**FACTS:** Rinden, a law firm entered into a lease-purchase agreement with Intertel pursuant to which Intertel installed a phone system for which Rinden was required to make monthly payments through 1982 when it could then purchase the phone equipment for one dollar. Intertel assigned its rights under the lease agreement to Chemical Bank. Before making the assignment, Rinden requested Chemical to sign a document in which Rinden, as lessee, agreed to pay the monthly rental payments directly to Chemical "'notwithstanding any defense, set-off or counterclaim whatsoever, . . . which you may or might now or hereafter have as against the Lessor [Intertel].'" After making three years' payments to Chemical, Rinden replaced the phone system because it had been malfunctioning and refused to make any further payments to Chemical. A lawsuit ensued, resulting in a master's report in Chemical's favor and a finding that the waiver clause was enforceable. **HOLDING:** On appeal, the court noted that the matter was governed by UCC Article 9 as adopted in Massachusetts because the lease between Intertel-Rinden fit the UCC definition of a security agreement. Having established the statutory basis, the court proceeded to the issue of whether there was an agreement by Rinden, who was not a consumer, "to waive defenses against an assignee and that the assignment was made for value, in good faith, and without notice of claim or defense. . . ." The court found that each of these requirements had been satisfied and therefore Rinden had waived his defenses against Chemical Bank. First, the court noted that Rinden was not a consumer but rather "a professional association, a law firm." Second, Chemical gave value when it took the assignment because it paid Intertel over $8,800 for the assignment of Intertel's rights. Third, the court rejected Rinden's contention that Chemical Bank was not a purchaser in good faith because Chemical and Intertel were "too closely connected." The court noted that the record did not contain anything to show that the Intertel/Chemical relationship "was anything other than an arm's-length commercial relationship." Further, a Chemical employee in charge of the Intertel account testified that the purchase of Intertel's rights "was typical of its

CASES	SUMMARIES
Chemical Bank, continued	transactions with hundreds of other clients with which it had entered into similar agreements." Finally, the court rejected Rinden's argument that there was a lack of good faith because the bank checked Rinden's credit rating and insisted on a waiver of defenses clause. According to testimony from a Chemical employee and Intertel's former president, these actions were standard bank procedure when extending credit. Rinden also argued that the waiver of defense provision lacked consideration. In response, the court stated that under UCC §2-209(1) consideration was not required. In so doing, the court noted that the provisions of Article 2 were applicable because "Article 2 does apply to transactions in goods which involve both a sales contract and a security agreement."

(C) Assignees in Contests With Third Parties

CASES	SUMMARIES
U.S. Claims, Inc. v. Flomenhaft & Cannata, LLC (2006) → (CB pg. 999)	**FACTS:** Both U.S. Claims (USC) and Stillwater Asset-Back Fund (Stillwater) claimed interests in the assets of a New York attorney and his law firm ("the other defendants"). The assets consisted of the future fees the other defendants expected to earn from pursuing their clients' personal injury claims. USC sought a declaratory judgment that its interest was senior to Stillwater's. USC had obtained from the other defendants a series of assignments in those fees. Subsequently, the other defendants borrowed money from Stillwater and gave all their assets as collateral. Although USC had never filed a financing statement with respect to its interests in the fees whereas Stillwater had done so, USC nonetheless claimed that it was entitled to priority because Stillwater knew of USC's interests when Stillwater took its security interest from the other defendants. USC also claimed that under UCC §9-309 its security interests were perfected when they attached because they were assignments of "payment intangibles." The trial court noted, however, that under Article 9 "'a creditor's subjective knowledge is wholly irrelevant to the question of lien priority.'" Further, the trial court held that the fees to be earned were not "payment intangibles" but were "accounts" which would not be automatically perfected. Consequently, USC should have filed a financing statement with respect to its interest in the fees. **HOLDING:** The court further noted that USC's attempt to rely on an exception to UCC §9-309(2) regarding "casual assignments" was not applicable. The court explained that since USC was a sophisticated financial enterprise and its interests were in excess of $3 million, it would be hard to believe that USC would have considered such a transaction to be "casual" such that it failed to think it necessary to file to protect its interests.

■ TABLE OF CASES

Alaska Packers' Ass'n v. Domenico, **70**

Allied Steel and Conveyors, Inc. v. Ford Motor Co., **28**

Austin Instrument, Inc. v. Loral Corporation, **72**

Balla v. Gambro, Inc., **126**

Bartus v. Riccardi, **168**

Bayliner Marine Corp. v. Crow, **2**

Bayway Refining Co. v. Oxygenated Marketing & Trading A.G., **38**

Beaver v. Brumlow, **58**

Bel-Ray Company v. Chemrite (Pty) Ltd., **214**

Black Industries, Inc. v. Bush, **110**

Bloor v. Falstaff Brewing Corp., **121**

Bollinger v. Central Pennsylvania Quarry Stripping and Constr. Co., **86**

Bovard v. American Horse Enterprises, Inc., **122**

Britton v. Turner, **170**

By-Lo Oil Co. v. Partech, Inc., **182**

Callano v. Oakwood Park Homes Corp., **16**

Campbell Soup Co. v. Wentz, **132**

Canadian Industrial Alcohol Co. v. Dunbar Molasses Co., **196**

Carlill v. Carbolic Smoke Ball Co., **28**

Central Ceilings, Inc. v. National Amusements, Inc., **53**

Channel Home Centers, Division of Grace Retail Corp. v. Grossman, **45**

Chase Precast Corp. v. John J. Panonessa Co., **201**

Chemical Bank v. Rinden Professional Association, **216**

C. Itoh & Co. (America) Inc. v. Jordan Int'l Co., **37**

Cohen v. Cowles Media Co., **14**

Colfax Envelope Corp. v. Local No. 458-3M, **99**

Columbia Nitrogen Corp. v. Royster Co., **97**

Corinthian Pharmaceutical Systems, Inc. v. Lederle Laboratories, **29**

Cosden Oil & Chemical Co. v. Karl O. Helm Aktiengesellschaft, **179**

Cotnam v. Wisdom, **16**

Crabtree v. Elizabeth Arden Sales Corp., **55**

C.R. Klewin, Inc. v. Flagship Properties, Inc., **51**

Cundick v. Broadbent, **67**

Cyberchron Corp. v. Calldata Systems Development, Inc., **44**

Dalton v. Educational Testing Service, **118**

Dave Gustafson & Co. v. State, **151**

De La Concha of Hartford, Inc. v. Aetna Life Insurance Company, **119**

Delacy Investments, Inc. v. Thurman & Re/Max Real Estate Guide, Inc., **215**

Delchi Carrier Spa v. Rotorex Corp., **148**

Delta Dynamics, Inc. v. Arioto, **89**

Detroit Institute of Arts Founders Society v. Rose, **208**

D&G Stout, Inc. v. Bacardi Imports, Inc., **15**

Dickinson v. Dodds, **31**

Dixon v. Wells Fargo, N.A., **43**

Doe v. Great Expectations, **113**

Dorton v. Collins & Aikman Corp., **36**

Douglass v. Pflueger Hawaii, Inc., **66**

Drennan v. Star Paving Co., **32**

Dyer v. National By-Products, Inc., **6**

Eastern Air Lines, Inc. v. Gulf Oil Corp., **196**

Elsinore Union Elementary School District v. Kastorff, **23**

Ever-Tite Roofing Corp. v. Green, **27**

Fairmont Glass Works v. Crunden- Martin Woodenware Co., **21**

Feinberg v. Pfeiffer Co., **7**

Feinberg v. Pfeiffer Co., **13**

Fera v. Village Plaza, Inc., **150**

Fiege v. Boehm, **6**

Frigaliment Importing Co. v. B.N.S. International Sales Corp., **92**

Gianni v. Russell & Co., **83**

Gibson v. Cranage, **163**

Gill v. Johnstown Lumber Co., **169**

Graham v. Scissor-Tail, Inc., **113**

Greenfield v. Philles Records, Inc., **89**

Grigerik v. Sharpe, **210**

Groves v. John Wunder Co., **142**

Hadley v. Baxendale, **147**

Hamer v. Sidway, **6**

Harrington v. Taylor, **7**

Harvey v. Facey, **21**

Hawkins v. McGee, **1**

Henningsen v. Bloomfield Motors, Inc., **105**

Herzog v. Irace, **214**

Hicks v. Bush, **163**

Hill v. Gateway 2000, Inc., **41**

Hochster v. De La Tour, **178**

Hoffman v. Red Owl Stores, **43**

Hopper v. All Pet Animal Clinic, **124**

Hurst v. W.J. Lake & Co., **94**

International Filter Co. v. Conroe Gin, Ice & Light Co., **26**

In the Matter of Baby M, **128**

Iron Trade Products Co. v. Wilkoff Co., **174**

Internatio-Rotterdam, Inc., v. River Grand Rice Mills, Inc., **160**

Jacob & Youngs v. Kent, **141, 167**

Jones v. Star Credit Corp., **115**

Kannavos v. Annino, **78**

Kanovos v. Hancock Bank & Trust Co., **178**

Kenai Chrysler Center, Inc. v. Denison, **68**

Kenford Co. v. County of Erie, **148**

K&G Construction Co. v. Harris, **173**

Kingston v. Preston, **166**

Kirkland v. Archbold, **171**

Kirksey v. Kirksey, **8**

Klein v. PepsiCo, Inc., **133**

Koken v. Black & Veatch Construction, Inc., **102**

Krell v. Henry, **199**

Laclede Gas Co. v. Amoco Oil Co., **134**

Lake Land Employment Group of Arkron, LLC v. Columber, **8**

Lake River Corp. v. Carborundum Co., **152**

Langman v. Alumni Association of the University of Virginia, **52**

Laredo Hides Co., Inc. v. H & H Meat Products Co., Inc., **139**

Lawrence v. Fox, **206**

Lefkowitz v. Great Minneapolis Surplus Store, **22**

Lewis v. Mobil Oil Corp., **103**

Lucy v. Zehmer, **19**

Luttinger v. Rosen, **160**

Market Street Associates v. Frey, **120**

Masterson v. Sine, **84**

Mattei v. Hopper, **10**

McCloskey & Co. v. Minweld Steel Co., **180**

McKenna v. Vernon, **163**

McKinnon v. Benedict, **109**

Mills v. Wyman, **7**

Mineral Park Land Co. v. Howard, **192**

Monarco v. Lo Greco, **60**

Morris v. Sparrow, **133**

Nanakuli Paving & Rock Co. v. Shell Oil Co., **95**

New England Structures, Inc. v. Loranger, **174**

Northern Delaware Industrial Development Corp. v. E.W. Bliss Co., **135**

Northern Indiana Public Service Co. v. Carbon County Coal Co., **202**

Northrop Corp. v. Litronic Industries, **39**

O'Callaghan v. Waller & Beckwith Realty Co., **112**

Odorizzi v. Bloomfield School District, **74**

Oglebay Norton Co. v. Armco, Inc., **47**

Ortelere v. Teachers' Retirement Bd., **67**

Oswald v. Allen, **98**

Owen v. Tunison, **21**

Pacific Gas and Electric Co. v. G.W. Thomas Drayage & Rigging Co., **88**

Parker v. Twentieth Century-Fox Film Corp., **146**

Peacock Construction Co. v. Modern Air Conditioning, Inc., **162**

Peevyhouse v. Garland Coal & Mining Co., **143**

Plante v. Jacobs, **142**

ProCD, Inc. v. Zeidenberg, **40**

Pyeatte v. Pyeatte, **17**

Raffles v. Wichelhaus, **98**

R.E. Davis Chemical Corp. v. Diasonics, Inc., **140**

Renner v. Kehl, **189**

Ricketts v. Scothorn, **13**

Rocheux Int'l of N.J. v. U.S. Merchants Fin. Group, **183**

Rockingham County v. Luten Bridge Co., **145**

Sally Beauty Co. v. Nexxus Products Co., **211**

Scott v. Cingular Wireless, **116**

Seaver v. Ransom, **207**

Selland Pontiac-GMC, Inc. v. King, **195**

Sheets v. Teddy's Frosted Foods, **125**

Simeone v. Simeone, **127**

Sisney v. Reisch, **209**

Sisney v. State, **208**

South Carolina Electric and Gas Co. v. Combustion Engineering, Inc., **104**

Speakers of Sport v. ProServ, **78**

Specht v. Netscape Communications Corp., **19**

St. Ansgar Mills, Inc. v. Streit, **61**

Stees v. Leonard, **188**

Step-Saver Data Systems, Inc. v. Wyse Technology, **39**

Stewart v. Newbury, **166**

Strong v. Sheffield, **10**

Structural Polymer Group, Ltd. v. Zoltek Corp., **10**

Sullivan v. O'Connor, **3**

Sumerel v. Goodyear Tire & Rubber Co., **186**

Swift Canadian Co. v. Banet, **200**

Swinton v. Whitinsville Sav. Bank, **77**

Taylor v. Caldwell, **193**

Tongish v. Thomas, **145**

Toys, Inc. v. F.M. Burlington Co., **47**

Transatlantic Financing Corporation v. United States, **193**

Trident Center v. Connecticut General Life Ins. Co., **91**

Tuckwiller v. Tuckwiller, **110**

United States Life Insurance Company v. Wilson, **34**

United States Naval Institute v. Charter Communications Inc., **3**

United States v. Algernon Blair, Inc., **141**

U.S. Claims, Inc. v. Flomenhaft & Cannata, LLC, **217**

Verni v. Cleveland Chiropractic College, **209**

Vitex Manufacturing Corp. v. Caribtex Corp., **138**

Vokes v. Arthur Murray, Inc., **79**

Walgreen Co. v. Sara Creek Property Co., **135**

Walker & Co. v. Harrison, **172**

Wasserman's Inc. v. Township of Middletown, **153**

Watkins & Son v. Carrig, **71**

Webb v. McGowin, **7**

White v. Benkowski, **4**

White v. Corlies & Tift, **27**

Williams v. Walker- Thomas Furniture Co., **115**

Wood v. Lucy, Lady Duff-Gordon, **11**

Wright v. Newman, **13**

W.W.W. Associates, Inc. v. Giancontieri, **90**

X.L.O. Concrete Corp. v. Rivergate Corp., **123**

Young v. City of Chicopee (1904), **203**